BLACK SHEEP

BLACK SHEEP

CHRISTOPHER SIMON SYKES

1982

CHATTO & WINDUS

LONDON

Published by
Chatto & Windus Ltd
40 William IV Street
London, WC2N 4DF
★
Clarke, Irwin & Co. Ltd
Toronto

British Library Cataloguing in Publication Data

Sykes, Christopher Simon
    Black sheep.
    1. Upper classes – Great Britain – History
    2. Deviant behaviour
    I. Title
    305.5'2 (expanded)   HT653.G7
ISBN 0–7011–2548–9

Printed in Great Britain by
Fakenham Press Limited,
Fakenham, Norfolk

To Jane

Acknowledgements

Throughout the writing of this book I have received help and encouragement from many people. Special thanks are once again due to the Marquis of Anglesey, who has helped me so much in the past, for introducing me to Lord William Paget, and for lending me all the family papers relating to him. These had been superbly catalogued by Mr. T. L. Ingram, whose hard work must have saved me hours of time. For other original material I am equally indebted to the Duke of Wellington for diverse material relating to the fourth Earl of Mornington. Others who have assisted me in various ways, and to whom I offer my unreserved gratitude, include Mr. Roger Adelson, the Marquis of Ailesbury, Miss Alexandra Alec-Smith, Colonel Rupert Alec-Smith, Mr. Mark Bence-Jones, Mr. Edmund Brudenell, Mr. Andrew Brudenell-Bruce, Miss Catherine Caulfield, Mr. Bruce Chatwin, the Hon. Robert Corbett, Mr. Philip Davis, the Duke and Duchess of Devonshire, Mr. Max Fairbrother, the Right Hon. Hugh Fraser M.P., the Knight of Glin, the Duke of Grafton, John Lister Kaye, Miss Marianne Lowther, Mr. Brian Masters, Sir Iain Moncreiffe, the Duke of Northumberland, Miss Diana Potter, Mr. Robert Temple, Lord Teviot, Mr. Christopher Wood, and Mr. Ed Victor.

Most of the book was written in the London Library, for whose staff and facilities there can be no praise high enough. My thanks are also due to Mrs. Wilson, librarian at Stratfield Saye, the staff of the National Portrait Gallery, and to Norah Smallwood and Alan Williams for having faith in me.

I am especially grateful to Mary, Countess Waldegrave, for her great generosity in allowing me to draw on her own privately published family history.

For permission to reprint copyright material, the following acknowledgements are made: The National Trust and Methuen London Ltd for an excerpt from a poem in *Barrack Room Ballads* by Rudyard Kipling; Doubleday & Co. Inc. for an excerpt from *The Pioneer Years 1895–1914* by Barry Broadfoot. Copyright © 1976 by Barry Broadfoot.

'We're poor little lambs who've lost our way,
  Baa! Baa! Baa!
We're little black sheep who've gone astray,
  Baa-aa-aa!
Gentlemen-rankers out on the spree,
Damned from here to Eternity,
God ha' mercy on such as we,
Baa! Yah! Bah!
. . . .
We have done with Hope and Honour, we are lost to Love and Truth,
We are dropping down the ladder rung by rung,
And the measure of our torment is the measure of our youth.
God help us, for we knew the worst too young!'

(Gentlemen-Rankers. RUDYARD KIPLING)

CONTENTS

INTRODUCTION

'There is a black sheep in every flock.'
(Proverbs)

WHEN I and my brothers and sisters were children, there was a family mystery which intrigued each one of us. As far as we were aware our father had one brother and three sisters, all of whom we knew well – Uncle Christopher, Aunt Freya, Aunt Petsy and Aunt Angela. Yet our childish ears would occasionally prick up at the mention of an Uncle Daniel. Who was this unknown figure, we wondered amongst ourselves. Why had he never been to stay? When we dared to ask our parents these things, our questions were either brushed aside or met with a wall of silence, and for many years all attempts to discover his identity proved fruitless. Then as we grew older we gradually began to glean small pieces of information about him. He was the youngest member of the family by five years, eleven years younger than our father. He was an interior decorator and painter. He was homosexual. He dyed his hair. He wore make-up. He drank. He took heroin. He was paid to stay away. He died while I was at school. None of us ever met him. I have never even seen his grave. He was the black sheep of our family.

Black sheep are sons or daughters who have, in the eyes of their parents or relations during their lifetime, or of their posthumous descendants, brought disgrace upon their family. It is an expression which derives from times of superstition when farmers believed that the black sheep in a flock bore the devil's mark. Such animals were considered worthless. To the outsider, the person whose welfare does not rely on all the wool being pure white, the black sheep of a flock is invariably the most interesting for the very reason that it is different. Thus in a family, whose morality is based upon certain standards, the child who breaks those standards for no apparent reason other than for the hell of it is likely to be cast out, while to others this is the one whose name will be remembered, and be whispered behind closed doors for generations to come.

INTRODUCTION

The characters who exemplify my theme are all from aristo-cratic families. There are two reasons for this. The first and most obvious is that the greater the escutcheon, the more violent the stain upon it. What is almost more to the point, though, is the fact that to the aristocracy the honour of the family was all-important. 'I have long doubted Lord William Paget's feelings of honour . . .', wrote the Marquis of Anglesey in 1829 of his way-ward son. 'All my kindness and forbearance has ever been thrown away upon him, and he has never made one effort to leave off his extravagance and disgraceful habits, but goes on defrauding everyone who has the folly to be deluded by his baseness and utter contempt of truth. I give him up. He is hardened in iniquity and lost to all sense of shame, and the feelings of a Gentleman and Man of Honour.'

Traditionally black sheep are somehow always associated with younger sons, a concept I found hard to accept since all children, young and old alike, are subject to the varied weaknesses of human nature, to the temptations of the Seven Deadly Sins. In fact it turned out that the heirs of families were just as likely to stray from the straight and narrow as were their younger brothers. Whatever course they took was influenced by two important factors.

The first was their upbringing, much of which was extremely harsh, particularly in the seventeenth and early eighteenth cen-turies. Children were swaddled after birth and farmed out to wet nurses; thereafter it was generally regarded that the key to the successful raising of the child was, as in the training of a favourite horse or hunting dog, the breaking of its will, and enforcing its total subjection to the will of its parents. One method of achiev-ing this was the administration of constant and severe corporal punishment. It was a severity which was continued in the schools to which they were sent from the age of seven onwards. In the early eighteenth century Edward Wortley-Montagu ran away from Westminster School on several occasions to escape the cruelty of his Latin master who 'grinned with a fiend's delight as he laid the lash across my naked flesh'. He reached home how-ever only to be locked in a large cupboard without food, beaten twice daily, and quickly sent back whence he came. This kind of upbringing was liable to produce adults who were cold, suspi-cious and violence-prone.

Even if children did not lose one or other of their parents at an early age, which was often the rule rather than the exception, they were still likely to spend most of their time in the hands of nannies and tutors, servants and boarding schools. The majority of fathers certainly took little personal interest in their offspring, whom they tended to regard at the best as pets. Lord Robert Spencer, for example, can hardly have seen much of his father at all, owing to the Earl of Sunderland's rather erratic diplomatic life – envoy to Madrid, 1671, Ambassador Extraordinary, Paris, 1672, Plenipotentiary, Cologne, 1673, Ambassador Extraordinary, The Hague, 1678. Modern psychiatric study has shown that patients from wealthy homes who have experienced parental deprivation suffer from an inability to maintain human relations, psychotic-like attacks of rage, and a paranoid belief that the world is against them. These are feelings that are common to many black sheep.

The second important factor which I believe contributed to the downfall of many a son was the principle and practice of primogeniture, which affected all families who owned property. This was a system, still widely in operation today, under which both the elder and the younger children suffered. As far as the latter were concerned, unless one of them was lucky enough to be heir to some property on the maternal side, they were extremely unlikely to inherit either title or estate. Their prospects in life were, therefore, not very good, especially as they were invariably brought up to enjoy a standard of living which they would never be able to afford on their own. The weak-willed among them, such as Lord William Paget, and John Knatchbull, whose inheritance in 1819 was only £300, got into severe debt, and ended up turning to crime.

As for the elder sons, the very knowledge of the certainty of the inheritance to come often deprived them of any motive to lead a useful life. Many of them were condemned to spend years, living a kind of shadow existence while they awaited the death of a father, during which time it was only too easy for them to become men of luxurious and idle habits, depraved tastes and corrupted morals. 'It requires a most gigantic resolution to suffer pain', wrote Thomas Lyttelton, who was in just such a position in 1766, 'when passion quickens every sense, and every enticing object beckons to enjoyment. I was not born a Stoic, nor am I made to be a martyr.' In the Autumn of 1688, Lord Robert Spencer drank himself to death fourteen years before the death of his father, while George, Earl of Euston's dissipation was such that his father disinherited him in 1743.

Those who did finally inherit often came into fortunes the immensity of which are only comparable today to those amassed by Arabs, or other oil tycoons. When the fifth Marquis of Anglesey came of age in June 1896, his income from his estates alone was the equivalent today of nearly three million pounds a year. He set about spending it at such a rate that when he died eight years later, his debts amounted to over twelve and a half million. Similarly, in 1891 at the age of twenty-eight the fourth Marquis of Ailesbury was bankrupt for eight million.

One category which does not conform to the general pattern, and which is therefore somewhat out on a limb, is that of homo-sexuality. I have included it, however, since no study of black sheep would be complete without it, it being the reason why, until comparatively recently, so many young men were ostra-cised both by their families and society.

Black sheep are by no means confined to men. I have included a number of black ewes. Frances Howard, Countess of Somerset, for example, is almost the wickedest person in the book. She is, however, something of an exception. Most of them were not evil, but were merely making a desperate effort to achieve some kind of independence. One cannot emphasise enough the extent to which women were treated as third-class citizens. Not only were they considered biologically inferior but any suggestion that they could be the intellectual equal of a man, or that they could be educated in any form of serious scholarship, aroused strongly hostile response. Their function was regarded purely as being to subject themselves to the will of man. The few women who defied this convention found it wise to keep quiet about it. Thus Lady Mary Worley-Montagu, who had taught herself the classics in the early eighteenth century in the deepest secrecy, advised her daughter to give her granddaughter a serious and scholarly education, but warned her 'to conceal whatever learn-ing she attains, with as much solicitude as she would hide crookedness or lameness: the parade of it can only serve to draw on her the envy, and consequently the most inveterate hatred, of all he and she fools, which will certainly be at least three parts in four of all her acquaintance'.

In a woman the concept of Honour was regarded as being her chastity. Those, such as poor Miss Sophia Howe, who were known to have broken the code were ruined for life. She died broken-hearted. Jane Digby, however, simply turned her back on society and went her own way. She didn't give a damn.

This book does not touch on modern times. Because in the society in which we live almost anything is considered normal, it is nowadays quite hard to be a black sheep. When the son or daughter of some distinguished family is had up on a drugs charge, or brought to court for non-payment of debts, or on a shoplifting charge, although it may cause their family some temporary embarrassment, there is little likelihood of its resulting in their ostracism from society. To achieve the besmirching of the family honour beyond redemption would require participation in some major crime for which there could be no excuse, such as robbery with violence, or child rape. Certainly murder does not always fit the bill. Consider the most prominent example of the latter to have occurred in recent times, in November 1974, when Richard John Bingham, 7th Earl of Lucan, better known to his friends as 'lucky', allegedly made an attempt on the life of his wife and, in doing so, allegedly murdered the family's nanny, the hapless Miss Sandra Rivett. He disappeared soon afterwards and has never been seen since. What surprised the police officers investigating the crime was that, amongst his circle of friends, rather than being denounced for the wicked thing he was alleged to have done, he was consistently held up as a man of honour who had been driven over the top by his wife's unreasonable behaviour towards him, particularly concerning his children. There is no doubt that, if he were able to return today without fear of arrest, he would be welcomed back warmly into the society he left behind.

One volume leaves room enough only to scratch the surface of this subject. As it is I have a file inches thick containing material which it has not been possible to include. I therefore beg the forgiveness of those readers who may feel there are certain omissions in this book.

I

A THORN IN THE FLESH

'For shame, for shame, you disgrace the name of Paget!'
(Lord Anglesey to his son)

'THE most perfect hero that ever breathed' was how a contemporary once described Henry William Paget, Earl of Uxbridge. It was an epithet bestowed on him after the brilliant victory at Waterloo in June 1815, in which he had greatly distinguished himself as Commander of the whole of the cavalry and horse artillery. He had also suffered a severe wound, and had subsequently conducted himself in a most courageous manner. Almost at the very end of the battle he had been struck by a piece of grapeshot on the right knee which had completely shattered the joint. (Popular legend has it that he at once exclaimed to Wellington, who was by his side, 'By God, sir, I've lost my leg!', to which Wellington replied in matter-of-fact tones, 'By God, sir, so you have!') His leg was amputated, an operation during which he never moved or complained, merely remarking once, perfectly calmly, that he thought the instrument was not very sharp. When he returned to England the Prince Regent, declaring him to be 'his best officer and his best subject,' created him Marquis of Anglesey in recognition of his services. 'Since the soldier's drawn sword first glittered in the sunshine,' wrote an admirer in *The Times*, 'never did a more fearless or more chivalrous officer support the honour of his country.'

It was not only the honour of his country that Lord Anglesey cared about so passionately. He spent much of the latter part of his life in a seemingly endless struggle to prevent that of his family from being irretrievably besmirched. The threat to it came from within. Anglesey had been married twice, first in 1795, at the age of twenty-seven, to Lady Caroline Villiers, a younger daughter of the fourth Earl of Jersey. She bore him three sons and five daughters. In 1810 he divorced her and married Lady Charlotte Wellesley, a step-sister of the Earl of Cadogan, by whom he had a further six sons and four daughters. It was the second son of his first marriage who was to grow up to be the thorn in his side.

Lord William Paget was born on 1 March 1803. Of his childhood little is known. He had four elder sisters and one elder brother. The family divided its time between three great houses: Beaudesert Hall in Staffordshire, Plas Newydd on the Isle of Anglesey, and Uxbridge House in London. William evidently adored his mother, referring to her in later life as 'my own angel mother'. His father was a more remote figure. So, at any rate, one of Paget's sisters, Louisa Erskine, described him in a letter to her husband:

'his indifference and cold manner upon all occasions must not a little astonish you who are so very much the reverse of what I am sorry to say he rather piques himself upon. How strange that anybody should effect what is so very unamiable. I am convinced that Paget au fond has great feeling but he studies so to appear devoid of it that I fear it will end in his being so!'

Certainly many years later William was to write:

'He never could *bear me* from a child. *I doted upon him*, but I *was* afraid of him. . . . He is the only being and thing I ever feared, and for this fear I ever deceived him.'

The divorce in 1810 split up the family. William's mother married the Duke of Argyll and went to live at Inverary Castle. William himself was sent off to Westminster School, from where he passed straight into the Navy as a First-Class Volunteer on board H.M.S. *Glasgow*. He was fourteen years and one month old.

Coming from as distinguished a family as he did, William's prospects for a successful career in the Navy were bright, and he seems to have made a promising start. After six years' statutory sea-service, first in the Mediterranean from 1817 to 1821, and then as a Midshipman in the Home Station and the West Indies from 1821 to 1823, he achieved rapid promotion. He was appointed Lieutenant in April 1823, Commander in April 1825, and Post-Captain in October 1826. Finally in November 1829, upon the appointment of his father as Lord-Lieutenant of Ireland, he received the command of the Vice-Regal Yacht, *Royal Charlotte*, at Dublin.

Yet, at precisely this moment, with so much opportunity open to him, William for some reason chose to launch himself along a

1. LORD WILLIAM PAGET

road to ruin that was eventually to lead to a debtor's prison, followed by permanent exile abroad. One can only surmise that a significant act of defiance against his father led to an obsessive desire to defy at every turn, blinding him to his own downfall. In March 1827 William married Fanny Rottenburgh, daughter of General Rottenburgh, a soldier who had served under Lord Anglesey at Walcheren in 1809. The marriage took place against the express wishes of his father, who considered it extremely unwise for a younger son to marry a woman who brought with her no fortune. He was soon to be proved right.

The first inkling that Anglesey received of the trouble that lay ahead came in March 1829. Having recently paid some bills on William's behalf, he received a letter from him explaining why it

19

had been necessary to ask for money. For the past two years, he said, he had been Commander of the Vice-Regal Yacht, the pay and allowances from which position had amounted to £1,000 a year. This had enabled him to run a considerable establishment in Ireland, fully staffed with footmen, coachmen, groom, knifeboy, odd man, women servants and gardeners, as well as two carriages and four horses. Unfortunately, his appointment to the *Royal Charlotte* had ended in March 1829, and with it all the additional income. It seems that for William this was no reason to cut down on his household. He had simply kept it going and sent the bills to his father. The letter ended with the assurance that 'I love my brothers and sisters too well to desire to enrich myself at their expense.' Anglesey's reply to his son contained the solemn warning that 'unless you reduce your expenses in proportion to your reduction of income, you will be involved in irretrievable ruin'. It was a warning that fell upon deaf ears.

By July, a mere four months later, William was in severe financial difficulties, with creditors pressing him on all sides. When it became clear that this time his father was less ready to help him out, he decided to retaliate, mindful of Anglesey's reputation and high position as Lord Lieutenant. Thus on 22 July he wrote to the family solicitor, William Lowe, saying that he would have to give up his seat in Parliament (in 1826 he had automatically succeeded his uncle, Charles Paget, as Member for the Welsh seat of Caernarvon) and to surrender himself as a debtor. He knew that this would have meant ending up in the debtor's gaol, the disgrace of which would have been too great for his father to bear. It was a crafty and ruthless move.

Lord Anglesey was indeed horrified when informed of his son's threats. He wrote to William Lowe:

'I have long doubted Lord William Paget's feeling of honour, and am, therefore, scarcely surprised at the circumstances you announce, altho' I could not anticipate that he would have the baseness voluntarily to place himself in such a situation as he might calculate would force me into a measure of relief, in pity and mercy to the rest of his family ... he might like many, many others have withdrawn to the Continent and lived sparingly, but honestly. But no! he first of all barefacedly deceived me by assuring me as he did, when in Ireland I remonstrated with him upon the extent of his establishment, that he had not a single debt and now he takes a course which he imagines will force me into a necessity of paying for his extravagances. . . . I acknowledge that he has me in his clutches and that I must tamely submit to what he has imposed upon me. I must now save him from Prison (not him but his family's name).'

He concluded with a warning which he was destined to issue time and time again, that 'if after the present relief he chooses again to play the rogue, he must incur the penalty'.

Lowe had the job of persuading William to make up a list of his debts. This proved to be no easy task. Eventually, after numerous cancelled appointments and lame excuses, the long-suffering Lowe received the following note: 'Dear Sir, my debts amount to £20,000, yours truly, William Paget'. There was no sign of a list. Considering the size of the debt, which was twice William's entire inheritance, it was a colossal cheek. Anglesey was outraged. He scratched across the note: 'I will not pay them. I do not believe it. The thing is impossible. But I will not pay even one shilling without an accurate account.'

When a full list of the debts finally did arrive, in late September, Anglesey was, in his own words, 'thunderstruck' by the catalogue of 'meanness, prodigality and selfishness' evidenced by the numerous and long-standing debts incurred in Dublin – tailors' bills exceeding £900, hosiers and hatters over £400, coachmakers £700.

'Why is he to have a carriage at all? After his infamous conduct in respect of his marriage, he and his wife should have been satisfied, like others more respectable than themselves, with public carriages or a Hack Chaise. . .'

William's total disregard for his situation was further shown by the fact that, on his return from Ireland, instead of taking up the offer of the loan of a house by his father's agent, John Sanderson, he had chosen instead to rent one near London.

'Is it to be believed', continued his father, 'that this disgraced and wretched young man, with all his difficulties staring him in the face, and knowing that his tricks and falsehoods must come to light ... with the *loan* of a house wherein he might have lived retired, and hidden his guilty head, he should have impudently taken a house near London, and have expended above £1,300 on the furniture!!! Here I stop. It would be endless to attempt to enumerate his extravagances – his folly – his falsehoods – alas what a word to write of one's own son!'

He went on to say that, regretfully, he felt that the only course he could take under the circumstances was to pay up. 'I solemnly protest', he concluded, 'it shall be the last assistance he shall ever get from me'. Had these words turned out to be less empty, William's subsequent career might have been different.

William's attitude throughout all this was outrageous. That he never for a single moment considered himself to be in the wrong is well illustrated by the fact that when he received a note which had been sent anonymously to his father, to the effect that 'nothing on earth can be going on more disgraceful than Lord William', he replied indignantly that 'I am as incapable of a disgraceful action as any other member of my *virtuous* family.' He took it as a matter of course that all his debts should be paid at once and in full. They were after all no fault of his. He was a younger son with inadequate funds to finance a lifestyle to which he had become accustomed. He expected everyone to commiserate with him. It was this that upset his father as much as the debts themselves.

Apparently not a day went by without Anglesey receiving in his post a letter of complaint concerning William from some desperate tradesman or other. The following serves as a typical example, and as an illustration of William's impudence. A Mr. J. Curwen of Dublin had for some time been owed a considerable amount of money by William. After many fruitless attempts by himself, he eventually got his lawyer, a Mr. George Thompson, to write insisting on prompt payment. Thompson received from William the following reply:

'Sir, on looking over some paper this day, I find one from you, dated 4 May last upon the subject of Mr. Curwen's bill. I do not recollect to have seen it before, and certainly a more laughably impertinent production I never received. Who you are, for you sign your name George Thompson (there are a great many George Thompsons in the world) dating your letter (if it deserves the name) Dublin, I am at a loss to guess; neither should I be at the trouble of finding out, excepting for the purpose of informing you, that the next opportunity you give *me*, I shall give *you* the benefit of the postage of your letter-back again. P.S. Mr. Curwen's bill (by the way) is an impudent extortion, whether I undertook to pay it or not.'

In desperation Curwen forwarded all the correspondence to William's father, along with a plea that 'your Lordship would make much representation to Lord William as would induce him to pay me'.

Lord Anglesey was determined that the payment of William's debts should have as hard an effect as possible on William himself. He saw no reason why the estate should bear the whole burden. The conditions he made were as follows: that William's inheritance of £10,000 should be put in trust for the payment of his most pressing debts; that his carriages, horses, and furniture should all be sold for the same purpose; that he should at once give up all communication with certain of his more undesirable associates; in return for all this his father would make him a small allowance of £500 a year, to supplement his naval half-pay. This would allow him to support himself in a simple manner. There was one 'indispensable condition' – he had to go and live abroad, though his residence was not to be in a capital city. 'If I could anticipate the time', he wrote, 'when Lord William's conduct may entitle him to further indulgence, I shall meet it with satisfaction.'

A further insight into William's spending followed:

'Jewellers, Perfumiers, Portrait Painters etc, £751, Hotel and Innkeepers and Wine Merchants £1,072, and many of Trades without names, and name without Trades, which may include several of the descriptions specifically stated; besides a large amount on loan extracted from personal friends, and negotiated with Money-Lenders. Considering all these things, it is impossible not to believe that many articles have been purchased on credit for resale to obtain ready money. This is the return I have received for my weak and early forgiveness of a marriage against my consent in a disgraceful and clandestine manner.'

If Anglesey expected a letter of apology from his son, an acceptance of his conditions, he was sadly mistaken. Instead his agent, Sanderson, received a letter from William's solicitor stating that, in his opinion, William should be allowed to remain in England, as this would give him a better chance of being appointed to a ship in a foreign station. His house should thus be kept on so that his wife and son (William, b. 13 March) should have somewhere to live during his absence abroad. As for the sale of his property, he certainly had no horses or carriages on which money could be raised – he had only one horse, for the pony carriage, and also one for a water-cart. 'The fact is', commented Anglesey, 'he is ignominiously fighting for his comforts, when he ought to be hiding his disgraced head!'

On 14 December, Anglesey received the news that William had been appointed to command H.M.S. *North Star*, and that he was on his way to Portsmouth to join her. The ship was to sail for the West Indies without delay. 'The *North Star*', wrote Sanderson, 'is a propitious guide to sailors, and God grant it may keep Lord William, for the future, on a steady course ...' How Anglesey would have loved to believe that: he had just heard from his wife that 'even *lately* Lord William has been purchasing extravagant articles of ornamental breakfast service ...'

Another plea for mercy on behalf of William arrived from Lowe on 31 December:

'I am to tell Lord William that until he has sailed from England, and his furniture, carriage, and horses are left for sale for the liquidation of debt and he has given some pledge that he will live on such allowance as your Lordship may deem reasonable in addition to his pay, your Lordship will not stir a step in regard to the discharge of his debts ... If I do and it is made known to Lord William, it will, I dread, drive him to distraction and in his despair he may commit acts of desperation such as resigning his seat in Parliament, giving up command of his ship and yielding his person to the creditors ... My dread arises from the violently alarming state of mind he has been long, very long labouring under ... Lord William appears now to be very zealously pursuing his profession, and it would be deeply deplored if he should be checked in so honourable a career ... my long cherished feelings of respect, esteem and regard for your Lordship ... lead me to implore you to afford relief and consolation to your son Lord William before he encounters the pestiferous climate of the West Indies, whence he may never return.'

The little twist at the end, designed to play on his father's emotions, leads one to believe that William almost certainly had a hand in the writing of this letter. It had no effect.

'I do not doubt', wrote Anglesey on 1 January 1830, 'Lord William is in the state you describe, and shocked am I to be compelled to declare that he fully deserves it. I shall not – I cannot bring myself to depict the frightful conduct of Lord William, or allow myself to describe my opinion of his character. What must not I have suffered, I, who love my children beyond my life – to find I have such a son! Alas! a disgrace to his name! ... As for the threat you hold out of his relinquishing his ship and his seat in Parliament and giving his person to his creditors ... He is his own master, and may do as he pleases ... I do hope you will spare me from this subject in future.'

To William this was a declaration of war. On 4 January he wrote to Lowe:

'The course for me to pursue is clear, and I shall forthwith act upon it, viz, to relinquish my present command, vacate my seat, and take the benefit of the Act [Insolvent Debtors Act] – a fig for Lord Anglesey's favours and protection!!!'

His father's reaction was swift and to the point: 'to deprive him of the fortune I have destined for him by my Will in the event of any one of the three threats being carried out'.

Faced with the probability of being cut out of his father's will, William now executed a complete about-turn. He first of all wrote Lowe a stinging letter:

'*you knew* full well that I never for *one instant* seriously contemplated the commission of any one of the acts threatened in my letter to you, but *you knew better* still that I love my father with an enthusiastic devotion to which your *lawyer's stone heart is a stranger*. My own reflections are to be envied, but so help me God, I would not change with you.'

On receiving this Lowe, who until now had been William's one ally, immediately dropped him as a client. He followed this up with a grovelling apology, addressed to his elder brother, Lord Uxbridge, in which he spoke of his 'very deep sorrow and contrition' for all that he had said, particularly with reference to his affection for his father. He ended by reaffirming that '... so help me God, I *never for an instant* seriously contemplated the commission of any one of the acts so ridiculously, but so wickedly, threatened by the letter in question.'

By the beginning of March, with bills of every kind continuing to pour in daily, the conditions imposed by William's father were starting to be carried out. The £10,000 was placed in Drummond's bank and made available to the trustees. The interest on this money, which in the past had constituted William's private income, could therefore no longer be employed for this purpose. Instead an allowance of £300 a year was to be paid to him in quarterly instalments of £75. He was also required to furnish the trustees with all his tradesman's bills, each one to be attested with his signature, his general account with his servant, and with his bank book.

At the end of April, William, realising that he had no chance of getting any more money out of the trustees, left home and set sail with the *North Star*. Before going he appointed a new solicitor to keep an eye on his affairs while he was away, a Mr. Thomas Minchin of Gosport, whom he left in no doubt as to the nobleness of his intentions.

'He wept expressing his deep regret at all the past, assuring me it would be his happiness to be restored again to the same share in the Marquis's confidence as he had in his affection.'

The *North Star* was away for nine months, visiting the West Indies, Bermuda and Halifax, Nova Scotia, returning to Portsmouth in January 1831. It was a journey that was not without incident, culminating in William standing trial by Court Martial. This took place as a direct result of circumstances involving one of the ship's company, a boy called William Heritage. At some point early on in the voyage Heritage left his hammock lying about and failed to tidy it away. Harsh though it may seem, this was an offence for which the regulations stipulated flogging as a punishment. The boy received twelve lashes. Soon after this he committed a second offence, failing to lock the fresh water tank after going for water. A second flogging was ordered. The prospect of this was too much for the boy, who threw himself overboard and was drowned. Pressed by Heritage's father, the Admiralty ordered an enquiry into the conduct of the ship's Captain. A court of enquiry was held in Halifax, and William was exonerated of all blame. When the *North Star* returned to Portsmouth a second court of enquiry was ordered to investigate the case, with the same result. When public outrage forced a third enquiry to be called, William refused to face it and demanded, instead, as was his right, trial by Court Martial. This opened on board H.M.S. *Vincent* at Portsmouth on 5 February. It lasted three days, at the end of which the court found that the boy had been rightly punished for the first offence, and that the second punishment was also justified. William was 'most fully and honourably acquitted'.

As William left H.M.S. *Vincent* after the trial he was arrested by the Sheriff on behalf of five creditors, for a total debt of £772. He at once wrote off to Thomas Beer, his father's under-agent and a man who was destined to play a great role in his later affairs, instructing him to inform John Sanderson of what had taken place, emphasising that:

'The writs ... are of that nature that nothing but *actual payments* can be of any use to me ... As he is so well acquainted with my pecuniary affairs, it is wholly unnecessary for me to observe that the liquidation of this would not serve me for an hour – as there are hundreds of other creditors ready to act in the same way – he is aware too how wholly impossible it is for me to address Lord Anglesey on the subject. The *crisis* however is at length arrived – I am unable to return to my own house where Lady William is not yet recovered from her confinement [this was the second son Frederick who must have been conceived just before William left for his first cruise in April 1830], nor yet to my ship. In a word I am in a situation which unless everything be immediately done for me, I shall be compelled to give up my ship, for she is ordered to sea on the 15th, and I unable to attend to her in any way ... He will see the necessity for not a moment's time lost ...'

Anglesey was in Dublin when he heard of William's arrest. He had been so delighted by the results of the Court Martial that he had at once written to express his willingness to forgive and forget, a move which apparently delighted William:

'I can find', he replied, 'no words to describe to you the happiness which your most kind letter has occasioned me ... I read it over and over again and again, and can hardly believe that I am once more friends with my dearest Father. I have no no more promises. I am to be judged henceforward by my actions alone ...'

Anglesey instructed Sanderson to pay off the debts to keep his son out of gaol.

Sanderson himself had the gravest misgivings both about William's motives and his father's generosity, feelings he expressed to Thomas Beer:

> 'I should be surprised if it had escaped his Lordship's penetration that Lord William's return was a premeditated and selfish contrivance to precipitate the very crisis which he knew would force Lord Anglesey to pay his debts ... I deeply deplore the success of such artifices, and that such a father should be made the dupe of such a son ...'

But in spite of the fact that Sanderson passed these suspicions on personally to Anglesey, as well as suggesting to him that his willingness to pay up could lead to 'an entail of distress and difficulty in the family which be wholly without remedy', he remained adamant that this promise should be carried out.

Meanwhile William, since his release from custody, had been virtually imprisoned in his own house, awaiting the sailing of his ship. This was to avoid a second arrest by further creditors. Eventually, on 27 February, Sanderson received the following note from Thomas Minchin, the new solicitor:

> 'I am happy to announce to you that with the utmost vigilance and care, Lord William ... has avoided further arrests. There are *many* writs out against him, and his house has been continually besieged with all sorts of contrivances and disguises to effect an entrance, but in vain; and at length this morning he has sailed in the *North Star* in perfect safety and is now quite out of the way of an arrest.'

Evidence as to how William spent the next few years of his life is sketchy. We know that on the 18 May 1831, he was appointed to H.M.S. *Winchester* as Flag Captain, under Admiral Sir Edward Colpoys. But in September 1832 he returned to H.M.S. *North Star*, which ship he brought home and paid off in the summer of 1833. O'Byrne's *Naval Biographical Dictionary*, published in 1849, records that 'He has not been employed since'.

Between leaving his ship in 1833 and 1836 William lived for the most part abroad, in France and in Belgium. Here, judging from correspondence received by his father, he continued to live well above his means and to borrow from anyone he could. A Mrs. Drummond, for example, of the Château D'Ouvran, near Atan, in Belgium, wrote of how early one morning in May 1834 she was

> 'much surprised by a visit from Lord William Paget ... I was the more surprised as I had no previous acquaintance with His Lordship. I found him suffering under great agitation and on enquiring the cause he informed me that he was placed in a most unhappy situation and unless he could procure the advance of £180, the consequences to him would be fatal.'

The rest of the story is typical. William promised to repay the advance in a few days. The woman lent him the money. He disappeared, and that was that. It was the last Mrs. Drummond ever heard of him.

In the summer of 1835 William returned to England, leaving behind him debts that were to add up to well over £2,000. In November he obtained himself a commission as a Lieutenant-Colonel in the unofficial British Auxiliary Legion which had been raised to fight, in the civil war that had broken out in Spain, on behalf of the infant Queen Isabella II. The commission carried with it three months' advance of pay, and William promised that he would join his regiment without delay. True to form, he completely ignored this request, and proceeded to squander the money elsewhere. By the time he was ready to leave the country 'he was destitute of the means of doing so'. So wrote Richard Kirkman Lane, another poor fool who had fallen into William's clutches. He had been persuaded 'by the representations he made of the indelible disgrace which would surely attach to his Lordship's name if he did not join' to part with the £250 which William needed. It was the last he saw of the money.

William joined his regiment in February 1836, and was at once promoted to Colonel in the Legion and appointed to the staff of the Commander-in-Chief, General Evans. The legion was made up mostly of mercenaries recruited from General Evans's constituency of Westminster. Many of its officers were financially embarrassed adventurers. William first saw action in May when he made a sortie with seven thousand men to raise the siege by the Carlists of the town of San Sebastian. According to Sir Charles Chichester, the commander of a brigade of infantry, he 'shewed himself in the business a capital officer'. He was mentioned in

General Evans's despatch, and was awarded by the Spanish Government the Cross of St. Ferdinand, 2nd Class.

Shortly after this William returned home and immediately set about using his record of good service to try and make his father look kindly upon him. Once again it was money he wanted. On 31 May he wrote from his sister Caroline, Duchess of Richmond's house in Portland Place:

'I have at this moment received orders to embark at ten tomorrow morning for San Sebastian, and to enable me to make some pecuniary arrangements absolutely necessary before my departure I have *ventured* to address myself *direct* to you for the temporary advance of £200. I will repay it in such instalments as will not subject me to a repetition of the dilemma I have placed myself in now – I beg of you to forgive my addressing you, and not to attribute to a wrong motive and *you may believe me* (notwithstanding all that has occurred), that I will not disappoint any hopes you may place in me, if you comply with my request. Want is a hard taskmaster, and economy and prudence are not to be learnt in a day nor a year ... I cannot with a wand make my difficulties pass away, but I can truly say I have exerted myself, since your ineffectual but generous effort to relieve me, to make you proud of me in other respects...'

His father paid the money, but he made it quite clear that he did so 'without the slightest hope that it will be useful in effecting any change in your hardened feelings'.

'I have too many damning facts before my eyes', he continued, 'too many undeniable proofs of your having at defiance all principle of honour and integrity, to expect any good result from this foolish weakness on my part ... for shame, for shame, you disgrace the name of Paget! Think not that gallant conduct before an enemy can compensate for unprincipled and dishonest actions. No one prizes valour more than I do, but I know what it is worth, and I prefer an honest man to the bravest hero of history ... You *may* amend, God grant it. But until you effectually reform, you will be a deep and lacerating thorn in my side, and a curse upon your family...'

In view of his father's quite remarkable patience and kindness towards him, paying up as he had done time and time again, William's continued reluctance to make even the slightest effort to live within his means or put his affairs in order makes it hard to have much sympathy for him, and leads one to feel that he fully deserved everything that was coming his way. He returned to Spain for a brief period, and in July left San Sebastian for France. From here he returned to England in November, with his eldest son, William, and the boy's tutor, Henry Kellner. Kellner gave the reason for his return to his father as being because he had been 'molested by some of his English creditors in France', and that he therefore no longer felt safe there.

He was no safer in England. On 11 November one Henry Rimell prosecuted a writ for William's arrest for a debt of £20, and, on the order of the Sheriff of Middlesex, William was committed to the King's Bench prison in Southwark. His father was in Paris when, on the morning of 18 November, a letter bordered in thick black was delivered to him on his breakfast table. It was from Kellner, informing him of what had taken place. 'It is very distressing to me', he wrote, 'to see him in such a situation, the associate of persons but little removed from thieves and forgerers, in a cold damp room without any comfort or decency around him . . .'

Anglesey was unmoved. His patience had been tried once too often.

> 'All my kindness and forbearance has ever been thrown away upon him, and he has never made one effort to leave off his extravagance and disgraceful habits, but goes on defrauding everyone who has the folly to be deluded by his baseness and utter contempt of truth. I give him up. He is hardened in iniquity and lost to all sense of shame, and the feelings of a Gentleman and Man of honour.'

He ended this letter, written to Thomas Beer, who had now succeeded John Sanderson as his chief agent, 'The subject sickens me. I can write no more.'

Rimell's prosecution of William opened the floodgates, and others followed suit. Because he found himself faced with at least sixteen such prosecutions, and the probability of subsequent prolonged detention, William finally decided to take advantage of the Insolvent Debtors Act. The procedure for this was as follows. First, Notice of Intention had to be published in the *London Gazette*. Then a Schedule, on oath, of all debts had to be produced in the Debtors' Court within a given time. Creditors, or indeed any person on payment of a shilling, were now free to inspect the Schedule. Needless to say, the Schedule drawn up by William, under the auspices of yet another solicitor, a man of doubtful reputation called Mr. Hamer, was wildly inaccurate, setting the total amount of his debts at no more than £5,300. For a start it failed to take into account any of the money which had been forwarded by his father, a sum which now amounted to at least £15,000.

'To take the benefit of the Insolvent Act', wrote Anglesey to Thomas Beer on 2 January, 1837, 'is so atrociously horrible, so cruelly unjust towards his dupes, that I am horrified at the idea. There seems a sad want of honourable and just feeling towards me that the £15,000 he has had from me is not noticed, but I do not mind that. It disgusts me, but it should not prevent me from making one further effort to reclaim him, if ... you advise it, and can devise some means of preventing him from practising further frauds upon tradesmen and dupes from whom he has obtained money...'

In his somewhat curious willingness to bail William out yet again, Anglesey may have been moved by another serious consideration. It was clear that the Schedule of Debts was so inaccurate that to produce it and swear to it in court would be perjury and could lay William open to a criminal charge, with consequent disgrace, the loss of his naval commission and a possible prison sentence. Beer evidently thought it best to get him out of the country as quickly as possible. He scribbled on a memo, 'Send him to Ostend. Enquire about steam boats. Can he be got off on a Sunday?'

With the help of the trustees, headed by his sister Augusta's husband Lord Templemore, the detaining creditors were paid off and William was extricated from the King's Bench. But before he had time to congratulate himself on his good fortune, he was presented with the following list of stipulations, drawn up by the trustees and approved by his father, which required his signature:

1. A solemn pledge that Lord William Paget will immediately upon being released from Prison go abroad and reside there upon his present yearly income of £680; but such residence shall not be either at Paris or Boulogne or any other place to which Lord Anglesey may take exception.

2. That he will give a devout promise of total reform.
3. That he will not incur more debts.
4. That the present allowance of £500 per annum from Lord Anglesey (part of the yearly income of £680) be put under control for the purposes of maintaining Lady William Paget and her children; and that Lord William shall give up all control over at least four fifths of it.
5. That if the aforegoing stipulations, or any one of them, be broken on the part of Lord William, Lord Anglesey will not only not pay another shilling of debt, but will withhold the said allowance of £500.

Why they seriously believed that his signature on a piece of paper would make his word more valid is a mystery. On 27 January 1837 William scrawled his name across the bottom of the document.

The next question was where William should go and live. Lord Templemore suggested 'Dresden, and Baden and parts of Germany highly spoken of for the '*cheapness* and *respectability*'. Lord Anglesey had merely banned Paris and Boulogne and various other places. William himself favoured Berlin or Potsdam, where his sons could be educated at a military academy and enter the German service. But the importance of his leaving the country was paramount and thus, even though no decision had yet been reached, on 16 February William sailed for Brussels where he wished to dispose of the house he had had there in 1835. He was to await orders.

By the time William heard that his father had chosen Pau, at the foot of the French Pyrenees, as his son's place of residence he was already in trouble again. When he left Belgium in 1835 he had apparently also left behind many creditors, and they were now seeking to have him put in gaol, which they thought his family would do anything to avoid. A solicitor in Brussels, a Monsieur Allart, was appointed by the trustees to cope with his affairs, with instructions to advance the necessary funds to get him out of the country with his family. Before this could happen William decided to escape to Chantilly, and on 17 May Allart wrote to Beer:

'It is of the most urgent necessity that you decide to come forward for the payment of the household debts. On all sides the creditors are crying out – already writs are out and, not-withstanding all my efforts, I fear that considerable expenses have been incurred. They know that my Lord is gone, and that he will not return again – they think that my Lady will follow him, and on all sides are coming tailors, bootmakers, butchers, bakers, etc, who mean to give publicity to all that has passed...'

But William's wife fell ill, and he was forced to return to Brussels. He managed to avoid arrest only by giving a solemn promise to the President of the Belgian Courts that he would not leave the country again before his debts were all settled. By July the President's patience was exhausted, and once again the threat of arrest loomed large. Lady William's carriage had to be sold to raise money to pay lawyers for her husband's defence. When her health deteriorated, and she had to go off to a Spa, William immediately pawned the few trinkets she had left in order to pay Allart, and retain his services.

As for the move to Pau, William prevaricated and three times changed his mind before Anglesey, in exasperation, took a firm line in a letter to Beer:

'Someone of weight and respectability should go to Brussels to *see* Lord and Lady William *off* to *Pau*, for which journey I authorise you to furnish the means. I will not listen to any other arrangement, and, if that is not carried instantly into effect, I peremptorily declare that I will not have any further communication whatever with Lord William...'

For this purpose Beer appointed Nicholas Weinhert, an Attorney with a large practice among foreigners in England. Before leaving for Brussels he was given strict instructions that should any act of William's make his task impracticable, then he should return home at once. On 21 August Weinhert reported from Brussels that William was willing to leave the city. The President of the Courts had been approached and had agreed that, providing all debts were settled, he would ensure that William's departure was not prevented by creditors. Weinhert wrote to say that William 'expressed himself truly sensible of his father's kindness in relieving him on the present occasion, and assured me of his serious determination in future to do all in his power to merit Lord Anglesey's approbation.' The letter had the usual sting to its tail. 'Since I wrote to you last I have found I was mistaken in supposing the amount of debts to be paid would not exceed the sum you imagined ... you will perceive the necessity of extending my credit ... to the extent of £700 to £800 more'.

William and his family set out for Pau on the morning of 24 August, leaving Weinhert to clear up the mess. He very soon discovered the kind of double-dealing he was up against. On 30 August he wrote to Beer:

'I am extremely sorry to have discovered a gross deceit on his part with regard to his horses, of which it appears he had altogether four, and which he said were held by some of his creditors and would be applied in liquidation of his debts, whereas I found that they were in a stable at his own disposal and that, on the very eve of his departure, he disposed of them to various persons without my knowledge, and put whatever he may have received in his own pocket...'

Such duplicity seemed to Beer sufficient reason for suspending any further dealings on William's behalf, but Weinhert felt obliged to finish what he had started, especially since he had given his assurance to the President of the payment of all debts. Lord Anglesey sent the extra £800.

Meanwhile William's journey to Pau was punctuated by all sorts of delays, invariably to do with lack of money. A letter written to Weinhert from Bordeaux shows William to have been suffering from acute paranoia about his situation: *I have always been left to struggle in the dirt!* and *always* shall be. *Good care will be taken of that ...*' It was not till the beginning of October that the family finally reached their destination, from where William wrote, somewhat cheekily:

'Here we are! we have taken the *only* vacant house in the town at the enormous rate of £136 per annum – without any exception we find it the most expensive place we have lived in since we were married – But I have obeyed orders!'

With William now safely at Pau, and with the chance of redeeming himself in the eyes of his family by quiet and economical living, the settlement of his affairs continued. In the summer of 1838 Lord Anglesey decided to take on and pay for the education of his eldest grandson, provided he was given complete control over the boy, a stipulation to which William readily agreed. Anglesey also, through a letter written to William by a friend of his, Sir William Gossett, reiterated that he was always ready to receive his son back into the fold:

'Lord Anglesey, although he will not communicate direct with you, has not abandoned you – I can promise that his heart yearns towards you ... to renew that bond of union which naturally exists between father and child. But ... this cannot be effected by professions and promises ... Acts and acts alone can restore you to that position which it would give me the greatest possible pleasure to witness.'

It comes as no surprise to learn that events did not follow the course that all had so earnestly wished for. On 26 August, 1839, William once again stood upon English soil, a direct breach of the stipulations. He came bearing the news that he and his wife had separated. He imparted this to Beer in an interview in which he also told him that his intention was now to 'seek employment in the Merchant Service ... to get a service at Sierra Leone, where generally the return ship carries news of the death of those who go there – which will be welcome intelligence in a certain quarter.' Beer went on:

'He then broke into a violent strain against his father and his family – that the former had loaded him with abuse and infamy – and had entertained the idea of confining him in a madhouse – that he never intended his debts to be settled, but kept a portion hanging over him ... and in short would neither listen nor believe anything to the contrary ... he mentioned also ... that I was quite at liberty to tell his father that he had separated from Lady William, that he would not go again to Pau, that he would not be dictated to as to where he should live, that Lord Anglesey could only withdraw the pitiful allowance placed monthly at his command, and that he defied him! That he did not wish his necessary debts to be settled or any more of them to be paid, he would manage them himself and act for himself henceforward; and that he would listen to nothing thro' any medium of communication whatever, but if Lord Anglesey would see him – only for a few minutes – and allow him to explain himself personally to him, to receive from him the assurance that he did intend and had always intended to assist him, he could not say what effect *that* might have upon him.'

36

Strong words, and they evoked from his father a strong reaction. He wrote to Beer on 1 September:

'Your letter has shocked and distressed me amazingly. Yet God knows I *ought* to have been prepared for mischief whenever Lord William's name came before me. He is certainly sent as a curse instead of a blessing to his family, which he has never ceased to disgrace. Here is the finale of a clandestine marriage contracted against the advice and remonstrance of all! At the moment when I had hoped that he was losing his evil ways, and that there was a faint prospect of reform, he comes and as it were intentionally destroys in one breath all further hope ... He *must* now take the consequences of his unworthy acts. I can help him in no way whatever ... I will *not* see Lord William. I had been looking forward with anxiety to the moment when I might again take him to my heart – but now it is impossible. After his peremptory decision to submit to no dictation it is forced upon me to discard him ... He has been so long incorrigible that I believe him capable of coming to England (from which he had bound himself in honour to absent himself until he had my sanction to return) to court incarceration for the mere purpose of distressing his family still further ...'

Beer told Lord Anglesey that William had seemed 'desperate' when he had seen him, a state of mind that was due, partly to his separation from his wife, which was the result of 'temper shewn by Lady William to some act of Lord William's', and partly to a renewal of hostilities from certain creditors, some of whom were 'a little savage', since his return to England. This was further borne out by the man with whom William lodged while he was in London, a Mr. W. H. Douglas. This gentleman informed Beer that William's health was at times in an alarming state:

'he becomes worked up to such a pitch of excitement that the first symptoms of delirium tremens has shewn itself.'

Douglas also suggested to Beer that, if William's father were to order him to return to Pau at once, he was sure that he would do so without delay. This is exactly what Anglesey did, yet again showing his generosity with a postscript to his letter to Beer:

'If to get him back to Pau, a little money is necessary, *lend* it to him yourself, and I will bear you harmless, but do not let it come from me. I must appear inexorable.'

William got no further than St. Malo. Here he received a letter from his wife expressing her willingness to see him with regard to a reconciliation, but warning him under no circumstances to return to Pau, where he would face instant arrest by creditors. It appeared that when he had left Pau in the summer William had given to these creditors the reason that he was going to England to raise money to pay them. They were now violent in their disappointment.

William thus found himself in the absurd position where he could neither return to Pau nor to England, the settlement of his affairs there having not yet been completed, as he faced arrest in both places. Beer informed Lord Anglesey of the situation on 31 October.

'I am quite at a loss to know', declared Anglesey, 'how to act with Lord William. Every kindness shewn him does but increase his extravagance, his impudence, and his disregard of every honourable feeling and pledge given. I believe him to be without principle and utterly incorrigible. What is the use of paying his debts at Pau? It will only encourage to incur more: he is a real scourge to me... No doubt he will incur other debts at St. Malo, and wherever he goes...'

But William did not stay in St. Malo. Instead, in early November he slipped back into England in secret, hiding himself at the home of his friend Mr. Douglas. Beer was furious when he found this out and, when on Boxing Day William attempted to see him, he refused an interview. William was indignant:

'I called at Uxbridge House this evening for the purpose of seeking an interview with you. The Porter, who (having I presume received his lesson) is always particularly impertinent to me, informed me *you were at home*; on sending my name in, however, he returned and informed me you could not be found. I thought it odd you should be lost in a house, but he persisted in driving me from the door. I wish to know whether it is your intention to give me an interview or not? Of course you will say I threaten you (which I deny) when I tell you that whatever be the consequences to myself, they will be equally disagreeable to Lord Anglesey if you do not... you are all so rude to me as so many bears...'

Soon after William had arrived in England, his wife had also come over, with Lord Anglesey's permission, to stay with her friend Lady Cardigan at Deene Park. In return for this permission, she had promised Anglesey that she would do her best to persuade William to return with her to Pau. They were both still in England at the beginning of 1840 when Anglesey decided to make one last grand attempt to alleviate the financial situation of his son, and to receive him once more into the bosom of his family. Exactly what motivated this move is hard to say. There are various possible reasons. On 13 January Beer had received a letter from William which contained the following plea:

'What I have is enough for existence, but nothing more. As for ever having five pounds in my pocket, or the means of paying a single extra anything beyond meat and bread and a very scanty supply of clothing, it is quite impossible...'

He may have been moved by this account of his son's poverty. It may have been because he felt that Lady William was making a special effort at a reconciliation, or that the settling of William's main debts was proceeding well enough to allow some room for hope.

Whatever the reason, on Sunday 16 February Anglesey summoned a 'solemn meeting' at Uxbridge House, with as many members of the family present as could be gathered together. They were Lord Arthur Paget (brother), the Hon. Berkley Paget (uncle), Lord Anglesey, Lord and Lady William, and, of course, Thomas Beer. Judging from the minutes of the meeting it must have been a painful occasion.

Anglesey opened the proceedings by stating 'some unpleasant truths'. After reminding the assembled company of what an 'improvident' marriage William had made, he 'recapitulated, in general terms, the dissolute and extravagant course of life which Lord William had led for many years past'. This catalogue of infamy ended with the fact that since 1830 the staggering sum of £26,916 had been paid to William in favour of his debts, or the equivalent of almost three times his inheritance.

'What right had he to expect this? Or that his extravagance should be fed at the expense of his brothers and sisters, and towards whom it were injustice to allow it. Promises had been made by Lord William, and on the last occasion, when taken out of the Bench, they were most solemnly made, but, as usual, broken. Again he has incurred debts at Pau, to the extent of upwards of £500 and had left his residence there, and come to England against his father's wishes.

And now this is what I will do – and for the last time, I here declare it most solemnly. Lady William asked some short time ago for an additional £20 per annum, on the score of house rent being high at Pau. I will increase that to £100 per annum, in addition to the present allowance of £500 – and I will pay the debts at Pau to the extent stated – nay I will go further and call them £600. This will put Lord William once more free at Pau, with an income of £780 per annum (including his half-pay of £180) having only himself, his wife and two children at present to maintain ... This is what I will do, in the hope yet of reformation: but I repeat it is all I will do – indeed that I can do – in justice to myself and others.'

Anglesey then approached his son, who had sat, head bowed, throughout the meeting, and said: 'And now, William, I will take you by the hand once more'. He then kissed him, saying: 'I freely forgive you all your past conduct in the hope you will yet prove worthy of my affection and regard'. And thus the meeting ended.

On the following day, 17 February, Lord and Lady William returned to France, and on 23 March Beer received a letter from Lady William in which she said:

'I think I can say with confidence that Lord Anglesey will never again have to find fault with Lord William. He seems quite changed, and I really believe having seen his father has had an effect on him which nothing else could have had ...'

On 7 April she reported that she had settled all the debts at Pau. William signed a document detailing the debts with the words:

'*nor will he ever again draw, or accept a bill, or give a cheque, either for himself or any other persons, without the knowledge of having funds to pay it*'.

This pledge delighted his father, and the reconciliation seemed complete.

But it was impossible for William to stay put for long. In October he returned to London to ask his father's permission to remove himself and his family from Pau, either to the north coast of France, or to England. The reason he gave for this was that he was very disturbed by the political instability of France and the possible emergence there of forces stronger than the King, Louis Philippe, and his government. He emphasised that he did not mind remaining at Pau himself, but he wished certainly to remove his family. His father considered this to be nonsense, and ordered him to return to France, unless he could suggest some place which would cost him less. It was a shortlived return. War clouds were gathering in the East, and when the news of the bombardment of Acre in Syria reached his ears, William was immediately on the way back to London, filled with fears of war sweeping across Europe, and the possibility of becoming a prisoner. The family followed in his footsteps. They moved to 51 Portland Place, and never returned to Pau.

In June 1841 William managed to get himself adopted as MP for the borough of Andover, a position which necessitated his remaining in England. It also put him beyond arrest. He wrote of his success to his father, whose reply suggests that the reconciliation had not been going as well as it might have.

'You are relieved from present arrest, and my dire apprehension is that you will launch out into new extravagances and follies ... I received and behaved to you with the warmest affection – and what was the return? How did you quit my house? What acts were you in the commission of all that time?, and how were you grossly misrepresenting me? For shame, for shame, my dear William. Your whole course and career seems to have been one of insanity ... And why am I thus writing to you? ... my poor son, it is in distress and pity for your sad errors ... that I may at length open your eyes to the folly – to the impolicy – to the wickedness of your conduct, and finally reclaim you, and again possess you as a cherished son...'

The 'acts' to which his father referred in this letter were simply the cases of more and more creditors which kept appearing, and whose debts William had said nothing about. He had also run up large debts over his election expenses, some of which involved yet another solicitor, a Mr. Joseph Bebb. In July William had written to this gentleman telling him that his father had promised to meet his expenses up to £200, but that as he was out of town it was impossible to get a cheque out of him. He had asked for £50, which Bebb had foolishly advanced in return for a Bill of

Exchange, payable by Lord Anglesey within fourteen days. Needless to say, when the time came, this was refused by Anglesey, who had never given any such promise.

In October, once again driven beyond the limits of his patience, Anglesey took the toughest line yet. On receipt of a claim from his brother-in-law, Lieutenant-Colonel, the Hon. Edward Cadogan, for the repayment of £120, loaned to William in Pau in 1839, he wrote to Beer:

'I shall take the only course to make him *feel* that I will be no longer trifled with. I desire you to put my annual allowance to Lord William under stoppages in the way of instalments, until the debt is liquidated, and to inform Lord William that this is the course that I shall in future pursue. I know of no other chance of checking the dishonourable practices of Lord William'.

William's reaction to this step was whining self-pity. 'I am afraid Lord Anglesey cannot look with mercy upon anything I do.'

These words evidently stung his father:

'It is very unfortunate that with all the sacrifices I have made for you, and wth all the efforts I have made to conciliate you (but accompanied at the same time with such comments upon your conduct as I felt it my duty as a parent to make) they should invariably have been met with ingratitude and reproach. Is it possible that you should think so lightly of a debt of honour claimed by a friend, as to pass his application by unnoticed, and to think you are ill-used by me in enforcing the payments out of your allowance? ... I have no angry or hostile feelings against you, but I have those of deep-rooted sorrow. I beg you for your own good, calmly to look back upon your whole conduct for many years past, and also calmly to look upon all that I have done for you ... Yet what have I gained by all this? Twice after complete forgiveness you flew from my house without the slightest shadow of reason! Call to your recollection the way in which you have misrepresented and maligned me. The language you have held about me! And how have I taken this? Did this exclude you from my roof? Were you less well received than if you had ever been my solace and my comfort? Never – I received you with open arms, and see the result! I suffered in all this for you, and not for myself, for I felt confident that my character could not suffer by what you have said of me – I will add no more, but give you my blessing, hope for amendment, and pray that your heart and spirit may be so softened as to make you anxious to live upon decent terms with your affectionate father...'

But Anglesey's words were wasted, for William never read this letter. He admitted to Beer, on 30 November, that:

'I have *never dared to break the seal* of his last letter to me – I felt sure that it must contain a well-deserved rebuke for the improper remarks I made ... I love my father better than anything in the world; *better than my children*, whom I worship, but I am driven half mad when he rows me, and when I allow my violent temper to get the better of me, I would say or do anything ...'

Anglesey stuck rigidly to his decision to put William's allowance under stoppage. As more and more debts came to light his whole attitude hardened. The 'distress and pity' which he had once felt for his son gave way to an unrelenting sternness. The result was that by 1843 William's finances were at their lowest ebb. He was living at the White Bear Hotel in Piccadilly, from where he wrote to Beer on 28 February:

'Will you ask Lord Anglesey to be so good as to give me £10 – I want some clothes, I am literally in rags. I would not ask for it if I did not want it very bad'.

A plea at the end of June for his allowance to be regranted fell on deaf ears:

'My Lord, all I can say is that your allowance is under stoppage ... and will remain so until the debt owed to Captain Travers is repaid [A naval captain who had lent William £23.6.8.] and then there is the debt to Monsieur Delage [a tailor from Pau to whom William owed £100 for clothes and for cash advanced] and Mr. Copeland [William's naval agent to whom he owed £80] also to be liquidated in like manner ...'

In August more unpaid bills forced William to leave the White Bear Hotel. It later transpired that in the thirty-seven weeks that he was living there, he had never paid his landlady, Mrs. Ball, a single penny. He moved into lodgings at 238 Oxford Street, from where, on 8 September, he made another desperate plea for money:

'I beg to call your attention to the fact that I have now been some months with any means at all of paying for my *very humble* lodgings and *very humble* daily fare. May I hope that under all the circumstances of my distress and sorrow (for really I am almost broken-hearted) you will feel authorised to advance me ten pounds? God knows it is only for the necessaries of life I want it ...'

The money was not forthcoming. In a letter to Beer, written at this time, the solicitor Joseph Bebb painted a pathetic picture of William's existence:

'I can answer for this last four months having been a punishment almost sufficient for any deserts; lodgings up three pair of stairs, a chop or steak and pint of porter for his almost daily meal, and without the Marquis's countenance and not a shilling in his pocket: I scarcely thought at times that his Lordship was safe from committing self-destruction...'

William's self-imposed privations were made less easy to bear by a new shadow that had crept slowly into his life. This was a mounting suspicion that his wife was being unfaithful to him. His suspicion had first been aroused in June of 1841 by an anonymous letter he had received from Pau, stating that his wife had been carrying on an affair with a Frenchman called Hamel, while he had been absent from Pau in the autumn of 1839. Lady William had admitted this to have been true, and after a short separation William had forgiven her. Then in April 1843 rumour had reached his ears of a flirtation she was said to be enjoying with a certain Lieutenant Packenham, whom she had met while staying with her brother and sister-in-law, the Duke and Duchess of Richmond. Although this seems to have been fairly innocent, no more than the occasional walk home from church, and the odd exchange of letters, William was furious and forbade any further correspondence with Packenham, ordering her to write to him for the return of all her letters. She refused to do this, showing 'much more violence and abuse ... towards her husband, which induced him to quit his house with a determination never to return to it'.

William did in fact return, on 5 May, though 'with feelings of great general suspicion'. He had placed all the facts of the

Pakenham affair before a friend in London. This friend had told him that, though he saw nothing particularly wrong in Lady William's conduct, he felt bound to tell William that her name 'had been the object of much distressing comment connected with Lord Cardigan...' William was now determined to put his wife's conduct to the test. The opportunity arose when, one morning, she told him that she had been invited to the Opera by Lord Cardigan, and she asked whether she could accept. Seeing that here was his chance to find out the truth, William gave his permission. He then employed a private detective by the name of Winter, a man whom it later turned out was of extremely doubtful reputation, to spy on the couple.

What followed, as described by Winter in a statement to Joseph Bebb, has all the elements of a French farce. Somehow or other Winter had been smuggled into Lady Paget's temporary London house, at 10 Queen Street, Mayfair, where he managed to hide himself under a sofa in the drawing-room to await the couple's return from the Opera.

'Witness then heard Lord Cardigan kiss Lady William, and he asked her how she had liked the Opera – Lady William said "She liked it very much", and asked Lord Cardigan "how he liked it?" Lord Cardigan replied "he liked it pretty well but should have liked it better had he been able to have had closer conversation with Lady William". Witness then heard a noise as of the pulling down of a blind in the front drawing-room... where witness then distinctly heard kissing again – shortly afterwards a hard short breathing and the seeming pressure by persons upon and noise from the sofa – and the rustling of silk as from a lady's dress. Witness had not the slightest doubt in his mind at this time that Lord Cardigan and Lady William were having connexion with each other and witness drew or moved himself forward upon the ground from under the sofa where he lay, and by so doing and altho' upon his belly ... saw the sofa in the front room upon which two persons appeared to be lying, the one on top of the other – distinctly saw the heels of Lord Cardigan's boots as he lay uppermost, and the straps which went under the boots – heard Lord Cardigan get off the sofa and witness returned to his former position under the sofa – Lord Cardigan then said, "There, that's some of the seeds of misery", and he moved about as if adjusting his dress...'

While all this had been going on William had apparently been waiting in Berkeley Square. As soon as he was able Winter escaped from the house and told him all that he had witnessed.

'Lord William', continued the statement, 'at once rushed to the house in Queen Street where Lady William was and upbraided her with the infamy of her conduct and told her how the discovery had been made; for at least ten minutes she was paralysed, sat down deadly pale and never uttered a word. At length Lord William left her, not however without having inflicted personal violence upon her.'

William was quick to seize the opportunities offered by the break-up of his marriage. For one thing it presented an excuse for more outpourings of self-pity.

'It is true I have got into debt', he wrote to Joseph Bebb on 30 October, 'but oh God if my father *could* know the life of *jealousy* and *misery* those *demons* have led me, he would not wonder I had done everything. *To live* all day and nights, to keep up a continual state of excitement was my only thought. My Father has said, when I am reformed he will not forget I am his son. *I am reformed.* . . . Wicked, *morally speaking*, I never was. Look how I have brought up my children. Have I ever gambled, drunk or whored? *Never!* Who can say I have? How have I lived for *months* past? What have I eat, what have I drunk, how have I passed my time, and I have had no money for nearly a year from my father, nor any from Lady William's allowance for three months, and if my expenses were now laid before my father, would he not say, "My son is again getting into debt, and leading a 'scandalous life'." No, I am not doing so. I am capable of being anything and everything my father can desire if he will but let me, but I seem on the brink of being ruined, sacrificed, lost, by the most *infamous whore* that ever breathed. But do pray beg of Lord Anglesey not to leave me without a farthing, but to give me an allowance. I cannot do impossibilities, but I can and will do and *am doing* all that is possible, but really I am driven to desperation...'

For another thing he saw a way of making some easy money. He was certain that Lord Cardigan could never bear the disgrace and scandal of a divorce case, and would pay handsomely to keep the whole affair out of court. He thus instituted proceedings for Criminal Conversation against Cardigan. Here he made a foolish mistake, for Cardigan vehemently denied the charge, and elected to defend himself against it. The trial, which was set for December, turned out to be a fiasco. William's entire case rested on the evidence of the private detective, Winter, who failed to turn up, and the trial was thus aborted.

A second trial was set for 27 February, 1844. A few days before, on 22 February, William wrote to Beer: 'am quite worn out with all the anxieties and annoyances I have gone through since August last, and I *really want* a few days change of air and scene. Will you ask Lord Anglesey to be so kind as to allow you to give me a *few* pounds *for that purpose* . . .' His father's reply was short and to the point: 'And you may tell Lord William that he has worn me out, and I can do no more for him.'

Winter did appear to give his evidence in the second trial, but the defence showed him to be an extremely disreputable man. Without so much as waiting for the judge's summing up, and without retiring, the jury returned a verdict for Lord Cardigan. Cardigan's defence lawyer, Sir William Follett, the Solicitor-General, made a public declaration that the sole object of the action had been in reality 'to extract money from a wealthy nobleman'.

William was deeply wounded by the jury's verdict, and par-ticularly by the statement of Sir William Follett, which he described as '*a cruel, wicked, infamous and unfounded charge*'. He wrote a pleading letter to his father, begging him to receive him back into his arms, this time, if not for his sake, then for the sake of his children:

> '*Try me once more!* It is never too late to mend. I have had great difficulties to contend with, of my own seeking, if you will, but withal . . . I am *an injured man*, and God is my witness, as far as Lady William is concerned *a most innocent one*. I will give up (*without any mental reservation whatever*) all my old associates, everyone of them. *Forgive this once*!! and shame and disgrace befall me if I disappoint you. Only don't make me afraid of you, the only thing I do fear! Once more for my children's sake . . . see me and be reconciled to me. *Try me!*'

But Anglesey was now quite indifferent to any appeal from William. The fact that, on top of everything else, his son had publicly dragged the noble name of Paget through the dirt, hardened his heart even further.

'Under present circumstances,' he wrote, 'it is quite impossible for me to replace you under my roof. How often have I not forgiven you, and how often have you not deceived, and even calumnated me. From henceforth I must have long and unequivocal proof of reformation before I can again take you by the hand. At present I am not unhappy to say that it is wholly out of my power to throw a shield over you; and I feel perfectly assured that your presence in my house would close my doors against every friend and relative I have...'

The 'unequivocal proof of reformation' that he so longed for was sadly to be unforthcoming. In a letter dated August 1844 Anglesey spoke of 'a continued recurrence of disgraceful facts quite sufficient to break down even parental affection', a reference to the continued discovery of yet more bad debts and dishonoured cheques. Incredible though it may seem, for, considering his long involvement with William he certainly should have known better, one of these was connected with Thomas Beer. It was Beer's strict rule that William's naval half-pay should never be paid in advance. On 30 March, however, he had received a letter from William asking for his half-pay for the quarter ending 30 June to be paid that very day. He gave the excuse, 'I want to pay for some mourning this evening which I have ordered and will be sent to me'. The mourning in question was for the death of his sister-in-law, Henrietta, Lady Uxbridge, who had died on 22 March. Beer, somewhat foolishly as it turned out, agreed to make an exception because of the circumstances, and advanced him the money as a personal loan. A letter he wrote to William on 6 May reveals the result of this action:

'My Lord, I beg *once* more to remind your Lordship that I have not received any reply to my two or three former letters ... And I have but to observe that, as I cannot afford to lose the money which I have advanced to you, on good faith and promise of repayment in a manner proposed by yourself, I have but one course open – namely to bring the matter under the notice of Lord Anglesey'.

A period had begun in which William's financial and moral state was to sink to a new low. At the beginning of 1845, in spite of his repeated assertion that he would no longer pay any of his son's debts, Anglesey was forced to intervene on William's behalf in order to prevent the ultimate disgrace of his being kicked out of the Navy. This was the result of a threat by a large City wine merchants, Messrs. Young and Co, to whom William had owed a considerable sum of money for many years, to turn over all the papers and correspondence concerning the case to the Admiralty. When Anglesey heard about this, he at once realised that 'the inevitable consequence will be dismissal from the service with disgrace', something that he could not have borne to see.

'From the experience I have had', he wrote wearily to Beer, 'of the total want of principle in Lord William Paget, I have now not the slightest hope of reclaiming him. He seems entirely given up to the most barefaced and vicious courses, and is abandoned by every man of upright character and principle... For once – for the last time – and to save him from being publicly disgraced by being dismissed from the Service, I have ordered this debt to be discharged ... but I hereby pledge myself that I will never again interfere in any way whatever with Lord William's concerns and transactions.'

It is hard to believe that, after so many years of malpractice, William's reputation did not to some degree go before him. Yet people continued to be taken in by his petty deceptions. One can only assume that he had considerable charm, and was expert enough at the hard-luck story to melt the heart of any person that he wished. This is well illustrated by the story related by Monsieur Edouard Vidocq, a high-ranking French policeman, who had been introduced to William in London when they had found themselves fellow guests at the Hotel de Provence in Leicester Square, William had told Vidocq the following tale. The proprietor of the hotel, Monsieur Deneulain, was in desperate financial straits. He had seven children to support and needed five pounds at once to save him from distraint by the bailiffs. If Monsieur Vidocq would kindly lend the money, William would guarantee repayment within two days from the monthly allowance given to him by his father. Moved by this tale of misfortune, Monsieur Vidocq paid up. Four months later he was still waiting for his money. 'I swear to you, my Lord,' he wrote to Anglesey, 'that during the twenty-five years that I directed the French police, I never, by the grace of God, came across an action as vile or as monstrous.'

The year 1846 saw William involved in new and even more

nefarious schemes, which ended in his having to leave the country once and for all. He defrauded a Mr. Charles Lightfoot of Harley Street by undertaking to obtain for him a position in the Commissariat Department for the sum of £300 with an advance payment of £100. Offering to obtain places in government offices in return for money was a highly profitable, though illegal, business. Advertisements regularly appeared in the press inserted both by those who wished to purchase such posts, and by those who had them at their disposal. William took advantage of the fact that his father was Master-General of the Ordnance, and his brother Clarence Secretary to the Master-General, to answer such advertisements as a purveyor of posts in the Ordnance Office. He also inserted his own advertisements, of which the following is an example from *The Times* of 18 September, 1846:

'A gentleman who has influence to obtain situation of £300 per annum legally saleable with a progressive salary would be willing to hear from a young man of good character and business habits. As the appointment must be filled within the present month no one need apply who has not a few hundred pounds at command...'

Between May and September of 1846 William deceived seven different customers by this means, taking altogether £900 for non-existent posts. It was perhaps his most lucrative period, but it did not last long. The net was closing in. To begin with Frederick Winter, the private detective, was pressing William for money which had been promised him in return for his giving evidence against Lord Cardigan. He had apparently been promised £100 a year for three years, and had received only the occasional trifling amount, and various worthless cheques. William realised that Winter knew far too much, and that he would have no scruples about making his knowledge public. Secondly, the Board of Admiralty was now finally pressing to remove him from the Navy. Thus pressurised on all sides, on 7 December 1846 William fled the country to Spain.

As soon as he was out of the way Lord Anglesey stepped in yet again to save his son from the ultimate disgrace of being thrown out of the Navy. On 15 February 1847, he wrote to him in Cadiz, where he had settled:

'You must be aware that all chance of your being again

employed in your profession has now ceased, and that you are precluded from being appointed to a ship. One single course is open to you by which you may, without public exposure, retire from the Service and secure permanent pay. It is that of accepting the retired allowance. This, under your circumstances, is a favour, and I am authorised to offer it to you, and let me implore you to bear in mind that one single further transaction such as those I saved you from suffering by, if again made known at the Admiralty will inevitably entail total dismissal from the Service. It is grievous to be compelled to write to you in such terms, I have always strained every nerve to save you from calamity. I write now in sorrow more than in anger, but I deem it to be my duty for the last time to make you thoroughly acquainted with the situation that your sad course of life has brought you to...'

William's first letter from Cadiz, written to Thomas Beer on 27 April 1847, expressed his desire to turn over a new leaf and his resolve to live within his means 'if enabled to do so'. He asked for his allowance to be paid to him in Cadiz. When he received no reply to this letter, he wrote again on 7 May repeating his request. This letter soon developed into a long ramble, philosophising on his own past troubles, and he finished with a reiteration of his desire to reform:

'I beg of you once more to assist in affording me the means of living peacefully and quietly and if such be done I shall give no further cause for complaint. I do not ask to be believed. I have often promised what I did not perform, but it is no reason why I should not do so now. Time will shew...'

As if in an attempt to arouse his father's compassion, he followed this up the next day with an account of the miseries of exile:

'I have been nearly three months here, with not one human being to converse or associate with. I dine I breakfast I walk I pass all my days and hours *alone*, oh, if you knew what it was to be *alone* as I am it is horrible, but I bear up as well as I can...'

Not 'wishing to put any obstacle in the way of so praiseworthy a purpose', Anglesey agreed to William's allowance being paid in Madrid, though he made it quite clear that he saw no reason why he should possibly believe William on this occasion, rather than on any other. 'Perhaps my father will be less disposed to doubt my resolve,' commented William, 'when I assure him that it is not for any love I bear to him but for my own personal comfort and convenience that I propose to adopt this moral course.'

Three months later, in September, William wrote triumphantly to Thomas Beer:

> 'I have been in Cadiz now six months and I do not owe a human being sixpence. I have not drawn a bill or a cheque, or borrowed a farthing or had any pecuniary transaction of any kind, directly or indirectly with any person ... and I am *saving money! I do not intend* that you should shew this letter to Lord Anglesey, nor the next at the same period, nor the next, but *when* I shall, with the same truth, have been able to make such a communication to you for, perhaps the sixth time, say, in three years, perhaps my father will then believe that I *am* reformed and as unwilling to do anything to displease and shock him as I have (under the influence of a set of villains, whose heads were better but whose hearts were worse than mine ever was) been indifferent to it heretofore. The past *cannot* be recalled, but for the future *he may rely*. I am naturally weak, I believe, but I feel I *can* be as determined for good as I have proved myself too often obstinate for evil.'

Difficult thought it must have been to believe, William did seem to be making a serious effort to control his spending. He certainly impressed his father enough to have his allowance increased, in April 1848, by £200 a year. He expressed himself to be 'completely overcome' by his father's kindness, reaffirming his determination to keep on the straight and narrow.

> 'I believe I know however the only return which can be really acceptable to him, and that is not to be conveyed in words, but by conduct. Well! it is not more certain that I am alive to make the assertion that he will *never again* hear of me to my prejudice.'

> 'Tell Lord William,' wrote his father to Beer, on being shown this letter, 'that I am so happy to learn he sees and feels the error of his ways, and devoutly hope it may lead to a total reform in his conduct, that I am willing to believe him sincere in his present professions of amendment – and that he may rely upon it, my kindness will keep pace with his repentance...'

A THORN IN THE FLESH

The next two years passed quietly enough, with William apparently sticking to his resolution. His only requests for money were to do with his health, an additional £10, for example in July 1849, in order that he might go to a Spa to take the mineral baths for his rheumatism. He was quick to add, however, that 'should my request be deemed unreasonable the thing itself is of no consequence whatever, and my bones can go on aching a little longer.' In March 1850 the money was required for a more serious reason. William wrote that he had to go to Madrid 'for advice in a surgical case'. When his father heard of this he was clearly distressed, and wrote a touching letter to his son, the first for many years not directed through Thomas Beer.

'My dear William, I grieve to hear of your suffering. I have sent Mr. Beer to Drummond's with a request that they will immediately place in the hands of Mr. Shaw of Cadiz, twenty-five pounds for your use, and when you arrive at Madrid, I shall be glad to hear that you are going on well. The use of chloroform is now so generally known, that in the case of an operation being performed, I should hope that you would have the benefit of it. Be assured that whilst you conduct yourself prudently, and without producing scandal, and thereby an injury upon your name and family, you need not have any scruple in addressing me. Long and severely as I have suffered on your account my affections towards you have never been deadened, and I have hoped and prayed for your reformation, and consequent restoration to favour. Alas! Alas! You have rendered it impossible that there should be personal communication, as your return to this country cannot be looked for: but do not imagine that you are totally cast off and forgotten, but believe that I take a lively interest in your welfare *here* and *hereafter*, and that nothing could give me greater happiness than to be certain that your health would be restored, and with it your spirits, and that sincerely repenting of your sad career (*and it is never too late to do so*) you are thereby obtaining a perfect calmness of mind and resignation to your fate, and a well-grounded hope for the future ... God bless you.'

The strain of living in permanent exile was now beginning to take its toll. Despite his brash assertions that he had no wish ever to return to England, William was obviously a deeply unhappy man. In December 1850 he wrote to his father asking to be allowed to change his residence:

'I am weary of my life here, and would fain change the scene. Sometimes I think of going to sea, to Barcelona or Malaga, or some other Spanish port in the Mediterranean, and sometimes I think of spending a year or so in Madrid ... I am *very*, *very* unhappy as I must needs be, and who can help me? but I look forward to an entire change of scene and faces as in some degree likely to improve my spirits, which are indeed sometimes fearfully depressed.'

Lord Anglesey's reply was the very embodiment of Victorian morality:

'I am very sorry to hear so bad an account of your health and spirits: but alas! I have no comfort to give you ... you must know that it is wholly out of my power, or indeed that of any human being, to restore you to the situation you have unhappily lost in Society, and your only resource is, without giving way to any weak feelings of despondence, to make peace with your God – to trust to his mercies, and to conduct yourself with entire submission to what is inevitable. I feel a perfect conviction that such a course as *that*, *steadily persevered in*, (and such a course alone will effect it) you will recover your spirits and with them your health.'

These words were evidently of little comfort to William, whose depression seems to have increased by the month. In May 1851 he wrote:

'I am well in health, but so greatly changed that persons who see me daily are shocked to see me ... My *troubled spirit* is my punishment here but it presses hard and sore upon me – think you that for now nearly five years I have *lived alone*, this *sounds* nothing but taken *literally* and *truly it is dreadful* and enough almost to deprive a man of his reason. There are in my house five other lodgers, they and I have without a change inhabited this house for two and a half years, yet so help me God I have never sat down to breakfast or dinner with them *once*, nor ever exchanged a word with them beyond the civilities of the day. *I live alone* day and night in a frightful solitude and instead of seeking to make it otherwise I avoid all connection or communication with anybody who could throw in my teeth what now cannot be undone, and can only be deeply repented of; and oh how deeply how sincerely do I repent apart from all selfish and interested motives to have thrown away the blessed advantages you have heaped upon me all my life.'

In the face of these pathetic outpourings his father, whose heart was long hardened by years of despair, merely repeated his assertions that William should search his own soul. But it was all in vain. In October William was in trouble again. First of all a Spaniard named Jose Fernandez wrote to Lord Anglesey claiming to have lent William £200 which had not been repaid. At the same time he also received a long, rambling account from William of how he had been blackmailed by an Englishman who had threatened to expose his past to his acquaintances in Seville, where he was now living. He had finally paid this man off with £20 which he had had to borrow, in order to avoid being 'morally destroyed'. He begged his father to pay off this debt, for otherwise, he said,

'I am a man wholly without expenses of any kind ... to this all Seville can testify. I have never been seen on horseback or in a carriage or theatre; I have no expenses of house or women ... it has always been so here, and this after more than thirty years of relentless extravagance of every sort and kind.'

But William had lied too often for his father to believe him.

'You have so often deceived me that I should be a fool to have faith in any thing you state. Yours has been an almost uninterrupted life of misery to all your family and disgrace to yourself. Kindness and repeated forgiveness is lost upon you. I dread the appearance of your handwriting for it never fails to disclose something which *must* give me pain...'

As for the £200 owed to Fernandez, he was adamant:

'I totally decline to have anything to do with it, and I desire you to understand that if I hear any more of your malpractices, I shall cease to have any further communication with you.'

He signed the letter 'Your afflicted father'.

From now on William sank back into his old ways, constantly

asking for money, and running up debts. A memorandum written by Lord Anglesey on 30 January, 1852, tells the whole story.

'The allowance I make to Lord William Paget is more by £100 a year than to any other of my younger children. I have moreover his sons in charge, to whose maintenance he does not contribute one shilling. I have also very frequently paid large sums of money for him. In justice to the other members of my family, I have received note of a bill drawn on Messrs. Drummonds which has been referred to me for payment – I decline to do this; and peremptorily determine never again to advance any money for him, beyond the stipulated allowance...'

But Anglesey's threats appear to have been as empty as his son's promises. In September, for example, we find endorsed, on a letter from William asking for £5, the words, 'This unhappy youth is incorrigible! Alas! Let him have it!' One cannot but wonder whether the story might have been different had he simply refused to pay years before.

During the period that followed, William suffered from a variety of illnesses. On each occasion he asked for money, and his father invariably paid up. It is more than probable that William saw in this an easy source of cash. Certainly in one letter, written from Valencia on 7 July, and in which he complained of a fever 'for which I had been bled ten times,' and which had been 'succeeded by a violent and obstinate bowel complaint,' he was quick to add that 'although much better, I am subject on the slightest occurrence to a return of the most violent and distressing disorder.'

Unfortunately for William his demand for £20 arrived at a time when his father had more important things on his mind. He was grief-stricken by the death of his wife Charlotte on 11 July. William's letter of condolence was one of the few communications between him and his father which contained not a single reference to money.

Lord Anglesey survived his wife by no longer than nine months. He died after a stroke, on 29 April, 1854, aged eighty-six. Six days later he was given the honour of a full State Funeral. 'It is questionable,' commented *The Times*, 'whether on any previous occasion so many immediate relatives and connections followed the head of a family to his last home.' There was one son, however, who did not attend.

At almost the very time that his father was being buried, William, who had not yet heard the sad news, was writing him his last letter.'

'I write to ask you to be so good as to give me twenty pounds more than my allowance on the first of June. I propose on the second to leave Valencia, and I desire to do so as your son should do – without leaving *a single farthing of debt* behind me ... I have always before me your advice to be *humbled* and resigned, and I am truly *humbled, penitent* and *resigned*, and God knows I need all my strength to combat against the sad and painful recollections which are forced upon me, by the sterling events which are taking place with our fleets, but if it is not a consolation, for me, it is something, to feel sure, as I do, that my local ailment would perhaps wholly incapacitate me from really active service; but this cannot lessen my poignant griefs and bitter sorrows, for having wasted my now useless life, and blasted all the brilliant prospects placed in my power. May God have mercy upon me, for I am heartbroken ... from your affectionate and grateful son.'

How William reacted when he finally heard the news of his father's death is not known. The mind conjures up a rather sad picture of the lonely exile, cut off completely from his family and friends, facing the reality of the death of the man who had never failed to bail him out. It is hard to believe that he did not shed a tear or two, if only for himself. Only one more letter from William exists in the Anglesey archives. It was written in June to his brother Henry, now the second Marquis:

'I write to you to tell you that fully aware of my altered circumstances, that I have no longer a father to whom to address myself, and knowing that it is not in the order of things for brothers to assist each other, I nevertheless pray for you to enable me to start fair in the new course which is before me and you may rest assured *that I will never trouble you again*. In three years nearly that I am here, I am owing about £529, *not a farthing more*, and it is true that I have nominally that sum monthly; I say nominally because I lose by the exchange *nearly £4* every month. If you would send me fifteen pounds or twenty pounds, you would perhaps have made me richer and given me more peace of mind than when upon former occasions you have given me hundreds. I hope your heart will

2. 'I was led astray by drink and bad companions'

be softened towards me, for this once and last time. If I have sinned I have *suffered*, and what more would you. What I ask you for *may be* of little consequence to you, and will certainly *assist me greatly*. From your affectionate and grateful brother...'

On this familiar note the story of Lord William Paget ends. No further correspondence between him and his family exists. Apart from the fact that he is known to have died in 1873, at the age of seventy, the rest of his life is a complete mystery.

2

LOOSE LIVING

> *but when lust*
> *By unchaste looks, loose gestures, and foul talk,*
> *But most by lewd and lavish act of sin,*
> *Lets in defilement to the inward parts,*
> *The soul grows clotted by contagion.'*
> (*Comus: 463–7*, MILTON)

LORD William Paget is the archetypal black sheep. Born into a distinguished family, brought up lacking nothing, and with the prospect of an active naval career ahead of him, he cast aside every opportunity that was laid before him, and chose instead to pursue a course of reckless self-indulgence, leading to his eventual ruin, and a sad and lonely exile. His father put the blame on an improvident marriage. This was only part of the story. The truth is that William was the victim of a system which actively discriminated against younger children, and often encouraged idleness and dissipation amongst their elder brothers: the system of primogeniture.

In the days of the Roman Empire land was considered primarily as the means of subsistence and enjoyment, and by the natural law of succession it was divided equally among all the children of the family, with no distinction made between elder or younger, male or female. But when the Empire fell, and all of Western Europe was overrun by the German and Scythian nations, land came to be regarded as the means not merely of subsistence but of power and protection, and it was then thought better that it should pass undivided from one generation to the next. In those disorderly times every great landlord was like a monarch. His tenants were his subjects, of whom he was the judge and legislator in peace, and their leader in war. He made war according to his own discretion, frequently against his neighbours, and sometimes against his sovereign. The security of a landed estate, therefore, the protection which its owner could afford to those who dwelt on it, depended upon its greatness, and hence on its remaining undivided.

59

The convention of primogeniture thus became established in the succession of landed estates for the same reason that it has generally taken place in that of monarchies. That their power and consequently their security might not be weakened by division, they had to descend entire to one of the children. To which of a man's children, assuming that he had several, so important a preference should be given had to be determined by some general rule which could admit of no dispute. The only indisputable difference among children of the same family is that of sex and age. The male sex was almost universally preferred to the female, and it is usual for the elder to take precedence over the younger.

The land laws which existed in England during the lifetime of William Paget were entirely based on this system, which had been introduced into England by William the Conqueror, and which had continued in force long after the circumstances which first gave occasion to it had disappeared. Under these laws the eldest son was invariably the sole beneficiary of the estate at the expense of the rest of the family, who were expected to fend for themselves on whatever their father was pleased to give them. Thus younger children of the aristocracy such as William who had acquired under their parent's roofs certain habits, tastes, and ideas of style grew up to find that these could not be gratified in later years without running into serious debt. Their education and prejudices, moulded by the rules of society, meant that their portions were rarely turned into capital for merchandise or manufacture. Instead their pittance was more likely to secure them from want, and serve to eke out the meagre incomes of the more aristocratic professions, such as the Church, the Army and the Civil Service, which thus became refuges for the privileged destitute.

But it was not just the younger children upon whom these land laws had such an adverse effect. The common practice of the entailing of an estate by the heir of one generation upon the unborn heirs of successive generations, thereby neatly tying up the property and protecting it from interference of any kind for years after his death, often led to unprincipled and careless land-lords being tenfold more negligent than they otherwise might have been about the education of the child who was to succeed to the ownership of the estate. They knew that however badly the child might be brought up, however extravagant, or reckless or dissipated he might turn out, he could not, however great his folly, lose or lessen the estates or the social status of the family. The land would go undiminished to the next owner mentioned in the deed or will. In this way these laws went a long way to setting up in influential positions, as examples to society, men of luxurious and idle habits, depraved tastes and corrupted morals.

The career of Mervyn Tuchet, Lord Audley, and 2nd Earl of Castlehaven, for example, did nothing to enhance the reputation of the peerage, and brought disgrace upon his family. It ended in May 1631 at the age of thirty-seven with his execution on Tower Hill and the forfeiting of his peerage. At his trial the picture that was painted of life in his household was deeply shocking, even in an age of immorality:

'Never poet invented', said the King's Attorney-General, Sir Robert Heath, 'nor historian writ of any deed so foul. And although Suetonius hath curiously set out the vices of some of the Emperors who had absolute power ... yet none of these come near this Lord's crimes ... they are all of such a pestilential nature that, if they be not punished, they will draw from Heaven a heavy judgement upon this kingdom.'

Lord Castlehaven was twice married. By his first wife Elizabeth, daughter of Benedict Barnham, an Alderman of London, he had six children, three sons and three daughters. He married secondly in July 1624, at the age of thirty-one, Lady Anne Chandos, the widow of Grey Brydges, 5th Lord Chandos, and the eldest daughter of the 5th Earl of Derby. Lord Chandos had died some three years previously leaving Lady Anne with four children to bring up. A reckless, extravagant, and luxury-loving woman, she had not looked forward to the prospect of a penurious widowhood, and had rushed into marriage with the first available husband. Had she, or her mother, the Dowager Countess of Derby, with whom she was living at Harefield, their family estate, made the slightest investigation into the character of Lord Castlehaven they would have discovered his reputation to have been so unsavoury as to make any thoughts of marriage to him quite out of the question.

In the seven years during which she was married to Lord Castlehaven Lady Anne suffered a life of such degradation and overwhelming profligacy that it almost certainly corrupted her, and her eldest daughter Elizabeth, as it did most of the others

3. MERVIN TOUCHET, Earl of Castlehaven

who lived under his roof. It was a story that only came to light in
1631 when the Earl's heir, James, whose education had been
utterly neglected, and his sensibility horrified at scenes he could
not avoid witnessing, 'appealed for protection from the Earl, his
natural father, to the father of his country, the King's majesty.'
The facts he unfolded before the authorities led to his father's
prompt arrest. After a preliminary hearing at Salisbury Assizes,
Lord Castlehaven was brought for trial before his peers, charged
with the crimes of rape and sodomy.

The testimony of Lady Anne bore witness to the indignities
and obscenities of an existence that was scarcely imaginable in
civilised society. Amongst the members of her husband's house-

hold to whom she was first introduced on her arrival after their marriage was a young man named Ampthill. A former page to a certain Sir Henry Smith, he had arrived in the service of Lord Castlehaven with no possessions other than the mare he rode. However during the eight years he served as a page he enriched himself greatly, and was allowed to keep horses in his master's grounds. In fact he eventually ingratiated himself so far as to be able to marry one of Lord Castlehaven's daughters, for whom he had received a dowry of £7,000 and the honour of being allowed to sit at his Lord's table. Another young page in the household was one Henry Skipwith, who was appointed as Lady Anne's personal servant.

At the trial Lady Anne told how, on the second night of her marriage, she and her husband were in bed when Ampthill suddenly entered the room. At this point Lord Castlehaven became somewhat excited and spoke to her 'lasciviously' and told her that 'now her body was his, and that if she loved him, she must love Ampthill; and that if she lay with any other man with his consent, it was not her fault but his; and that if it was his will to have it so, she must obey and do it.' She was thus introduced to an extraordinary life of sexual abandon, in which she was expected at her husband's bidding to sleep with all and sundry. Both Ampthill and Skipwith became her lovers. Not only that; her husband was also in the habit of calling up his other servants to their bedroom 'to shew their privities; and would make her look on and commend those that had the largest.' At one point he even kept a common whore in the house named Blandina. Another page, Lawrence Fitzpatrick, bore witness that 'His house was a common brothel-house, and the Earl himself took delight not only in being an actor, but a spectator while other men did it. Blandina was once abused by himself and servants for the space of seven hours together, until she got the French pox.'

Apparently not content with merely turning his wife into a strumpet for the use of his servants, Lord Castlehaven's attention then fell upon his step-daughter, Elizabeth Brydges, his wife's eldest daughter by her first marriage. In 1628, when she was only twelve, he had her married to his son James, himself a boy of only thirteen. Within the shortest possible time however he had persuaded her to commit adultery with Henry Skipwith by telling her that his son bore her no love, and that he would anyhow rather that she had a son by Skipwith than by any other. He also threatened that if she did not agree to do exactly as he asked he would tell her husband she had slept with Skipwith whether or not it were true. In his evidence Skipwith related how 'she was only twelve years of age when he first lay with her, and that he could not enter her body without art; and that the Lord Audley fetched oil to open her body, but she cried out, and he could not enter; and then the Earl appointed oil the second time; and then Skipwith entered her body, and he knew her carnally.' Another servant, Brodway, told how when Skipwith 'got upon her, the Lord Audley stood by, and encouraged him to get her with child.'

For his services Henry Skipwith was well rewarded. Like Ampthill, he too had come into his master's service quite penniless, being of very poor parentage, but was soon earning £500 a year, and receiving gifts of land, and on one occasion £1,000. These services almost certainly included sexual relations with the Earl. Lawrence Fitzpatrick also admitted under oath that 'the Earl had committed sodomy twice upon his person . . . and that the Lord Audley made him lie with him at Fonthill and at Salisbury . . . and that he heard he did so with others.'

Against this background the exploit that perhaps damned the Earl most may not seem to have been so outrageous. This was the arranging of, and the watching and assisting in, the rape of his own wife. Lady Anne described how Lord Castlehaven 'one night being a-bed with her at Fonthill, he called for his man Brodway, and commanded him to lie at his bed's feet; and about midnight called him to light a pipe of tobacco. Brodway rose in his shirt, and my Lord pulled him into bed to him and her, and made him lie next to her; and Brodway lay with her, and knew her carnally, whilst she made resistance, and the Lord held both her hands, and one of her legs the while; and that as soon as she was free, she would have killed herself with a knife, but that Brodway forcibly took the knife from her and broke it; . . . and she cried out to have saved herself.'

Lord Castlehaven was found guilty on both counts and sentenced to death. On hearing the sentence passed upon him he asked for their Lordship's pardons 'in that he had been so great a stain to honour and nobility.' He was beheaded on Tower Hill on 14 May, 1631. The two servants Fitzpatrick and Brodway were sentenced along with him. At their execution by hanging at Tyburn in July they spoke publicly of the events in which they had been involved, referring at one point to Lady Castlehaven as being 'the wickedest woman in the world'. But if her character was ruined by her experiences, then so was that of her daughter Elizabeth, who was reputed to have become by the age of fifteen such a 'whore' that her husband refused ever to live with her again. (As late as August 1655 Elizabeth is referred to, in a letter from Kenelm Digby to the Earl of Dorset, in a manner which suggests she had not abandoned her dissipated habits: 'Lady Peters and Lady Castlehaven were, by the constable in the common garden, carried to the cage where they lay all night.') Certainly after the trial the Dowager Countess of Derby refused to receive either her daughter or her granddaughter at Harefield, so 'perplexed and afflicted with grief' was she 'in that they have so infinitely offended God, and the King, by their wicked crimes.' She had another good reason. She was already taking care of all of Elizabeth's remaining brothers and sisters, and was especially unwilling to have them exposed to an influence that might possibly have proved corrupting. 'I am fearful,' she wrote to Lord Dorchester, the King's secretary, 'lest there should be some sparks of my grandchild Audlie's misbehaviour remaining, which might give ill example to ye young ones which are with me.'

The Derbys and the Castlehavens did not suffer alone in their shame. The trial had been far too sensational to escape the attention of lewd publishers marketing catchpenny sheets, and no side of the family was spared the mortification arising from the widespread advertisement of the terrible scandal. Lady Anne's sister Frances was married to the 1st Earl of Bridgewater, one of the richest men in England, and his family too felt the disgrace acutely, particularly as he was about to take up his new vice-regal position as Lord President of the Council of Wales. But Lord Bridgewater was cleverly to use the celebrations to honour this appointment to try and repair the reputation of his family.

He commissioned the young writer John Milton to write a Masque, in which his last unmarried daughter Lady Alice Egerton would be seen publicly to act out her resistance to dangerous sexual temptation. Milton knew all about the Castlehaven affair. Some time after the trial he had been commissioned by Lady Bridgewater and another of the Dowager Countess of Derby's daughters, Lady Huntingdon, to write an 'entertainment' for their mother to help take her mind off past events.

He wrote for her, in collaboration with Henry Lawes, the Bridgewater children's tutor, *Arcades*, and it is more than likely that amongst those who performed in it were some of those children of Lady Castlehaven whom the Dowager Countess had taken into her home.

For the Earl of Bridgewater's celebration at Ludlow Castle in September 1634, Milton wrote *Comus*, again in collaboration with Henry Lawes. In the beginning of the Masque three aristo-cratic children, the Lady, the Elder Brother, and the Younger Brother (acted by 15-year-old Lady Alice Egerton, 11-year-old John, and 9-year-old Thomas Egerton) are lost in a wood. The Virgin has become separated from her brothers. She is dis-covered by an enchanter, Comus, who tempts her to drink his magical potion, and to submit to his sexual offers. The Lady easily refuses his temptations because she knows so little about the pleasures described in them. There was no attempt to disguise the identity of Lady Alice. In the Masque her character was glorified and idealised. It was a bold statement to the audience of her absolute purity in contrast with that of her cousin Elizabeth.

Public reaction to the Castlehaven case was one of shock and disbelief. Puritan households were filled with all the indignation of the righteous suppressed. 'It is well yet the land is cleared of so vile a monster,' wrote a friend to Doctor Ward, Public Professor of Divinity and Master of Sidney Sussex College in Cambridge, 'and yet the pack of them is discovered and dissolved. For horrible things are acknowledged to have been commonly prac-tised among them, and much more in likelihood was than is disclosed.' The King ignored a plea from Lord Castlehaven for a pardon. This was because he knew he could not afford to outrage public opinion. Two years previously he had closed Parliament abruptly because its members were attacking his prerogative to raise money as he chose. To pardon a shockingly perverted aristocrat at this particular time would have caused a further outcry. Besides, in many people's minds sexual scandals involv-ing members of the aristocracy, who were still meant to define all virtues and so to exert a superior moral authority over the rest of the population, had for too long gone unpunished.

The popular association of sexual licence with the aristocracy and with the Court had gained great strength during the reign of James I, who ruled over a Court in which morals were loose and drunkenness rife. It is reported by Gardiner in his history of

England that at a feast given by the Earl of Salisbury for King James and his brother-in-law, Christian the Fourth of Denmark, in the summer of 1606, English ladies who were to have taken part in a Masque reeled about the hall in a state of intoxication, and the King of Denmark was carried off to bed when he was no longer able to stand. James also both swelled and debased the ranks of the nobility by the large-scale issue of peerages and, thriving on favourites as he did, surrounded himself with men whose positions were all too often attained through sycophancy and bribery. The resulting atmosphere of moral decay gave birth to an affair of so infamous a nature as to cause untold damage to the prestige and popularity of the Stuart monarchy.

Frances Howard, Countess of Essex, was one of the greatest beauties of the Court. The second daughter of Thomas Howard, 1st Earl of Suffolk, she had been married to Robert Devereux, Earl of Essex, in 1606, at the age of fifteen, an age when she was, wrote Arthur Wilson in his *History of the Reign of James I*, 'too young to consider, but old enough to consent.' The Howards were one of the most ancient and powerful families in the land whose lines dated back to the time of William the Conqueror, and whose influence had been maintained throughout the Tudor reign by a combination of occasional loyal service with restless and unscrupulous intrigue. Charles, Lord Howard of Effingham had commanded the fleet against the Armada in 1588, and was now Earl of Nottingham and Lord High Admiral. Frances's father, Lord Thomas, was a younger son of the Duke of Norfolk. He too was one of the heroes of the Armada, and had earned the gratitude of Queen Elizabeth I, who always referred to him as 'Good Thomas', by bringing his squadron safely back from the Azores in 1591. His younger brother, William, 'Bould Willie', spent a lifetime keeping King James's peace along the Scottish Border. It was services such as these which had kept the family prominent under Elizabeth in spite of the treason of Frances's great-grandfather, the fourth Duke of Norfolk, who was executed for plotting with Mary, Queen of Scots in 1572.

When James I acceded to the throne in 1603, Frances's father was created Earl of Suffolk. He gave up the sea and became a courtier, a move which was to lead to his downfall since, as Lord Chamberlain of the King's household, a post he held till 1614, he succumbed to temptation. Finding himself at the head of a vast patronage, he used it unscrupulously for personal profit. Bribery was rife, and offices were openly put up to the highest bidder. His career in fact ended in disgrace in 1619 when he was accused, fined and imprisoned for gross embezzlement of public funds. His wife was little better. She was notorious for her greed, and had an insatiable appetite for gold, which she spent on jewels and dresses. It was she who generally received those 'presents', amounting to enormous sums of money, which were really bribes to her husband. These were hardly the sort of parents to give any education or sense of responsibility to a young girl, and thus Frances grew up thoroughly spoiled, and used to getting her own way. Yet however bad they may have been, even their sins pale into insignificance compared to those that were to be committed by their daughter.

Almost as soon as her wedding to Essex was over Frances and her new husband were parted. Essex was sent back to Oxford to finish his M.A., and from there went abroad to learn soldiering. Frances, after returning home for a short while, took her place among the great ladies of the Court. Her charm and her 'sweet and bewitching countenance' soon made her eagerly sought after, something that she did not fail to take advantage of in every way. She was, wrote Wilson, the historian who was the Earl of Essex's secretary, 'of a lustful appetite, prodigal of expense, covetous of applaus, ambitious of honour, and light of behaviour.' It was not long before she made her first conquest, becoming the mistress of the Prince of Wales, Prince Henry. Their affair, however, lasted only until the day she set eyes on the man who was ultimately to be the cause of her downfall, and with whom she fell instantly and passionately in love. This was the King's favourite, Robert Carr, Viscount Rochester.

To begin with Rochester, a Scot who came to England on the accession of James I, conscious of the delicacy of his position as Royal favourite, was wary of the dangers of such an intrigue, with the Prince of Wales on one side, and a husband soon due home on the other. What he needed was a confidant to help him carry on the intrigue away from the prying eyes of the Court. For this purpose he engaged a brilliant young man whom he had befriended in Scotland, when he had once served as a page to the Earl of Dunbar. His name was Thomas Overbury. He was a scholar, and a writer of prose and poetry. Rochester himself was an ill-educated man, with little talent for correspondence, and Overbury fitted the bill perfectly. Not only was he able to act as a secret messenger between the lovers, but, according to a letter later written to Rochester by Overbury in 1613, he actually wrote Rochester's love letters for him: 'you fell in love with that woman, as soon as you had won her by my letters.' Overbury also served another purpose. He acted as secretary to Rochester who was employed by the King as a Privy Councillor, and his superior brain was invaluable to the Royal favourite in giving him advice, and helping him trace out his career. For some time the two men were seen to be almost inseparable, and in June 1608 Thomas Overbury was knighted.

Unfortunately for Frances her carefree days of flirting were about to come to an end. Early in 1609 her husband returned, expecting to claim his wife. She had no intention of surrendering to him. The overwhelming passion she bore for Rochester made his advances quite repugnant to her. She had also become accustomed to the gaiety of Court life, and could not bear the thought of life in a lonely country house. She simply refused to go with him, forcing Essex to approach her father, who also ordered her to leave. The situation was further complicated by the fact that Rochester was aware that any kind of open scandal could jeopardise his position with the King. Thus on one side was a husband whom she did not love, who was eager to claim her as his wife, whilst on the other was a lover who might well have dropped her.

Frances attempted to remedy this uneasy situation by the use of witchcraft. In spite of the hideous punishments which faced those who were caught, there were still many practitioners of the Black Art in London at this time who were willing to risk all for the considerable financial profits to be gained from telling the future for Court ladies, or administering love potions. One such specialist was a certain Mistress Turner, a woman who had once held a position in society, but had ruined herself through riotous extravagance and loose living. Frances approached her and promised her any money if she could quench the ardour of Lord Essex, and secure for her the love of Lord Rochester. To assist her, Mistress Turner introduced a more sinister figure into the picture, Doctor Simon Forman, a trained apothecary and self-styled Master of the Magick.

To these two arch-quacks Frances unburdened her soul. Mistress Turner raised her hopes by telling of how, when she herself had desired the love of a certain gentleman at Court called Sir

Arthur Mainwaring, Dr. Forman had given her some powder which, when secretly administered to Sir Arthur, had 'wrought so violently with him, that, through a storm of rain and thunder, he rode fifteen miles one dark night to her house, scarce knowing where he was till he was there.' Dr. Forman, 'to amuse them, frames many little pictures of brass and wax, some like the Viscount and Countess, whom he must unite and strengthen; others like the Earl of Essex, whom he must debilitate and weaken; and then with philtrous powders and such drugs he works upon their persons.' The day finally came when Frances could no longer resist her husband's orders to accompany him home to Chartley. She left the Court in a state of abject misery. 'When she came thither,' wrote Wilson, 'tho' in the pleasantest time of summer, she shut herself up in her chamber, not suffering a beam of light to peep upon her dark thoughts. If she stirred out of her chamber, it was in the dead of night, when sleep had taken possession of all others but those about her.'

In the hours she spent alone at Chartley, Frances schemed at ways of administering all the strange potions which she had smuggled with her from London. No doubt she bribed certain servants to help her, for according to Wilson, 'no linen came near his body that was not rinsed with their camphire compositions, and other faint and wasting ingredients; and all inward applications were foisted on him by corrupted servants to lessen and debilitate the seminal operations.' The powders, however, seemed to do little good, in however great quantities they were administered. 'My Lord is lusty,' she wrote to Forman, 'and merry, and drinketh with his men; and all the content he gives me is to abuse me and use me as doggedly as before.' To Mistress Turner she wrote of how she was also under considerable pressure from her family:

'Sweet Turner, I am out of all hope of any good in this world, for my father, my mother, and my brother all said I should lie with him ... My father and mother are angry, but I had rather die a thousand times over; for besides the sufferings, I shall lose his [Carr's] love if I lie with him ... As you have taken pains all this while for me, so now do all you can, for never was I so unhappy as now; for I am not able to endure the miseries that are coming on me, but I cannot be happy so long as this man liveth...'

Trying to tame the shrew proved too great a task for Lord Essex, and in the winter of 1611 he finally gave up and returned to London. According to Wilson there was a widespread opinion 'that he was not much debilitated, but that she got (by her virtuous agents) an artifice, too immodest to be expressed, to hinder penetration. And thus she tormented him, till he was contented to let her steer her own course.'

Rochester was now at the height of his power. 'Now all addresses are made to him,' wrote Wilson, 'he is the Favourite in Ordinary: no suit or reward but comes by him: his hand distributes and his hand restrains ... the Lords themselves can scarce have a smile without him.' He was also unknowingly being dragged deeper and deeper into the web that Frances was spinning for him. The very fact that he was so afraid of jeopardising his position with a scandal made her even more brazen in her desire for him.

No sooner was she back in London than she was once again in touch with Turner and Forman. She made frequent visits to Forman's house in Lambeth where she took part in various Black Magic ceremonies. The evil apothecary produced strange parchments, upon one of which was fastened a little piece of the skin of a man. In others were written the names of devils who were to be conjured up to torment Rochester should his love for the Countess in any way diminish. In addition to the parchments he prepared other instruments with which to bewitch the Favourite and Lord Essex. There was 'one picture in wax, very sumptuously apparelled in silks and satins, as also one other sitting, in form of a naked woman, spreading and laying forth her hair in a looking-glass.' There were also leaden figures representing Rochester and Frances making love. These spells gave Frances complete confidence that she could ensnare Rochester, which is exactly what she succeeded in doing. He became caught in her 'net of adulation.'

The lovers met wherever they could; at Mistress Turner's lodgings in Hammersmith, for example, and at a house in Hounslow bought by Frances for just such a purpose from Sir Roger Aston. With spies everywhere, however, their meetings remained a secret known only to one man, Sir Thomas Overbury. But Overbury, who had gone into the affair lightly in the beginning, as a means of finding a little amusement on behalf of a friend, now, as he became more involved, began to see that

Rochester was sufficiently serious in this matter as to endanger his reputation and power. He saw also the true nature of Frances Essex, whose obsessive desire for Rochester had turned her into a vicious woman who would stop at nothing to get what she wanted. He began to be afraid of where it all might lead.

Now that Frances finally had Rochester in her power she was more determined than ever to become free of her husband. She touched on the subject of divorce. Although this was extremely difficult to obtain, she knew that her chances were certainly improved by the fact that she had the influence of her own powerful family, the Howards, whom she was confident could be persuaded to support her, and that of her lover, over the King. She had little difficulty in convincing Rochester of the feasibility of this step, since she had almost certainly told him that she had never enjoyed any carnal relations with her husband and thus the divorce could be obtained on the grounds of nullity. Her great-uncle, the Earl of Northampton, who was hand in glove with Rochester, took on the task of winning over her family to the idea. He also approached the King on the subject, at the same time revealing to him his favourite's interest in the affair.

When Thomas Overbury heard the rumours that were beginning to circulate of the proposal of a divorce for Frances Essex, he was horrified. He realised that this was only a preliminary to her marriage to Rochester. At once he made no secret of his feelings to his friend: 'if you do marry that filthy, base woman you will utterly ruin your honour and yourself; you shall never do it by my advice or consent.' He made his opinion of the matter well known in Court circles, and also published a poem entitled 'The Wife', which pointedly praised all the virtues that Frances lacked, and was taken by one and all as a moral lesson for her. When she herself became aware of what he was saying about her behind her back, and of his determination to thwart the divorce in any way he could, she became inflamed with hatred against him. Rochester still believed her to be innocent and virtuous, except in her love for him, but Overbury knew better. She was afraid that if he continued to go about talking scandal, it might put poison into her lover's brain, and turn him from her. There was another even greater danger. The King was merciful towards her, and sanctioned the plea for divorce. But if he were to be made aware that she was not so virtuous as her friends made out, that she had persistently refused her husband's love, and that she had schemed against his health and life, it was certain that James would at once quash the divorce proceedings, and punish her by public disgrace.

In her mind there was only one solution. Somehow or other Overbury had to be got rid of. The first thing she did was to try and have him killed. She offered a bribe of £1,000 to a certain Sir David Woods, a gentleman in attendance on Queen Anne, whom she knew to have a particular quarrel with Overbury, if he would kill him in a duel. When this plan failed she tried another scheme. With the help of Northampton, who needed little persuasion to join in the plot, being exceedingly jealous of Overbury's position, she set about poisoning the mind of her lover against his friend. She said she could no longer endure such open insults as Overbury had spoken against her, and which were an affront to her whole family. If Rochester were not careful he would find Overbury trying to step into his shoes, '"Unless you either curb his greatness, or abate his pride," said my Lord Northampton, "he will in time be your equal in power and greatness."'

The worm turned. A plan was concocted to get Overbury sent to the Tower. It so happened that the King was intending to send Ambassadors to the Low Countries and France, and it was discreetly suggested to him that Overbury might be an ideal choice for such a mission. In the meantime Rochester dissuaded Overbury from accepting such a post, at the same time promising that he would put in a good word for him with the King. On 21 April, 1613, Overbury was officially offered the Embassy of the Low Countries, or either France or Russia. When he refused the post outright, James was so angry that he had him committed to the Tower 'for a matter of high contempt.'

Once she had her enemy safely locked away in the Tower, Frances set about seeing that he should never again emerge alive. She went to Mistress Turner and poured out her vitriolic hatred of Sir Thomas, 'that negro', 'that scum of men', that devil incarnate'. She made it quite clear that she wished to see him die. 'Ay, that he should,' said Mistress Turner, 'and it is pity that he should live to defame so honourable a Lady, so well descended, to the utter disparaging of her house, and that rather than he should pass with life, she would be his Death's man herself.' After a cold-blooded discussion of the various ways and means of accomplishing this, the two women realised that neither of them could do the deed without discovery. They came to the conclusion that the only safe way of bringing about his death was by poison. Dr. Forman having died some time previously, a man called Weston, who had been an apothecary's assistant, and formerly in the service of Mistress Turner's husband, put them in touch with a Dr. Franklin, who was reputed to be exceptionally skilful in the art of slow poisoning. For the promise of a large reward he agreed to supply the poisons, and it was decided that Weston should be employed as the agent to administer them.

Frances had little difficulty in arranging to get Weston a position in the Tower. She approached Sir Thomas Monson, who was the Master of the Armoury, and asked him for a letter recommending Weston to the Lieutenant of the Tower as a suitable servant for Sir Thomas Overbury during his imprisonment. Monson was only too happy to do a favour for such a great lady who was so close to the royal favourite. He wrote immediately to Sir Gervase Elwes, the new Lieutenant, and a friend of Rochester. Suspecting nothing, Sir Gervase made the appointment, and in so doing signed the death warrant of an innocent man.

On the very day of Weston's appointment Mistress Turner went to Dr. Franklin and begged him to provide something 'that would not kill a man instantly, but would be in his body for a certain time, wherewith he might languish away little by little. At the same time she gave him four angels with which he bought some Aquafortis (nitric acid), and sent it to Mistress Turner who, to try the operation thereof, gave it to a cat, wherewith the cat languished, and painfully cried for the space of two days, and then died. Afterwards Mistress Turner sent for Franklin to come to the Countess, who told him that Aquafortis was too violent a water; but what think you (quoth she) of White Arsenick? He told her it was too violent. What say you (quoth she) to Powder of Diamonds? He answers, I know not the nature of that. She said that he was a fool, and gave him pieces of gold, and bade him buy some of that powder for her.'

The first attempt to poison Sir Thomas, on 6 May, 1613, was a failure. On the way to his lodgings with a phial of Roselgar, a green and yellow liquid, Weston was caught red-handed by Sir Gervase. Believing the Lieutenant to be involved in the plot, he blurted out 'Sir, shall I give it to him now?' Sir Gervase, who at this stage knew nothing, asked 'What? Give him what?' To which Weston replied 'Why, Sir, know you not what is to be done?' Sir Gervase then forced a confession out of Weston. Instead of arresting him, however, he kept silent. This was undoubtedly because he was afraid of what might happen to him if he breathed a word to anyone about a plot which, for all he knew, the King himself might be behind. He decided instead to keep a close watch on his prisoner, and if possible to prevent any further attempts on his life.

When Weston returned to Mistress Turner he pretended that he had in fact given the poison to Sir Thomas, and demanded the reward. But she was too clever for him, and told him that there should be no reward until Sir Thomas was dead. Thus fresh poisons were obtained from Dr. Franklin, seven varieties altogether: Aquafortis, White Arsenic, Mercury, Powder of Diamonds, Lapis Costitus, Great Spiders, and Cantharides.

'All these,' Dr. Franklin was to testify, 'were given to Sir Thomas Overbury at several times ... Sir Thomas never ate white salt, but there was Arsenic put in it. Once he desired pig, and Mistress Turner put into it Lapis Costitus. At another time he had two partridges sent to him from the Court, and water and onions being the sauce, Mistress Turner put in Cantharides instead of pepper; so that there was scarce anything that he did eat but there was some poison mixed...'

It is highly unlikely that much, if any, of this poison did in fact get through to Sir Thomas. Had it done so he would surely have died much sooner than he did. What is more likely is that it was intercepted by Sir Gervase, who continued to keep silent. He admitted, for example, that on one occasion, when some tarts and jellies had been sent in for the prisoner, 'I saw them so black and foul and of such strange colours that I did cause my cook to throw them away, and to make other tarts and jellies for him.'

So Sir Thomas lived on, and Frances never gave up. It was a rumour circulating in August that there was a strong possibility that he might be released from the Tower at any time which inspired a final attempt to get rid of him once and for all. She sent for Weston and 'was very angry with him that he had not despatched Sir Thomas Overbury.' A new source of poison was tried. They approached a young man called William Reeve, who was assistant to Dr. Paul de Lobell, the French physician who was in attendance on the prisoner in the Tower. For a reward of £20 he stole from his master a solution of Mercury Sublimate 'and put the same into a clyster mingled with the said poison; and the said clyster the said apothecary . . . did put and minister (as good and wholesome) into the guts of the said Sir Thomas.' This took place on the night of 7 September. On 13 September, after a week of indescribable agony, Sir Thomas Overbury finally died. His death was attributed to natural causes.

While Overbury was dying in the Tower, on the outside the final act of the farce which was the divorce was being played out. The grounds presented were that:

'the said Frances Howard, in hope of lawful issue, and desirous to be made a mother, lived together with the said Robert at bed and board, and lay both naked and alone in the same bed . . . and desirous to be made a mother, from time to time, again and again yielded herself to his power, and as much as lay in her offered herself and her body to be known; and earnestly desired conjunction and copulation. And also the said Earl, in the same time very often, again and again, did try to have copulation, as with his lawful wife, which she refused not, but used the best means she could; notwithstanding all this, the said Earl could never carnally know her, nor have that copulation in any sort which the marriage bed allowed.'

It was even alleged, after an examination by seven great ladies of the Court, that Frances was a virgin.

The whole matter stank of a conspiracy rather than a trial. Certainly the Archbishop of Canterbury, Dr. Abbott, a man of great honesty, was deeply suspicious of the truth of the evidence that was brought forward. It upset him deeply that the King was bringing all his influence to bear to force a favourable outcome of the trial for his favourite. He pleaded with James to throw the case out of court.

'It is nothing to me,' he said, 'that the Lady Frances remain wife to the Earl of Essex, or be married to another man. But I may not give a sentence where I saw no proof. I have lived fifty-one years almost, and had my conscience uncorrupted. I know not how soon I am to be called before God, and I am loath, against that time, to give a wound to mine own soul. All my grief is that your Majesty's hand is in this . . . You Majesty must never afterward expect true service of us, for how could I be true to him that is false to God?'

4. FRANCES, Countess of Somerset

They were brave words, but they fell upon deaf ears. The King
was now too much under the influence of the Howards, and too
keen to please his favourite to change his mind. When the com-
missioners finally voted on the annulment of the marriage, the
nullity was carried by seven votes to five.

The marriage of Robert Carr, Viscount Rochester, now
created Earl of Somerset, a fit title to match a great bride, and
Frances Essex, took place on Sunday 26 December 1613. It was a
truly magnificent occasion, attended by the King and Queen, and
all the great Lords and Ladies of the Court. 'Seldom,' wrote

G. M. Trevelyan, 'had a triumph, so shamefully won, been so openly celebrated.' As a masterpiece of hypocrisy it was hard to beat. The bride appeared dressed in white. Her hair was loose down her back, the symbol of innocence and virginity. The marriage sermon was preached by the Dean of Westminster. As Frances stood at the altar, with all the sanctimonious phrases echoing around her, praising her virtue, one wonders how many people were aware of the current anagram of her name: 'Carr finds a whore.'

For some while after the wedding Frances's health was in a very poor state, as a result of which her husband took a house for her at Isleworth, in order for her to be near Dr. Burgess who was one of the Court physicians. Although no mention is made of the nature of this illness it is not too hard to speculate that it may have been mental rather than physical. She was living, after all, under considerable strain. Somerset still had no idea that the wife who shared his bed each night had murder on her conscience. She was living a lie with him. She also lived in perpetual fear of discovery by the authorities should one of her accomplices squeal, all of whom were blackmailing her. Dr. Franklin, for example, was being paid £200 a year for the services he had rendered. There could be little peace for her with so many black secrets to hide.

Somerset too had his own fears. The death of the Earl of Northampton in 1614 raised the spectre of the possibility of the discovery of the part he had played in the plot to put Sir Thomas Overbury in the Tower. Dangerous letters had passed between them which he could not risk falling into the hands of his enemies. He managed to retrieve all those that had been in Northampton's own hands, and to destroy them. But other equally incriminating letters which lay in different hands, he failed to obtain, and these remained a constant threat to him. Another shadow on the horizon was the emergence in the Court of a new young favourite, George Villiers, whose rise to power was being supported by all of Somerset's enemies. Thus the first two years of marriage for the Somersets was not a particularly happy time. In fact they were a prelude to a far greater unhappiness that lay ahead.

In the autumn of 1615, when the name of Sir Thomas Overbury was almost forgotten, a rumour reached the King's Secretary, Sir Ralph Winwood, that he had met his death in the Tower by poison. The story came from abroad. An English boy,

William Reeve, that very apothecary's boy who had administered to Sir Thomas the poisoned clyster, having fallen sick at Flushing, and being at death's door, had unburdened himself of the deadly secret he had since carried with him. The British agent at Brussels heard of the confession and informed Winwood. Sir Ralph, who was an enemy of Somerset's, then approached Sir Gervase Elwes to find out what he knew of the matter. Elwes was taken by surprise and, believing that Sir Ralph knew a great deal more than he in fact did, gave him the name of Weston. Eventually the facts were laid before the King who, knowing that it would be fatal to attempt to hush the affair up, directed that the law should take its course. Once the matter was in the hands of the Lord Chief Justice, Sir Edward Coke, a notoriously tough investigator, it was not long before the whole vicious tale was revealed, and the trail of guilt led slowly but surely to the Earl and Countess of Somerset. On 18 October 1615, they were both arrested on a charge of murder.

Frances was brought to trial on 24 May 1616. She pleaded Guilty, 'with a low voice and wonderful fearful,' and was sentenced to death. On the following day Somerset himself stood in the dock. Though he maintained his innocence throughout, he too was found guilty as an accessory and was also condemned. Sir Anthony Weldon, a contemporary historian, wrote: 'Many believe the Earl of Somerset guilty of Overbury's death, but the most thought him guilty only of the breach of friendship (and that is a high point) by suffering his imprisonment which was the highway to his murder, and this conjecture I take to be of the soundest opinion.' Neither party in fact suffered the extreme penalty. The King chose, as was his prerogative of mercy, to grant pardons from execution for both. Instead they were imprisoned in the Tower. The news of the pardons was not well received by the public. When the Queen, with Lady Ruthin, the Countess of Derby, and Lord Carew were driving in a coach through the town, there was a rumour that it was Lady Somerset and her mother, and the people flocked together and followed the coach in great numbers, 'railing, reviling, and abusing the footmen and putting them in great fear.'

The Somersets remained in the Tower until January 1621, when the King granted them their freedom. It was, however, a restricted freedom: 'That the Earl and Countess of Somerset do repair either to Grays [Greys Court] or Cowsham [Caversham], the Lord Wallingford's houses in the County of Oxon, and remain confined to one or other of the said houses, and within three miles compass of either of the same, until further order be given by his majesty.' Lord Wallingford was her brother-in-law and it was to Greys Court that they went. According to Arthur Wilson they lived their final years 'as strangers one to another (tho' in one house).' Somerset's love had long since turned to hatred for a woman who had been the cause of his disgrace and downfall. He was constantly haunted by the memories of the terrible revelations of the trial: 'yet he and she were doomed to live together in close confinement at a country house, as they had lived together in the Tower ... if the King had been a fiend of cruelty, he could not have devised a more subtle punishment for two erring souls.'

Nor could he have devised a more cruel death for Frances than that which she suffered in August 1632. She died, wrote William Lilly, from 'an impediment in that very member she had so much delighted in and abused.' Wilson, believing that she got only what she deserved, was more explicit:

> 'that part of her body which had been the receptacle of most of her sin, grown rotten, the ligaments failing, it fell down, and was cut away in flakes, with a most nauseous and putrid savour... Pardon the sharpness of these expressions, for they are the glory of God who often makes his punishments (in the balance of his justice) of equal weight with our sins.'

The remaining years of her husband's life were lived in obscurity. He died in 1645.

The Puritan gentry, brooding in their country manor houses upon the evils of the day, had long memories, and the Somerset case was not forgotten. Although the Court of Charles I was on the whole a far more respectable place than that of his father, they continued to be regaled with news of aristocratic scandal. One such story concerned Lord Henry Jermyn, a man described as 'at once a bully and a coward; a hypocrite and a bungler; a gamester who haunted the card table ... a glutton ... a spendthrift loaded with ill-gotten gains, and yet with all the avarice of the mister ... a loathsome monument of decayed debauchery.' Having seduced Eleanor Villiers, the sister of Lord Grandison, 'a young man of so virtuous a habit of mind that no temptation or provocation could corrupt him,' when she gave birth to a child in 1633, he publicly refused to marry her on the grounds that she had already been the mistress of himself, Lord Newport, and Lord Feilding.

That these were the kind of men whom kings delighted to honour caused the godly preaching pastors to tremble with fury. They harboured their resentment until their moment of glory arrived. When the Puritan forces had triumphed in the Civil War, and Charles I's head had fallen, they gleefully set about wiping out all that they had despised. It was not only Royalists who suffered under Cromwell, though they were subjected to the notorious 'decimations', special taxes exacted to maintain the system of military police and to conduct the Spanish War, which drove many of them into states of extreme poverty. The military censors also moved through the country closing down large numbers of public houses, banning race-meetings, cockfights and bear-baitings, and sweeping away, in the words of G. M. Trevelyan, 'Rogues and jolly companions; wandering minstrels, bear-wards, and Tom Goodfellows; tipsy loquacious veterans, babbling of Rupert and Goring; and the broken regiments of stage-players whose occupation was now gone; all the non-descript population that lived on society in olden times and repaid it in full by making it Merry England.'

In accomplishing these things the Puritans failed to realise that not only were they ensuring their future exclusion for ever from the governing and fashionable society, but that the end result was to be the opposite of all that they had hoped to achieve. On the very first night of his return from a long and weary exile Charles established the moral atmosphere of Whitehall by installing the notorious Barbara Villiers as mistress of himself and his Court. Little resentment was shown on moral grounds to her splendid presence, and that of the suites of ladies with whom she was to share the Royal favours. This was the Happy Return and Cromwellian austerity was swept away with gay abandon. 'Debauchery was loyalty, gravity rebellion.' Thus the seal was set on a new age, an age of disbelief where there reigned supreme an air of cynical disregard for traditional ideals.

3

MAD DRINKING LORDS

'Insolent Children of Hell; ruiners of so many persons and families.'

(OBADIAH WALKER)

ON 20 August 1688, the diarist John Evelyn made a visit to Althorp in Northamptonshire, the home of his friend and frequent correspondent, Anne, Countess of Sunderland and her husband Robert Spencer, the second Earl. Althorp, recently rebuilt by the Earl from a simple Elizabethan mansion which had served as home for generations of Spencers, into a late-Renaissance palace which he considered a more worthy seat for a man of his standing, was a favourite haunt of Evelyn's, and he wrote of it and its great hostess in glowing terms:

'The Hall is well, the staircase incomparable, the rooms of state, galleries, offices and furniture such as become a great Prince. It is situated in the midst of gardens exquisitely planted and kept, and all this in a park walled with hewn stone; planted with rows and walks of trees; canals and fishponds, stored with game; and, what is above all this, governed by a Lady, that without any show of solicitude, keeps everything in such admirable order both within and without, from the garret to the cellar; that I do not believe there is any in all this nation or any other, exceeds her; all is in such exact order, without ostentation but substantially great and noble; the meanest servant lodged so neat and cleanly, the services at the several tables, the good order and decency, in a word the entire economy perfectly becoming a wise and noble person, and one whom for her distinguishing esteem of me from a long and worthy friendship I must ever honour and celebrate...'

His unsparing praise was next lavished on the Spencer's young son, Charles, 'a youth of extraordinary hopes, very learned for his age and ingenious, and under a Governor of extraordinary worth.' But then a dark note crept in to cast a blemish on his joy. 'Happy were it,' he continued, 'could as much be said of the elder brother, the Lord Spencer, who, rambling about the world, dishonours both his name and family, adding sorrow to sorrow, to a mother who had taken all imaginable care of his education: but vice, more and more predominantly, gives slender hopes of his reformation...'

Lord Robert Spencer was the black sheep of the Spencer family. Born in 1666, the eldest of five children, he was, by the time he went up to Oxford in September 1680, already showing signs of bad character. In February of that year his grandmother, Dorothy, Lady Sunderland, wrote to Lord Halifax complaining of his behaviour. 'He has no good nature, nor good humour: he is scornful and too pretending... He comes to me seldom, seems weary in a minute, talks of my company as if I picked them up off the streets. My Lord Sunderland at his age did nothing like it. He will be spoiled, I can see it.'

Spoiled he was. His mother could do no more than coo that her darling Robert was 'the prettiest boy in town,' while his father, who had spent much of his time, while the boy was growing up, abroad on various diplomatic missions, was inclined to defer to his somewhat over-indulgent wife when it came to discussions about the best way of bringing him up and educating him. In May 1681 the Countess exerted all her wiles to try and arrange a marriage for Robert to Jane Fox, the staid daughter of the millionaire financier Sir Stephen Fox. In addition to her hope that marriage might go some way to help calm down her wayward son, this particular match also had other advantages. Robert's father was, for various reasons, deeply in debt, among others to Sir Stephen, and the possibility thus loomed of a fat dowry that might free the Spencer estates. She approached John Evelyn, a close friend of Sir Stephen's, to make the arrangements. He declined, declaring 'the honour' to be 'too great.' He wrote his real reasons in his diary on 16 May:

'Come my Lady Sunderland to desire that I would a match to Sir Stephen Fox for her son, Lord Spencer, to marry Miss Jane, Sir Stephen's daughter. I excus'd myself all I was able for the truth is I was afraid he would prove an extravagant man: for though a youth of extraordinary parts, and had an excellent education to render him a worthy man, yet his early inclinations to extravagance made me apprehensive that I should not serve Sir Stephen by proposing it like a friend: this now being his only daughter, well bred, and likely to receive a large share of her father's opulence.'

5. Althorp, Northamptonshire

The marriage never took place.

The subsequent career of Lord Robert Spencer shows Evelyn to have been accurate in his assessment of the young man's character. By the year 1685, which is when we next hear of him, he had already developed into a rake-hell of the worst type. Sir Edmund Verney, writing in August from East Claydon in Buckinghamshire, told of how 'our country talk is that my Lord Scarsdale, Lord Spencer, Mr. Thomas Wharton and his brother Harry went to Ethrop, and whipped the Earl of Carnarvon in his own house, and did some other peccadillios in his castle besides... Captain Bertie was sent for to relieve the castle and I hear he did come accordingly, but the Bravos were all gone first.' Robert was banished abroad; but not for long. 'My Lord Spencer,' wrote Sir John Reresby on 11 May 1686, 'is not well by the ill usage he and the rest of his company received from the constables and watch three nights ago, being upon a high ramble.' When Robert's friends complained to Sunderland about the sound thrashing his son had received, all he could bring himself to say was 'it was pity it was not worse.' He bought him a commission in the Guards and as he thought washed his hands of him. But there was worse to come.

In March 1687 Robert marched into a church in Bury St. Edmunds in the middle of a service, drew his sword and, cursing and swearing all the while, attempted to drag the preaching parson from his pulpit. He had failed, however, to reckon on the congregation who, incensed with fury at this violent interruption, 'made a severe example of his roystering honour, beating, disrobing and dragging him through the kennel, and, worse...' Whatever this 'worse' may have been, it left Robert a severely wounded man. When news of the incident reached Sunderland he immediately pleaded with King James to have his son cashiered, and begged him to take no notice of certain rumours circulating that, believing himself to be close to death, Robert had sent for a Roman Catholic priest. He knew that little credence could be given to these stories unless his son returned to give an account of himself in person. But Robert did in fact recover enough to return home to beg his father's forgiveness, and confirm that he had indeed been received into the Catholic Church. For a short while the prodigal son's past sins were forgotten.

His new-found religion, however, did little to change Robert. After his conversion, King James entrusted him with a diplomatic mission to Modena to present the King's condolences to his brother-in-law, the Duke, on his mother's death. But passing through Paris, he found the temptations there too great to resist. He succumbed, and by the time he reached Turin the stories of his profligacy were widespread. It was here that, in the Autumn of 1687, he fell seriously ill, brought on, no doubt, by the Paris debauch, and remained so until March of the following year when he somehow managed to drag himself back to Paris. He was taken ill again in August, and on 16 September he died, victim of one final bout of over-indulgence. The Marquis de Dangeau recorded his death in his journal as follows: 'Milord Spencer, fils aîné du Comte de Sunderland, est mort cette nuit à Paris pour avoir trop bu d'eau de vie.'

The life of Lord Robert Spencer is not untypical of the lives of countless young men of his day. In many ways they were the victims of the age in which they lived, an age in which the upbringing of children seems still to have been rooted in the Middle Ages.

85

Firstly, upper-class babies were almost invariably taken from their real mothers at birth and put out to wet-nurses, women who were by no means always reminiscent of the nurse in Romeo and Juliet, but were often cruel and neglectful. If their milk ran out the baby was passed from one mother-substitute to another. Sometimes the baby would stay with one wet-nurse, to whom it became deeply attached, in which case, when the weaning process took place at about eighteen months it suffered the trauma of being wrenched away from the woman it had come to love and being returned to an alien world. Whatever the case this practice almost certainly inflicted psychological wounds.

Secondly, there was the practice of tight swaddling in the first months or even year of life, whereby babies, almost immediately after birth, were tightly bound in bandages so that they were unable to move either head or limbs. The medical reasons for this were to keep the limbs of the child straight. There was also a widespread popular belief that, unless restrained, the child might tear off its ears, scratch out its eyes, or break its legs. Also, swaddling was convenient for the adults concerned since a swaddled child had a slower heartbeat and thus tended to sleep longer and cry less. Furthermore it allowed the infant to be moved about and stored like a parcel in any suitable place, or even quite safely to be hung from a peg on a wall, a practice which Dr. William Cadogan, in a book on child care published in 1748, was later to deplore:

'At the least annoyance which arises, he is hung from a nail like a bundle of old clothes and while, without hurrying, the nurse attends to her business, the unfortunate one remains thus crucified. All who have been found in this situation had a purple face, the violently compressed chest not allowing the blood to circulate... The patient was believed to be tranquil because he did not have the strength to cry out.'

It is widely held nowadays that such total sensory deprivation in the first months of childhood would probably lead to a cold personality in adulthood.

Many children suffered the loss of one or other parent at an early age. Even if both parents survived, they would often inflict on their offspring an upbringing the key to the success of which was regarded as being, as in the case of breaking in a favourite horse or a hunting dog, the breaking of the will of the child, and enforcing its utter subjection to the will of its parents. Constant and severe corporal punishment was seen as one method of achieving this. John Aubrey wrote that when he was a boy parents 'were as severe to their children as their schoolmasters: and their schoolmasters as masters of the House of Correction,' as a result of which 'the child perfectly loathed the sight of his parents as the slave his torture.' Though Aubrey was inclined to exaggerate, Gilbert Burnet, Bishop of Salisbury, who was born in 1643, when writing of his youth, supports this view. He was, he recalled in old age, subject to 'much severe correction ... the fear of that brought me under too great an uneasiness, and sometimes to hatred of my father.' Such severity increased in the schools to which they were sent where, reported Henry Peacham, scholars were 'pulled by the ears, lashed over the face, beaten about the head with the great end of the rod, smitten upon the lips for every slight offence with the ferula.'

There is no doubt that these extraordinary methods of child-rearing often produced adults who were cold, suspicious, distrustful and cruel, unable to form close emotional relationships with others, and liable to sudden outbursts of aggressive hostility towards each other.

Once he was grown up it is easy to understand how a young man, even if he were remote from contact with Court life, could be affected by the immorality which penetrated so much of the society of the day and which had its source in the depraved atmosphere of Whitehall and St. James's. He would have heard again and again the stories that were told of the gay and reckless doings of the King and his courtiers, and undoubtedly, at some time or other, read some of their licentious writings. He would have witnessed the wild orgies that took place in taverns, and in the brothels which abounded.

There was also a kind of desperation, so evident in the exploits of Robert Spencer, which pervaded their lives, a philosophy of 'eat, drink, and be merry, for tomorrow we die.' The truth is that they very often did die. It can never have been far from the mind of any young Englishman that he could be struck down by an epidemic such as the Bubonic Plague, of which there were major outbreaks in London in 1603, 1625, 1636, and 1655, not to mention many even more lethal outbreaks in country towns. There was a constant danger of smallpox, which even if it did not so frequently kill, often left many of its survivors either blinded or pockmarked and disfigured for life. Then the almost total ignorance of both personal and public hygiene meant that contaminated food and water were an equally constant hazard. This was just as true of the top end of the social scale as of the lower end. Anthony Wood wrote of how, when in 1665 the Court of Charles II fled from the Great Plague in London to take refuge in the Oxford Colleges, they left behind them, on their return to London in the following year, 'their excrements in every corner, in chimneys, studies, coal-houses, cellars.' As for the streets of towns, they were rarely little better than open sewers, while open mass graves, or 'poor holes', abounded. In 1742 Dr. Johnson described London as a city 'which abounds with such heaps of filth as a savage would look on with amazement.'

Even if he were to survive disease, the well-being of a young man could be equally sadly affected by the general incompetence of the medical profession of the day. Strange and fearful were some of the remedies which our ancestors prescribed, often hardly differing from the magical formulas of witch-doctors. 'Take a silk thread,' runs one for a quinsey, 'dipped in the blood of a mouse, and let the party swallow it down with the pain or swelling in the throat, and it will cure him.' Another recommends oil of vitriol for toothache, with a timely caution not to confuse oil with spirit of vitriol, 'for if you do it will make foul work.' For apoplexy a glass of urine mixed with salt was recommended, to induce vomiting; for gout, live earthworms were to be applied to the affected part until they began to swell; while blowing dried and powdered human excrement into the eye was advised as a remedy for cataract. In most cases medical treatment did more harm than good. As for surgery, if it were required to save a man's life, it all too often ended in death from septicaemia. Add to this ever present threat of death and disease the fact that most young men ate and drank to excess, thereby ruining their digestion, and the high incidence within their ranks of venereal disease, with its alternating moods of violence and aggression and weakness and self-pity, and one understands why so many of them were unbalanced.

There was a whole group of talented young blades who were drawn to and welcomed at the Court of Charles II, yet, aspiring playwrights and poets though many of them were, it is for their scapegrace ways that they are now best remembered. The most celebrated of them, John Wilmot, 2nd Earl of Rochester, is forever 'Rake Rochester', and the same can be said for the rest of the coterie with which he associated. This included among its leading members Charles, Lord Buckhurst, Sir Charles Sedley, and Harry Killigrew. It was a bawdy and malicious clique, and was nicknamed 'the Merry Gang' by Andrew Marvell, a title which could be said to have been something of a misnomer.

Charles Sackville, Lord Buckhurst, was the son and heir of Richard Sackville, Earl of Dorset, whose father Edward had been one of the closest friends and supporters of Charles I. The Sackvilles were an illustrious family in more ways than one. Charles's great-great grandfather Thomas Sackville, who was created Earl of Dorset by James I in 1604, and was Lord High Treasurer, was one of the most celebrated of the early English poets, and a pioneer of English drama. With Thomas Norton he was the joint author of *Gorboduc*, which is regarded as one of the first great tragedies of the English language, and which was acted by the Gentlemen of the Inner Temple before the Queen on January 18, 1561. The poet Spenser referred to his poetry as 'golden verse, worthy immortal fame'.

Buckhurst is a good example of someone whose ruin was almost directly attributable to the advent of the Restoration and all that went with it, for, until it occurred, he appears to have been a more or less sedate young gentleman, judging from the lack of contemporary gossip about his early life. However when Charles came to power in 1660, Buckhurst, who was then 22, was, as heir to a great title, and being both clever and good-looking, singled out by the King for Courtly honours. Within a short while his name was notorious.

In 1662, for example, he found himself and various friends, who included his younger brother, on trial for murder. The story was reported in the *Mercurius Publicus* of the day as follows:

'Charles Lord Buckhurst, Edward Sackville Esq., his brother, Sir Henry Belasyse K.B., eldest son of Lord Belasyse, John Belasyse, brother to Lord Falconbery, and Thomas Wentworth, only son of Sir George Wentworth, whilst in pursuit of thieves near Waltham Cross, mortally wounded an innocent tanner named Hoppy, whom they had endeavoured to secure, suspecting him to have been one of the robbers; and as they took away the money found on his person, under the idea that it was stolen property, they were soon after apprehended on the charge of robbery and murder.'

6. JOHN WILMOT, Earl of Rochester

7. SIR CHARLES SEDLEY (Kneller)

8. LORD BUCKHURST

After a period of imprisonment in Newgate the charge was eventually changed by the Grand Jury to one of manslaughter, and they were acquitted. Although they claimed that the tanner, Hoppy, had confessed to robbery, the evidence suggested that he was probably innocent, and that they had run him through first, and asked questions afterwards. Certainly Samuel Pepys wrote in his diary that he was 'much troubled and for the grief and disgrace it brings to their families and friends.'

The honour of the family name evidently meant little to Charles Buckhurst, for the following summer he was involved in a disgraceful episode which ended in a riot, and a subsequent court case. It all came about as a result of an evening's drinking with Sir Charles Sedley at the Cock Tavern in Bow Street. Pepys heard the story one night after dinner from a friend, William Batten, a barrister of Lincoln's Inn, who

> 'told us of a late trial of Sir Charles Sedley the other day before my Lord Chief Justice Foster and the whole bench for his debauchery a little while since at Oxford Kates; coming in open day into the balcony, and showing his nakedness – acting all the postures of lust and buggery that could be imagined, and abusing of Scripture and, as it were, from thence preaching a mountebank sermon from that pulpit, saying that there he hath to sell such a powder as should make all the cunts run after him – a thousand people standing underneath to see and hear him. And that being done he took a glass of wine and drank the King's health.'

To put the seal on their fun and games, the party 'excrementised in the street'.

The crowd were so incensed by this behaviour that they attempted to storm the tavern. Finding the doors firmly bolted, however, they took to hurling stones, breaking all the windows and driving the exhibitionists inside where they were eventually seized and indicted for inciting a riot. They ended up before the Lord Chief Justice, Sir Robert Foster. Sir Charles Sedley, as ringleader, was the first to receive a verbal lashing.

> 'It seems,' wrote Pepys, 'my Lord and the rest of the judges did all of them round give him a most high reproof – my Lord Chief Justice saying that it was for him and such wicked wretches as he was that God's anger and judgements hung over us – calling him Sirrah many times... It being told that

my Lord Buckhurst was there, my Lord asked whether it was that Buckhurst that was lately tried for robbery; and when answered "Yes" he asked whether he had soon forgot his deliverance at that time, and that it would have more become him to have been at his prayers begging God's forgiveness than now running into such courses again.'

To Sir Robert, an old-fashioned and high-minded Cavalier of the school of Ormonde and Clarendon, such escapades were particularly odious.

He then turned to Sir Charles Sedley and asked him whether or not he had ever read *The Compleat Gentleman*. This work, by Henry Peacham of Trinity College, Cambridge, was one of the most popular and influential books of the time, and was devoted to the instruction of the gentleman, 'fashioning him absolut,' as the title page runs, 'in the most necessary and commendable qualities concerning mind or body. Perhaps the passage which Sir Robert had in mind when he asked this somewhat foolish question was the following:

'There is no one thing that setteth a fairer stamp upon nobility than evenness of carriage, and care of our reputation, without which our most graceful gifts are dead and dull, as the Diamond without his foil; for hereupon as on the frontispiece of a magnificent palace are fixed the eyes of all passengers, and hereby the height of our judgement (even ourselves) is taken... The principal means to preserve it is temperance, and that moderation of the mind, wherewith as a bridle we curb and break our rank and unruly passions, keeping as the Caspian Sea ourselves even at one height without ebb or reflux.'

Sir Charles's impudent reply was that 'set against his Lordship, he had read more books than himself.' With great pleasure Sir Robert fined them each £2,000, imprisoned them for a week without bail, and bound them over for good behaviour for three years. All Sir Charles could find to say was that 'he thought he was the first man that paid for shitting.'

Charles Sedley was the youngest son of Sir John Sedley Bt, of Southfleet in Kent, by his wife Elizabeth, daughter and heiress of Sir Henry Savile, Provost of Eton and one of the most learned Englishmen of the Elizabethan age. The Sedleys themselves were an ancient family from Romney Marsh who had moved to Southfleet and built a mansion there in the reign of Edward III.

Under normal circumstances, having two older brothers, William and Henry, the law of primogeniture would have restricted Charles's prospects. But at the age of sixteen, within a few weeks of his entering Wadham College, Oxford, he found himself the successor to the title and estates after both his brothers had died unmarried. Thus at an age when most young men crave pleasure and excitement he was suddenly and unexpectedly placed in a position to amuse himself beyond his wildest hopes. When he returned to London he immediately assumed the place that his brother, Sir William, had held in the fashionable society of the period, a society in which, wrote Clarendon, 'the tenderness of the bowels which is the quintessence of justice and passion, the very mention of good nature was laughed at and looked upon as the mark or character of a fool; and a roughness of manners, or hard-headedness and cruelty was affected.' It was the ruin of many a young man.

It is worth quoting here a letter from a country lady to her brother-in-law in London, worrying reports of whose behaviour in this very society had reached her, and who was quick to warn him against the disgrace he was in danger of bringing to his family.

'My Lord,' wrote Elizabeth Countess of Essex to the second Earl of Chesterfield, 'though I live here where I know very little of what is done in the world, yet I hear so much of your exceeding wildness, that I am confident that I am more cessible of it than any friend you have; you treat all the mad drinking Lords, you swear you game, and commit all the extravagances that are incident to untamed youths, to such a degree that you make yourself the talk of all places and the wonder of all those that thought otherwise of you, and of all sober people; and the worst of all this is I hear there is a very handsome lady (to both your shame) with child by you.'

Sir Charles Sedley fitted well into the company of these 'mad drinking Lords' who filled the Court of Charles II and who 'abhorred all discourse that was serious, and, in the liberty they assumed in drollery and raillery, preserved no reverence towards God or man, but laughed at all sober men, and even at religion itself.' They were soon to be joined by Rochester, also fresh from Wadham College. The Restoration was a great age of experiment, and Wadham was the cradle of the Royal Society, and a centre of scientific rationalism. Rochester, Sedley, and their fellow students had all read and admired the works of Thomas Hobbes of Malmesbury, the materialist philosopher who had been tutor to the King, and was much admired at Court.

Hobbes taught that there was no such thing as 'soul', 'spirit' or 'mind', and that thought and perception were purely mechanical processes. For him 'good' and 'evil' were merely convenient names with no permanent meaning and no divine sanction:

'Whatever is the object of any man's appetite or desire, that is it which he for his part calleth "good", and the object of his hatred and aversion "evil", and of his contempt "vile" and "inconsiderable." For those words of good, evil, and contemptible, are ever used in relation to the person that useth them, there being nothing simply or absolutely so.'

It is easy to understand how attractive doctrines such as these must have been to any intelligent, hot-blooded young aristocrat, scattering, as they seemed to do, all the dark and unpleasant connotations surrounding such words as 'evil' and 'sin'. In Hobbes' world men would no longer live in fear of a jealous and avenging God, but would explain and master the universe by means of the infallible laws of mathematics. It was the perfect roué's philosophy.

Rochester directed all his energy and passion into the experiment of living the life of pleasure. Fresh from the Grand Tour, he had arrived at Court at the age of seventeen-and-a-half, where he was looked upon with great interest. His rather beautiful, almost child-like face, and his boyish charm made him an instant favourite. He had considerable self-confidence after his travels, and his 'strange vivacity of thought and vigour of expression', together with his gaiety and ready wit, led to his being a much sought-after companion, not least by the King and his current favourite, George Villiers, Duke of Buckingham, then perhaps the most depraved and extravagant rake in Europe. They flattered and spoiled him, and soon he was roaring and frolicking with the rest of them. 'He gave himself up,' wrote Burnet, 'to all sorts of extravagance, to gross impiety and profaneness, and to the wildest frolics that a wanton wit could devise.' The result was that he was to end his short life with both his reputation and his health in ruins. Like many of his kind, his was a sad story, for his endless quest for pleasure brought him little happiness. A man of great brilliance and charm, he despised himself for wasting his true talents. His poem 'The Debauchee' is an unsparing self-portrait:

'I rise at eleven, I dine about two,
I get drunk before seven, and the next thing I do,
I send for my whore, when, for fear of a clap,
I dally about her, and spew in her lap;
There we quarrel and scold, till I fall asleep,
When the jilt growing bold to my pocket does creep;
Then slyly she leaves me, and to revenge the affront,
At once both my lass and my money I want.
If by chance then I wake, hot-headed and drunk,
What a coyl do I make for the loss of my punk?
I storm and I roar, and I fall in a rage,
And missing my lass, I fall on my page;
Then crop-sick all morning, I rail at my men,
And in bed I lie yawning till eleven again.'

What destroyed Rochester in the end was drink.

'He told me,' wrote Burnet after his death, 'for five years together he was continually drunk: not all the while under the visible effects of it, but his blood was so inflamed that he was not in all that time cool enough to be perfectly master of himself. This led him to say and do many wild and unaccountable things.'

This is borne out in a letter written by Rochester to his close friend Henry Savile:

'Oh that second bottle Harry is the sincerest, wisest, and most impartial downright friend we have; tells us the truth of ourselves, and forces us to speak truths of others, banishes flattery from our tongues and distrust from our hearts, sets us above the mean policy of Court prudence, which makes us lie to one another all day for fear of being betrayed by each other at night.'

But Rochester did not drink alone, for drunkenness was the scourge of the age. It filled the veins of many a wild young rake, whole gangs of whom, imbued with false courage, were wont to scour the streets in orgies of mischief. One of these, a close friend of Rochester's and brother-in-law to Sir Charles Sedley, was Harry Killigrew. Harry was a younger son of a famous

Cornish Cavalier family. His grandfather, Sir Robert Killigrew of Arwennack, was knighted by James I at Hanworth, on July 23, 1603, and was Member of Parliament for several Cornish seats. His father, Thomas, was one of the most celebrated of the Restoration dramatists, and was manager of the Theatre Royal, Drury Lane. He had three brothers, all of whom had respectable careers. The eldest, Robert, served with distinction in the army, rising to the rank of Brigadier-General. The second, Charles, was a Gentleman of the Privy Chamber to three kings, Charles II, James II and William III, and was also Master of the Revels. The youngest, Thomas, followed in his father's footsteps as a dramatist, and was the author of 'Chit Chat, a Comedy in 5 Acts', which had some success.

Harry was one of the worst rogues amongst all the Restoration rakes and scoundrels. An intimate of the Duke of Buckingham, he was notorious at Whitehall as 'Lying Killigrew'. 'He will never leave his lying,' Charles, Prince Palatine, once wrote of him 'as long as his tongue can wag'. His whole life was one long succession of brawls, duels, and intrigues.

Sometime between 1663 and 1665, 'having nothing better to do,' as Gramont put it, he became involved in an affair with Anna-Maria Brudenell, Countess of Shrewsbury, one of the most admired and sought-after beauties of the Court. For Harry's taste, however, she chose to conduct their intrigue in far too discreet a manner. 'He was amazed,' wrote Gramont, 'that he was not envied, and offended that his good fortune raised him no rivals in Lady Shrewsbury's affections.' He thus proceeded to brag of his conquest and, when drunk, to give 'luxurious descriptions of Lady Shrewsbury's most secret charms and beauties.' The man he chose endlessly to bore on this subject was his friend Buckingham, who responded just as Harry appeared to hope. Buckingham, 'deafened with descriptions of Lady Shrewsbury's merits, decided to examine into the truth of the matter himself.' He set about the attempted seduction of Lady Shrewsbury, a task in which he was more than successful. 'No amour in England,' commented Gramont, 'ever continued so long.'

Harry was furious. 'Without ever considering that he was the author of his own disgrace, he let loose all his abusive eloquence against Lady Shrewsbury: he attacked her with the most bitter invective from head to foot, he drew a frightful picture of her conduct; and turned all her personal charms, which he used to extol, into defects.' Buckingham could only listen incensed to these caddish outbursts. He could not challenge Harry without giving away his own interest in a married lady. Fortunately for everyone, fate now took a hand, in the form of Harry's loose tongue. He made the foolish mistake of slandering the King's mistress, Barbara Villiers, in public, saying that she had been 'a little lecherous girl when she was young.' True though this sneer may have been, for at the age of fifteen she had been the mistress of Philip Stanhope, second Earl of Chesterfield, who was the first in a long succession of lovers, when word of it reached the ears of the King, he banished Harry from the Court, and ordered the Duke of York to dismiss him from his post as Groom of the Bedchamber. He was thus temporarily off the scene. He blamed Buckingham, who was a cousin of Barbara Villiers, for his dismissal, and during his banishment his hatred for Buckingham increased.

In July 1667 Buckingham took his wife and Lady Shrewsbury, who somewhat surprisingly were good friends, to the theatre. By ill chance the next-door box to theirs happened to be occupied by Harry, who was just able to show his face again. When his gaze fell upon Lady Shrewsbury with Buckingham, he immediately gave way to 'abusive eloquence', loudly enough to be heard all over the theatre. Quietly and coldly Buckingham 'told him he might govern his tongue and his face better.' Then, before anyone knew quite what was happening, Harry struck Buckingham twice over the head with his sheathed sword, and ran away 'most nobly over the boxes and forms, and the Duke after him, and cut him well favouredly, he crying, "Good, Your Grace, spare my life!", and fell down, some say to beg for his life . . .' The theatre was in an uproar; the Duchess 'swounded', Lady Shrewsbury was 'hugely frighted', and Buckingham lost his blond periwig in the scuffle.

Harry was not seriously hurt, and when he came to his senses and realised what he had done, he saw that there was no course left him but to leave the country. There was already a warrant out for his arrest, and the King had ordered that when taken he should be sent to the Tower, and be banished from Court for ever. After borrowing £30 from one of the under-Secretaries of State 'which if not given will be followed with a gaol and a million of other miseries' – he fled to France, where he obtained a post at the Court of Henrietta Maria, who had always favoured him. Some three months later, in a letter to his sister, the Duchess of Orleans, the King wrote:

'For Harry Killigrew, you may see him as you please, and though I cannot commend my Lady Shrewsbury's conduct in many things, yet Mr. Killigrew's carriage towards her has been worse than I will repeat; and for his démêlé with my Lord of Buckingham, he ought not to brag of, for it was in all sort most abominable. I am glad the poor wretch has got a means of subsistence, but have one caution of him, that you believe not one word he says of us here, for he is a most notorious liar and does not want wit to get forth his stories pleasantly enough.'

The trouble with Harry was that he could not keep himself out of trouble even in France. Bent on seducing a young woman of his fancy, whose mother guarded her too closely, he lured them to his house, where he drugged them both, and then raped the daughter. He was captured, convicted, and sentenced to hang, but, due to the direct intervention of the Duchess of Orleans, was reprieved and banished. Early in 1668 he crept back to England where he haunted the London underworld as one of the 'Ballers', a company of wild young bloods who made their headquarters at a well-known brothel kept by 'Lady' Bennet. In his diary of 30 May 1668, Pepys wrote of a meeting with some of this gang, including Harry:

'To Fox Hall, and there fell into the company of Harry Killigrew, a rogue newly come back out of France, but still in disgrace at our Court, and young Newport and others, as very rogues as any in the town, who were ready to take hold of any woman that came by them. And so to supper in an arbour; but Lord! their mad talk did make my heart ache. And here I first understood by their talk the meaning of the company that lately were called 'Ballers': Harry telling of how it was by a meeting of some young blades, where he was among them, and my Lady Bennet and her ladies: and there dancing naked, and all the roguish things in the world. But, Lord! what loose company was this that I was in tonight...'

It was not long before Harry once again resumed his boasting about his affair with Lady Shrewsbury, gossip which soon enough reached her ears. This time, she decided to teach him a lesson once and for all. She laid her plans with care, noting his habits, and the route he always took at night to his home at Turnham Green. On the night of 18 May 1669, a black mourning coach drawn by six horses and attended by four footmen armed with knives and cudgels halted in the shadows beside the highway to Hammersmith. The figure silhouetted inside was Lady Shrewsbury herself. After a while Harry's coach appeared on his way home and, as it drew abreast, the footmen leaped out in ambush and dragged him from his coach. Cudgels rose and fell, and blades flashed. When the mourning coach finally pulled away, they left behind a senseless figure, bleeding from nine wounds.

The next day all of London was ringing with the news, and Lady Shrewsbury's name was on everyone's lips as prime instigator of the attack. It was even rumoured that she had her children with her in the coach as she watched. Pepys, on that day, was in the Queen's bedchamber with the King and, among others, Tom Killigrew, Harry's father, when Buckingham ('still passionately in love with this virago', said Ambassador Colbert) arrived and 'therein discourse did say that he had spoke with some that was by (which all the world must know that it must be his whore, my Lady Shrewsbury), who says that they did not mean to hurt, but beat him, and that he did run first at them with his sword – so that he doth hereby clearly discover that he knows who did it, and is of conspiracy with them, being of known conspiracy with her.' Lady Shrewsbury went into hiding, and, had Harry died, she might have found herself in very deep water. A few days later, however, the word went round that 'Harry Killigrew is better this morn; so as the Countess (if he continues thus) may leave her retreat and appear again.' The beating he received evidently had a sobering effect on Harry, as from this time no more was heard of him.

The 'Ballers' were only one of a number of wild gangs who roamed the streets in search of amusement. Their existence may be traced back to a company in Elizabethan times known as the 'Damn'd Crew'. By 1604, according to contemporary reports, the streets of London were full of quarrelling, rioting sets of young men calling themselves Roaring Boys, Bravadoes, Roysters and so on, whose ranks were, in many instances, made up of impoverished young gentlemen who had gambled away or otherwise dissipated their fortunes, and were being maintained at the expense of some still solvent noblemen. They became the

Bugles and the Tityre-tues, the Mums and the Ballers of the Restoration, circles whose sole purpose was to scour the streets in a state of drunkenness, lusting after women, and committing outrages which they termed 'Frolics'.

'He was quite the thing,' commented the Oxford Magazine, in a portrait of a typical member of one of these gangs, 'either for kicking up a riot, or keeping it up after he had kicked it up. This was a very high fellow: he would toss a beggar in a blanket; chuck a waiter out of the window ... hop round the room with a red-hot poker between his teeth ... He was a man of infinite fancy, for one day he kicked an old woman's coddling kettle about the streets, because he loved fun ... and not a long time since he pushed a blind horse into a china-shop; that was damn'd jolly!'

Wherever they went, gangs such as these spoiled for a fight. A poem by John Gay refers to their night-time revels:

'Now is the time that makes their revels keep;
Kindlers of riot, enemies of sleep ...
Was there a watchman took his hourly rounds,
Safe from their blows or new-invented wounds?'

Rochester, for example, was continually involved in this kind of incident. On 26 June 1675, it was reported that 'My Lord Rochester in a frolic after a rant did yesterday beat down the dial which stood in the middle of the Privy Garden, which was esteemed the rarest in Europe.' His companions were Lord Middlesex, Lord Sussex, and Henry Savile, and they had been 'deboshing all night with the King.' When they came to the sun-dial on their way to their lodgings, with shrieks of 'Kings and Kingdoms tumble down and so shall thou,' they took it in their arms and flung it down.

'But the highest frolic,' wrote another contemporary journalist, 'is a genteel murder; such as running a waiter through the body, knocking an old feeble watchman's brains out with his own staff, or taking away the life of some regular scoundrel who has not spirit enough to drink and whore like a gentleman. The noblest frolic of this kind I ever remembered happened a few years ago at a country town. While a party of Bucks were making a riot at an Inn, and tossing the chairs and tables and looking-glasses into the street, the landlady was indiscreet to come upstairs, and interrupt their merriment with her impertinent remonstrances; upon which they immediately threw her after her own furniture. News was soon brought of the poor woman's death, and the whole company looked upon it as a very droll accident, and gave orders that she should be charged in the bill.'

Rochester escaped being tried for murder by the skin of his teeth. Charles Hatton, writing to his brother in June 1676, told the whole story.

'Mr. Downes is dead. The Lord Rochester doth abscond, and so doth Etheredge and Captain Bridges who occasioned the riot Sunday sennight. They were tossing some fiddlers in a blanket for refusing to play, and a barber, upon the noise, going to see what the matter was, they seized upon him, and to free himself from them he offered to carry them to the hand-somest woman in Epsom, and directed them to the Con-stable's house, who, demanding what they came for, they told him a wench, and, he refusing to let them in they broke open his doors, and broke his head and beat him very severely. At last he made his escape, called his watch, and Etheredge made a submissive oration to them, and so far appeased them that the Constable dismissed his watch. But presently after the Lord Rochester drew upon the Constable, Mr. Downes, to prevent his pass, seized upon him, the Constable cried out murder, and, the watch returning, one came behind Mr. Downes and with a spittle staff cleft his skull. The Lord Rochester and the rest ran away, and Downes, having no sword, snatched up a stick and striking at them, they ran him into the side with a half-pike, and so bruised his arm that he was never able to stir it after.'

The Earl of Anglesey, in a letter to Lord Essex on 27 June, stated that Rochester was to be tried, and on 1 July Harbord, also writing to Essex, reiterated this news: 'Yesterday the Lord Cornwallis was tried by his Peers ... my Lord Rochester's turn will be next.' But Rochester absconded, and the trial never took place.

Another contemporary of Rochester's who was involved in murder, and who was also an infamous drunk, was Philip Herbert, 7th Earl of Pembroke, described by the historian David Ogg as 'the most violent homicide of his age.' This unworthy scion of one of the greatest houses in England had succeeded to the title in 1674, at the age of twenty-one, on the death of his half-brother William, who left no family. He had already abandoned himself to a life of total self-indulgence, and was evidently so notorious for his drunken and violent habits that people were afraid to sit near him in a tavern. When, for example, Sir Francis Vincent refused to join him for a drink, on some occasion in 1676, Pembroke threw a bottle of wine at his head and then drew his sword upon him. In this case it appears he had chosen the wrong man, for Sir Francis managed to overpower and disarm him, and then gave him a sound thrashing.

Others were not so lucky. There is an account in the Hatton correspondence of 27 November 1677, of Pembroke's insulting when drunk a Mr. Vaughan, who subsequently, and somewhat foolishly, challenged him to a duel. At some point during this duel Vaughan got the better of Pembroke and had him on the ground, whereupon Pembroke's footman, no doubt by prior arrangement, came up from behind and cut Vaughan over the hand, thereby disabling him. Pembroke then got up and ran him through the belly. Only a few months later, in February 1678, one Philip Rycaut petitioned the House of Lords to protect him from Lord Pembroke's violence. Rycaut complained that one evening, as he was leaving a friend's house in the Strand, Lord Pembroke, who happened to be passing, 'came up to the door, and with his fist, without any provocation, struck him such a blow upon the eye as almost knocked it out; and afterwards knocked him down, and then fell upon him with such violence that he almost stifled him with his gripes in the dirt; and likewise his Lordship drew his sword, and was in danger of killing him, had he not slipped into the house and the door been shut upon him.' This incident took place only one week after Pembroke had been released from the Tower, after having been committed there by the King in January 'for uttering such horrid and blasphemous words, abuse of the celebration of the Sacrament of the Lord's Supper, and other actions proved upon oath, as are not fit to be repeated in any Christian assembly.'

After the Rycaut affair Pembroke was bound over for a sum of £2,000 to keep the peace for twelve months towards Rycaut 'and all his Majesty's other subjects.' This was something he was quite incapable of doing. One month later a Grand Jury, headed by Sir Edmund Berry Godfrey, a notoriously tough magistrate, sent him for trial for wilful murder. The story was a sordid one by any standards. Late on the evening of Sunday, 3 February, two friends, Nathaniel Cony and Henry Goring, paid a visit to Long's tavern in the Haymarket to drink some wine. There they came across Pembroke and a party of revellers. Pembroke knew Cony and, as was his usual convivial habit, insisted that the two new-comers joined his group. It was not long before Goring became involved in a drunken argument with Pembroke who then threw a glass of wine in his face, and kicked him out of the tavern. When Cony dared to ask why he had behaved in such a manner to his friend, and attempted to go and help him, Pembroke, without any warning, immediately set upon him, felled him with one blow and, when he was down, jumped upon his back, his stomach, and his side, before proceeding to kick him uncon-scious. His body was then laid out on some chairs, and there the revellers left him. The beating he received must have been for-midable. At the trial, which opened on 4 April, Sir William Jones, the Attorney General, told the Court that 'there was so much blood forced out of his veins, and gathered into one place of his body, by those blows and bruises, that he could not be recovered, and so after a week's time passed in intolerable pain, died.'

Pembroke was found guilty of manslaughter, but escaped justice by claiming the benefit of the Statute. This was a privilege that had been granted to peers in the reign of Edward VI by which they might claim 'benefit of clergy' for manslaughter, if it was a first offence. He was thus discharged by the Lord High Steward, the Earl of Nottingham, who granted this, though with trepidation.

> 'You must have it, my Lord,' he said, 'it cannot be denied you ... But your Lordship must give me leave to tell you, that no man can have the benefit of that Statute but once, and so I would have your Lordship take notice of it as a caution to you for the future.'

It was a warning that he did not heed. Two years later Pem-broke was on trial for murder a second time. Towards midnight on 18 August 1680, attended by six servants, he was returning by Hackney coach from a dinner in London. He was 'somewhat high-flown with wine.' As they crossed Turnham Green they were stopped by the Chiswick watch, the constable of which was on his way to the Cock and Half Moon Tavern, along with a friend, Smeethe, and another constable of the parish, Halfpenny.

The constable asked who was in the coach and where was it bound. While the watch were thus questioning the other occupants of the coach Pembroke crept out and, without the slightest provocation, drew his sword and ran it right up to the hilt through Smeethe's stomach. He then wheeled about and ran through Halfpenny. At this point Smeethe, in a last desperate effort, cried out bravely, 'I will not be thus killed like a dog,' and seizing a staff from one of the watch felled Pembroke with a blow on his head, who was then taken prisoner. Smeethe died soon afterwards, while Halfpenny lingered on seriously ill. This time a Middlesex jury found Pembroke guilty of murder. Once again, however, he escaped justice, on this occasion through a Royal Pardon. This was no doubt due to the influence upon the King of his French mistress, the notorious Duchess of Portsmouth, whose sister Henriette de Keroualle was married to Pembroke.

Not even this second escape was enough to sober up the Earl. In November of the same year Lord Dorset complained to the House of Lords of a violent assault made upon him by Pembroke over a dispute about some land. After examination by the House, he was eventually persuaded to apologise, and they released him on the condition that he retired to his home at Wilton. Here he returned to drink himself into the grave at the age of thirty. Though Pembroke was brought to trial only twice for assault it is asserted by David Ogg, in his book *England in the Reign of Charles II*, that in the coffee houses of the time he was credited with no less than twenty-six murders. It has also been suggested that he may have murdered Sir Edmund Berry Godfrey in October 1678, in revenge for his part in bringing him to trial in the Cony affair, for which crime three other men were executed.

In his book *Of Education, Especially of Young Gentlemen*, Obadiah Walker, Master of University College, Oxford, made a particular point of warning parents of the dire consequences of their offspring associating with such wild young men as have been described. He referred to them as 'insolent children of Hell; ruiners of so many persons and families.' Half a century later his words were to be echoed by Philip Stanhope, 4th Earl of Chesterfield, who was only too ready to admit that, as a young man, he had once been just such a reprobate, as a result of which he confessed that 'my future impaired and my constitution shattered are ... the just punishment of my errors.' He was determined however that under no circumstances should his own son,

Philip, follow the same path, and much of his celebrated correspondence with the boy was devoted to warning him against such
a course:

March 17, 1747.

'Dear Boy,
    Pleasure is the rock which most young people split upon;
they launch out with crowded sails in quest of it, but without a
compass to direct their course; or reason sufficient to steer the
vessel, for want of which, pain and shame, instead of pleasure
are the returns of their voyage. Do not think that I mean to
snarl at pleasure like a Stoic, or to preach against it like a
parson; no, I mean to point it out, and recommend it to you
like an Epicurean; I wish you a great deal; and my only view is
to hinder you from mistaking it.
    The character which most young men first aim at is that of a
man of pleasure; but they generally take upon trust; and
instead of consulting their own tastes and inclinations, they
blindly adopt whatever those, with whom they chiefly converse, are pleased to call by the name of pleasure; and a man of
pleasure, in the vulgar acceptation of that phrase, means only a
beastly drunkard, and abandoned ... and a profligate swearer
and curser.'

October 12, 1748. Bath.
'... But the company of all others you must carefully avoid, is
that low company which in every sense of the word is low
indeed – low in rank, low in parts, low in manners and low in
merit. You will perhaps be surprised that I should think it
necessary to warn you against such company; but yet I do not
think it wholly unnecessary, after the many instances which I
have seen of men of sense and rank discredited, vilified and
undone by keeping such company. Vanity, that source of
many of our follies, and some of our crimes, has sunk many a
man into company in every light infinitely below himself, for
the sake of being the first man in it; there he dictates, is
applauded, admired; and for the sake of being the Coryphaeus
of that wretched chorus, disgraces and disqualifies himself
soon from any better company. Depend upon it, you will sink
or rise to the level of the company which you commonly
keep...'

4

THE SPIRIT OF PLAY

'*Is there a guilty deed I have not done,*
What say you, Coz? The Captain answered "None".
Have I not acted every villain's part?
Have I not broke a noble parent's heart?
Do I not daily boast how I've betrayed
The tender widow and the virtuous maid?
By deeds of ill have I not seemed to live?
The Captain gave a bold affirmative.'

('To the Worst Man in His Majesty's Dominions',
from Diaboliad, *by* WILLIAM COMBE)

LORD CHESTERFIELD was exceptional in the trouble he took to steer his heir away from the evils of the society in which he lived, and his wise words quoted on the previous page could have served as a lesson to many another unruly son had their fathers taken so keen an interest in their moral upbringing. In most cases, however, relations between fathers and children were far more remote. By the age of seven, when they were old enough no longer to be treated as pets, boys were usually sent away to school, from which they often did not return for years, spending their holidays instead with close relatives, uncles and aunts, or grown-up brothers and sisters. Frequently the schools to which they were sent were more conducive to rebellion than to good learning, for, until Thomas Arnold made a start on sweeping reforms in the early nineteenth century, the English public school system was extremely disorganised.

Public schools in England in the early eighteenth century were places where boys associated only with one another, with almost no adult companionship or supervision outside the hours of class. Thus cut off from their parents and ignored by their masters, the boys often turned hostile and vented their feelings in violence against each other, in attacks on outsiders, and in organised rebellions against authority. At Westminster, for example, to which in this period twenty-five per cent of the aristocracy sent their offspring, there were in 1690 only two full-time assistant masters to supervise all the boys, while those masters who came in from outside drifted in in the morning without any apparent regard for punctuality. Idleness and truancy were rife, and the younger boys were terrorised by bullies 'sending gentleman's sons on their errands to fetch them strong drink, buttered ale, cakes, custards, and tarts etc. to the school door; and not only to fetch, but to pay for them too; and if they refuse to go, they are abused and beaten with ropes ends and sometimes with sticks, and cudgels: not only to bruises and bloodshed, but often even to wounds and scars that remain all the days of their life.' Nor could they expect any protection from the Monitors and Seniors who 'esteem it a privilege belonging to their places to strike and abuse … their juniors; without any manner of provocation or just cause: sometimes flinging them on the ground, dragging them by the hair, treading them under foot, only to show their authority; which the inferiors dare not complain of, for fear of worse usage and therefore must be contented to endure it, unless they can rescue themselves by money or some present of tart, fruit, or such like gratification.' At night the boys wandered round the school unsupervised.

Violence was endemic, particularly against any outsider who might have strayed into the territory. In July 1679 a bailiff took possession of a house within the precincts of the school, and arrested the owner. The boys, regarding this action as an infringement of ancient privileges, such as that of Sanctuary, raced to help the owner of the house. When they came upon the bailiff, they clubbed him to death. Eleven of them, who were picked out of an identity parade of the whole school, were indicted for murder. These included Charles Montagu, later Earl of Halifax, and Francis Gastrell, the future Bishop of Chester. It was only the granting of a Pardon under the Great Seal that saved them all from the gallows. In 1722 three lives were lost in a battle against boys from other schools, while in 1779 six boys were tried and sentenced to a month's imprisonment for assaulting a man whom they had brutally beaten and wounded after threatening to 'rip him up' if he would not kneel down and ask their pardon.

Westminster was by no means alone in its shortcomings. Lord Ashley complained that although his brother had spent seven years at Winchester he was still unable to translate Latin. Instead he had learned to drink. The masters were over-indulgent, eventually allowing the boys to keep both horses and dogs, and seemed to bother little about teaching. At Harrow, in 1771, there were riots following the appointment of an unpopular headmaster, in the course of which the coach of one of the Governors was dragged out of the Yard to the King's Head, stoned, rolled down the hill to the Common, and smashed to pieces. In order to defuse the situation, the whole school was sent home for a week.

It was Eton, however, that was the home of organised rebellion. As early as 1729 Lord Bristol, in a letter to his wife, wrote of an uprising of the boys. 'The whole government of the school,' he reported, 'was in a state of anarchy.' He described the headmaster, Dr. George, as being 'so weak as to invite another'. The most serious rebellion at Eton took place in 1768 when the whole of the Sixth Form, and some of the Fifth and Fourth forms – one hundred and sixty boys in all – threw their school books into the Thames, and marched away from the school over a dispute over Sixth Form privileges. It was a badly organised affair, however, and after spending a night in Maidenhead the rebels returned and attempted to make a bargain with the Headmaster, Dr. Foster, whereby they would agree to capitulate in return for his assurance that they would all be treated equally. Their solidarity was broken when he resolutely refused to comply with their wishes, and discipline was restored within a few days.

In November 1783 there was a mass resignation of the Assistant Masters following some differences with the then Headmaster, Dr. Davies. For two days he was left as the only master in charge of the Upper School, a situation which certain of the boys tried to take advantage of to press various grievances. Dr. Davies's refusal to relax in any way the discipline of the school was the signal for the outbreak of another serious riot. He was driven out of the Upper School by a mob which proceeded to smash every window in sight, and to break up all his furniture and destroy all his papers. They seized the whipping block which they proceeded to carve up with red hot pokers, the wood being too hard for their knives. The situation was only prevented from getting out of hand by the return of the Assistant Masters to help re-establish law and order, and by sending the boys home for Christmas at the beginning of December.

When Keate took over Eton at the turn of the nineteenth century, discipline was at its lowest ebb. The boys' regard for authority was well demonstrated by an incident that took place in his first year. After the refusal of a hundred or more boys in the Fifth Form to conform to an extra roll-call he had instituted, he announced his intention to flog every one of them, a punishment he duly carried out in public on 2 June 1810. He had birched only twenty of them, however, when the spectators began to pelt him with rotten eggs, forcing him to abandon the operation until he had recruited enough Assistant Masters to control the mob.

The most serious trouble which faced Keate took place in October 1818 when he decided once and for all to put a stop to the illegal extra-curricular activities of the boys which were rife at the time, in particular hunting, shooting, and tandem-driving. He thus ordered a five o'clock curfew in the houses. For several days following the enforcement of this new law the school was in an uproar. 'Detonating balls bought at Windsor Fair were thrown about during lessons, the windows of one of the Masters' houses were smashed, and part of the wall of the Long Walk was thrown down.' When a boy called Marriott was expelled for driving a tandem, the whole of the Upper School booed and hissed Keate at a poetry reading on the following day, and pelted him with rotten eggs. His great desk was broken up, and placards were affixed to the doors of the Chapel and other conspicuous places in the school which read 'Down with Keate', 'No Five o'Clock Absence', and 'Floreat Seditio'. The rebellion lasted about a week, at the end of which Keate once again had the boys under control, though he continued to have great difficulty controlling the riding and tandem-driving.

In his history of Eton College, Christopher Hollis remarks that it is hard to understand why parents sent their sons to public schools at this period when riots of all sorts were common-place. He concludes that rather than take any interest in the scholastic education of these young aristocrats, their main concern was to get their tiresome offspring out of the way while they were at a difficult age. Hollis quotes William Cory who said that 'The squires who knew how hard it was to rule the peasants wished no doubt to have their beefy brats coerced sharply.' It is certainly true that the state of anarchy that existed in many public schools was nevertheless accompanied by the harshest system of discipline. This usually consisted of two forms. The first was to strike the hand or mouth with a ferula, a flat piece of wood which expanded at the end into a pear shape with a hole in the middle, one blow with which was enough to raise a most painful blister. The second and most common was either to lay the child across a whipping-block, or to horse him onto the back of a companion, and to flog his naked buttocks with a bundle of birches until the blood flowed. Punishments such as these were a normal and daily occurrence, and some of the most famous Headmasters were notorious for their savagery.

Keate, for example, seemed to take an almost sadistic pleasure in the use of the birch. Whether it was for shirking a roll-call, or for some far graver misdemeanour, he flogged on the slightest excuse. It seems as if sometimes he must have flogged all day. W. H. Tucker, in his *Eton of Old*, relates how, on one occasion, when a large number of boys were found cheating, 'Keate made short work of it. He devoted the whole seventy-two to the block after the next school time. It was a grand scene in the Library ... The floor was covered with victims; the benches and tables with spectators; upwards of a hundred present ...'

Men who endured brutal schooldays thought it only right that their sons should too. To them a flogging was in a way similar to the blooding ceremony on a hunt. It initiated the boys into his first venture into male society. One cannot however but feel that the men who emerged from these violent schools, although they may have been extremely independent and self-assured, had little love left in their hearts, even for themselves.

George, Earl of Euston, is a good example of the worst kind of vicious bully that was produced by this system. There is virtually nothing that can be said in his favour, for he heaped misfortune not only upon his own distinguished family, but upon the great family of Boyle into which he married. The eldest son of the second Duke of Grafton, he was born in August 1715, and was educated at Eton, during the period of the 1729 rebellion. By the time he reached his early twenties he was so widely known and despised for his wanton exploits that, when his engagement was announced to the beautiful heiress Lady Dorothy Boyle, daughter of the third Earl of Burlington, society was scandalised. In a letter of 15 October 1740, Frances, Countess of Hertford wrote to Henrietta Louise, Countess of Pomfret, of

'such conduct ... in my Lord Euston that formed a great part of the conversation of all companies last winter. Your Lady-ship undoubtedly knows that a marriage was agreed on for

9. LADY DOROTHY BOYLE (Zincke)

him and Lady Dorothy Boyle ... But though Lady Dorothy, besides her large fortune, is said to have all the sense and gentleness of temper that can be desired in a wife; and has so fine a face that, were her person answerable to it, one could scarcely imagine any thing more beautiful; yet he takes every opportunity to show his contempt, and even aversion for her;

whilst she entertains very different sentiments for him; and which, notwithstanding the great modesty of her temper, she cannot always conceal. Amongst the many balls that were given last Spring, there was a very magnificent one at the Duke of Norfolk's; where I saw so many instances of the slighting manner in which he treated her, and of her attention to him, as raised both my indignation and pity. But I heard that at another, where I was not present, he carried his unpoliteness much further; for when the company were sitting at supper (he being placed next to her), after looking upon her sometime in a very odd manner, he said, "Lady Dorothy, how greedily you eat! It is no wonder you are so fat!" This unexpected compliment made her blush extremely and brought tears into her eyes ... It was only a few days before I left London that this happened; and I knew of nothing since, but they are not married; and indeed I hope they never will be so ... were she my daughter, I should with less reluctance prepare for her funeral than such a marriage.'

These were chillingly prophetic words. The marriage took place on 10 October 1741. On 22 October, Horace Walpole wrote to Sir Horace Mann: 'I wrote you word that Lord Euston is married; in a week more I believe I shall write you word that he is divorced; he is brutal enough.' As soon as Euston had Lady Dorothy legally in his grasp he literally imprisoned her in his house, and refused entry to her mother, Lady Burlington. As a result of this, 'The whole family,' wrote Walpole, 'is in confusion; the Duke of Grafton half-dead, and Lord Burlington half-mad. The latter has challenged Lord Euston who accepted the challenge, but they were prevented; there are different stories ... in short one cannot go into a room, but you hear something of it: don't you pity the poor girl? Of the softest temper, vast beauty, birth and fortune! to be so sacrificed!'

Five months later, on 2 May 1742, Lady Dorothy was dead, 'delivered', in the words of the inscription written by her heartbroken mother on her portrait at Chiswick house, 'by death from misery'. Officially she died of smallpox. The truth is somewhat different. It is laid down in an obscure book, *Anecdotes and Biographical Sketches* by Elizabeth, Duchess of Devonshire, wife of the 5th Duke, according to whom, soon after his marriage, Lord Euston became obsessed with the idea that no child of this union should ever inherit his title and fortune. Thus 'when Lady Euston was with child, he drove her through the worst paved streets in

London: he made her walk till exhausted; she has been seen to sit fainting on the steps before the doors of people's houses. Sir Harry Englefield told me that Mr. Churchill, who is now alive, told him that he had seen her; and my aunt Lady Mary Fitzgerald, gave me the same account. When Lady Euston was in labour, he suffered none but the midwife to come, and after her death, for she died in labour, the same thing. The birth was premature, and the child died.'

As far as Euston was concerned, Lady Dorothy was well out of the way, for all along he had had designs on the wife of his brother, Lord Augustus Fitzroy, who had died in the West Indies in 1741. The haste with which he pursued this amour, with his wife still warm in the grave, shocked everyone. Mrs. Delaney wrote to her sister Mrs. Dewes, in January 1743: 'Now I talk of worthlessness, I must tell you the present discourse of the town is that Lord Euston is certainly going to be married to his sister-in-law, Lady Augustus Fitzroy ... What a monster he will show himself to be and his co-partner in wickedness no less so!'

In the event the marriage never took place. Perhaps Lady Augustus saw the error of her ways. Whatever the truth may have been, one thing is certain. Lord Euston's behaviour was going from bad to worse. In January 1743 Lady Hertford had written to Lord Beauchamp, of how 'Lord Euston has very near murdered two of his servants by beating them,' while in June Walpole wrote of how, when on a visit to Euston, he found the Duke of Grafton 'so unhappy in his heir apparent, that he checks his hand in almost everything he undertakes.' In October 'at Tunbridge with a Captain Wynne' he 'got drunk and went about the Wells and beat every man and woman they met, broke the church windows, and committed every disorder that drink and their own folly could inspire them with.'

At this point the Duke, finally driven beyond the limits of his endurance, disowned his son once and for all. It was an act which Lord Euston had not bargained for, but there was to be no reconciliation. Writing to Lord Beauchamp in December 1743, Lady Hertford told how:

'Lord Euston forced himself into the Duke of Grafton's house the other morning at eight o'clock, and would have gone to his bedside if the valet de chambre (who was waiting in the next room) had not prevented him. The Duke rose, and as soon as he was dressed, came out to him. Lord Euston threw himself at his feet, professed great remorse for his past conduct, and promised an entire reformation for the time to come. But the Duke told him he had tried him too often to be deceived any more, and that God was his witness that no man had ever loved a son more tenderly, or seen him lost with greater pain; but that was over now, and that he attempted in vain to move the bowels of a father who had long since looked upon himself to have no son. Thus they parted...'

There is one last piece of documentary evidence relating to the subsequent career of George Euston. On 4 October 1744, the Countess of Denbigh writing to her friend Lady Townshend, told of how:

'Lord Euston is gone off with a young lady into Italy, whose name is Nevill, of a very ancient family in Lincolnshire, with £11,000, for her fortune and a celebrated beauty; they fell in love with one another this season at the Hot Wells at Bristol, where she agreed to run away with him ... She has one brother who has a good estate and they say is a man of honour, spirit, and resolution, who, as soon as he heard of this affair, went pat after them, declaring that he would never come back to England, till he had forced Lord Euston either to marry her or to fight...'

He certainly did not marry the lady. More than that history does not relate. He died in Bath in July 1747, aged thirty-one. It may be imagined that the Duke breathed a sigh of relief. He was not alone in his filial problems, however. His political opponent John Carteret, 2nd Earl Granville, had an equally deplorable son Robert who made, according to Mrs. Delaney, 'but a poor figure, and is not a favourite with any of the family.' Walpole, writing in July 1744, tells of how 'about a fortnight ago he was at the Duke of Bedford's and as much in his few senses as ever. At five o'clock in the morning he waked the Duke and Duchess, all bloody and with the lapel of his coat held up full of ears; he had been in the stable and cropped all the horses.' 'The Duke,' wrote Elizabeth Wyndham to the Countess of Denbigh in July 1744, 'was so shocked [by this behaviour] that he made it known to his father through one of his friends that he ought to be looked after, as he had every sign of having a disturbed brain, which may well be the case as he drinks brandy from morning till night.'

Apart from the odd reference to him in contemporary letters, very little is known of the life of Robert Carteret. The best testimony as to his career is from a memoir of him published shortly after his death in 1776. It describes him as having been

'rather deficient in his intellects; fond of low company, profuse, fickle, and debauched. Though he had travelled in France, that country celebrated for elegance of manners, and brilliancy of dress, imitated by all its neighbours, Lord Carteret appeared constantly in the mean garment of a groom or a coachman, shunning his equals, and rioting in taverns with pimps and prostitutes. The conclusion of his inglorious amours was a Fleet marriage with one Molly Paddock, a woman of vile extraction, bold, loose and vulgar. She was the superintendent of a bagnio when his Lordship began an acquaintance with her, and though the charms of her person were no more than those of her mind (being coarse, short and clumsy) he gave her the preference above the stale beauties of this seminary of antivestals. His noble parent, who had to do everything in his power to reclaim him from disgrace and infamy, on receiving intelligence of a match that reflected an indelible reproach upon his family, disowned and abandoned him; allowing him merely what was necessary for food and raiment. With this scanty pension Lord Carteret could not afford long to drink Burgundy and Clarets to excess; his creditors' impatience being worn out, and the bailiffs growing troublesome, he threw himself within the verge of the court of green cloth with his wedded dame. My Lord walked regularly every day four or five hours in the Mall of St. James's Park, and now and then joined conversation with servant maids, street walkers and needy adventurers; no gentleman was ever seen with him, thinking it beneath them to associate with such a character. He wore commonly a large coachman's hat, with the flaps down, a jockey-striped waistcoat, and his garters below his knees.

'When he had money enough to invite three or four hungry parasites to dine with him, they remained in his Lordship's company till about one o'clock, that he went to bed scarce ever sober. He spoke French fluently, but was in other respects extremely illiterate as he never read anything but the jockey's calendar. He lived eight or nine years in this contemptible indolence and obscurity.

'After the death of his father he resided chiefly at his country seat in Bedfordshire; where he entertained all the grooms and jockeys of the county, without any change in his dress and manners. The jolly Countess survived but a little time her additional title and fortune. He seldom attended the House of Peers, and when he came to London, it was to diversify his amours, always in the humble and despicable class of chambermaids and women of pleasure.'

Carteret died in February 1776.

'In him,' continued the memoir, 'is literally extinct the lustre of his family, of which he was the last. He had been long sunk into oblivion, and dead to the polite world before he paid the last debt to nature.'

In oblivion he has remained ever since.

But oblivion is rarely the fate of the wicked, whose lives invariably hold a far greater fascination for their descendants than those of the blameless. In later generations, however evil they may have been, a certain romance becomes attached to their names. Maud Wyndham, in her introduction to Blunt's life of her ancestor Thomas, Lord Lyttelton, published in 1936, wrote:

'In his family "Naughty Tom" stands out as a spectacular figure, for although in Victorian days the nefarious doings which earned him the sobriquet were not disclosed to the younger sons, and in fact were only vaguely known to their elders, we were all familiar with the strange story of his death, and that it was on his account that the name Thomas, which had been a favoured family name since the days of Thomas Lyttelton the judge, was forthwith dropped like a live coal. Thus a certain glamour was shed over the personality of "Naughty Tom", and his portraits were gazed at, not only by the young, with an interest which those of more respectable forbears failed to excite.'

'A very bad man – downright wicked' was how Fox described Thomas, 2nd Lord Lyttelton, while other chroniclers of his day, in their efforts to portray his character, exhausted almost every epithet in the category of infamy. He was branded at once as a monster, scoundrel, madman, coward, and an abandoned wretch. His 'detestable character,' wrote Horace Walpole, 'was devoid of every principle and sentiment that became a man and his ingratitude, profligacy, extravagance and want of honour and

10. THOMAS, 2nd Lord Lyttelton (Richard Cosway)

decency seemed to aim at nothing but afflicting his father, shocking mankind and disgracing himself.'

The story of Thomas 'The Wicked Lord' Lyttelton is a good illustration of how someone was ruined by the fact that he was an only son, and heir to a great house and fortune. His mother died in 1747 when he was just three years old, and he and his sister spent most of their childhood with their maternal grandmother, Mrs. Fortescue, who lived in Gloucestershire. As the hopes and aspirations of the whole family were concentrated on him, he was thoroughly spoiled.

'Being the only boy, and hope of the family,' he later wrote, 'and having such an hereditary and collateral right to genius, talent, and virtue, my earliest prattle was the subject of continuous admiration; as I increased in years, I was encouraged in boldness ... while sallies of impertinence, for which I should have been scourged, were fondly considered as marks of an astonishing prematurity of abilities ... I suppose such a hotbed of flattery was never before used to spoil a mind and to choke it with bad qualities, as was applied to mine.'

Of his father, George, the first Baron Lyttelton, a great scholar and orator, who was to be known to history as 'The Good Lord

11. Hagley, Worcestershire

Lyttelton', he saw comparatively little. He was too engrossed in politics to pay much attention to the upbringing of his son, a fact which prompted Elizabeth Montagu, a close friend of the family, to write to him chiding him for neglecting the boy during the most impressionable years: 'Your public life will raise a high expectation of your son; it is but just that you should give some of your private hours to qualify him to answer it.' That he failed to heed this advice is evident from the fact that by the time Thomas was sixteen he was already going against society. In a letter written in September 1760, after the great ball which had been held to celebrate the family's moving into their fine new mansion, Hagley Hall, designed by Sanderson Miller as a worthy seat for the young heir from whom so much was hoped and expected, Lord Lyttleton described how Thomas, 'destined to have opened the ball with the first person of the first class, mutinied, and would dance only with a smart girl he had brought in the morning from a neighbouring village.'

In 1758 Thomas went up to Eton, where he showed himself to be a good scholar, the Headmaster, Dr. Barnard, even going so far as to compare his abilities with those of Charles James Fox who was his contemporary there. From there he went up to Oxford in 1762, the second stage of a typical progression for a young nobleman, which was aimed, in his case, at leading to a career in Parliament. Part of that progression was also the marrying of a suitable wife, and while he was still at Oxford just such a bride was found for him by his father in the person of Anne Warburton, a considerable, and not unattractive, heiress from Cheshire. Judging from a set of rather feeble verses which he dedicated to this young lady, entitled 'From the Squirrels in Hagley Park to Miss Warburton's Squirrel,' Thomas was rather taken with her. However, since he was only nineteen, and no marriage settlement could be made until he attained his majority, it was strongly recommended by his uncle, Sir Richard Lyttelton, that the marriage should wait, and that he should be sent on the Grand Tour. Sir Richard even offered to bear the expense of the trip himself.

> 'It was determined,' Thomas was to write, 'for me to make the Tour of Europe, previous to my marriage . . . But this was not all. For the better enabling of me to make a proper and becoming appearance, or, in other words, to give me very means of gratification, the family purse was lavishly held forth; I was left almost without control in point of expense, and every method pursued to make me return the very reverse of what expectation had painted me.'

The Grand Tour was part of the education of every young gentleman. The idea being that the young man emerging from boyhood should be conducted by some suitable person, usually a tutor, around all the most interesting places in Europe. These journeys, however, were not without pitfalls. Philip Thicknesse, writing in 1777, warned parents that all the great towns between London and Home abounded with

> 'artful, designing, wicked men, and profligate, abandoned, and prostitute women . . . and they are principally set to catch the young Englishman of fortune, from the age of eighteen to five and twenty . . . I have seen and heard of such wicked artifices of these people, and the fatal consequences to the unfortunate young men they have ensnared, that I really think I could never enjoy a single hour of contentment, if I had a large fortune, while a son of mine was making what is called the Tour of Europe.'

It is quite evident that many Grand Tourers returned from their travels, not as educated and well-mannered gentlemen, but rather as fully fledged rakes and spendthrift gamblers. 'Thus finished and adorned by their travels,' wrote Chesterfield, to his son, in a letter warning him against the dangers of keeping bad company while abroad, 'they become the disturbers of Play-houses; they break the windows, and commonly the landlords, of the taverns where they drink; and are at once the support, the terror, and the victims of the houses they frequent. These poor mistaken people think they shine, and so they do indeed; but it is as putrefaction shines in the dark.'

The Grand Tour certainly did little to improve Thomas Lyttelton. He left England in October 1763, travelling first to Paris, and from there to Turin, and then to Venice, carrying with him all the way a lock of his fiancée's hair as a talisman. If this was expected to protect him against the temptations of fashionable society in Italy, the intrigues and the vice, then it signally failed to do so. Hardly had he arrived in Venice than he lost so heavily at the gaming tables that he was forced to write to his uncle to beg him for more money. On a visit to Bologna he was involved in two duels, one with an Englishman, with whom he had been at Eton, while his 'affairs of gallantry' were soon notorious. There is no doubt that Sir Horace Mann, the British envoy in Florence, was less than favourably impressed by him.

'We have here a very odd young man,' he wrote to Horace Walpole on 11 August 1764, 'the son of Lord Lyttelton, one who has already taken a resolution to make himself consider-able by opposition, and whose ambition will bear no control. If he does succeed, it must be by the force of that and the harshest means only, for his contradictory temper makes it impossible for him to agree with anybody, and his behaviour in general disobliges and offends so that he is shunned by both the English and the Italians, whom he in return despises . . . On his return he must soon make himself talked of, as he has given occasion in every place he has passed through, much to his disadvantage.'

The gambling leases in Venice were evidently on sufficiently large a scale to bring the wrath of the whole family down upon him. When his uncle finally paid up Thomas wrote a grovelling letter of thanks filled with the usual shallow sentiments of spendthrift youth:

'Nothing I can ever do can balance the account, but no future ill-conduct of mine shall, at least designedly, lower me in your opinion and affections. In respect to the cursed transaction that raised your just anger at me at Venice, I do give you the most solemn and sacred assurances that you have nothing to fear on that account. Gaming I hold in detestation, and if again I ever relapse in that absurd vice, I will forfeit my life, my estate, or what is as dear to me as either, the good opinion of men, and will allow myself to be treated with universal contempt.'

If drink was the scourge of the Restoration era, then gambling was that of the eighteenth century. Society was like one vast casino. On whatever pretext and under whatever circumstances, if half a dozen people of fashion found themselves together, whether for music, or dancing, or politics, or drinking the waters or each other's wine, the box was sure to be rattling, and the cards being cut and shuffled. In 1750 Thomas's father had written to Dr. Doddridge:

'The Dryads of Hagley are at present pretty secure, but I tremble to think that the rattling of a dice box at White's* may one day or other (if my son should be a member of that noble academy) shake down all our fine oaks. It is dreadful to see, not only there, but almost in every house in town, what devastations are made by that destructive fury, the spirit of play.'

He did not exaggerate. Men and women gambled on a scale which has never been equalled. 'The gaming,' wrote Horace Walpole in 1770, 'is worthy the decline of our Empire. The young men lose five, ten, fifteen thousand pounds in an evening. Lord Stavordale, not one and twenty, lost eleven thousand last Tuesday, but recovered it by one great hand at Hazard. He swore a great oath, "Now if I had been playing deep, I might have won millions".' Millions were lost daily. Wriothesley Russell, for example, the third Duke of Bedford, a thoroughly dissatisfied and bored young man, who died at the age of twenty-four, sustained losses that were so enormous that they put into jeopardy even the vast estates and fortune he had inherited from his father, who was said to have been the richest man in England.

---

* White's Chocolate House in St James's was, along with Almack's and Brookes, one of the most notorious gambling clubs of the day, where many a fortune was thrown away on games like Hazard and Faro.

In one session at Newmarket, playing from ten o'clock on Saturday night till eight o'clock on Sunday night, in a shuttered room so that he would not give offence by being seen to play on Sunday, by the light of candles, he lost thirty thousand pounds, the equivalent today of over a million pounds.

Thomas Lyttelton's contemporary, Charles James Fox, was perhaps the greatest gambler of the age. Considering that he was almost weaned on the pastime this is not so surprising. When he was about fourteen his father, Lord Holland, who believed that a bright child should be indulged in every possible way, took him away from Eton to join the fashionable at Spa. Here, every night for four months, he was given five guineas to lose at the gaming tables. As a result of this, when the boy returned to Eton, he managed to turn the school into a gambling den.

Fox's love of play was desperate, and before he had reached the age of thirty he had completely dissipated everything he could get his hands on. Horace Walpole records that in the debate on the Thirty-Nine Articles on 6 February 1772, Fox did not shine,

'nor could it be wondered at. He had sat up playing at Hazard at Almack's, from Tuesday evening the fourth till five in the afternoon of Wednesday the fifth. An hour before he had recovered £12,000 that he had lost, and by dinner, which was at five o'clock, he had ended losing £11,000. On the Thursday he spoke in the above debate; went to dinner at past eleven at night; from thence to White's, where he drank till seven the next morning; thence where he won £6,000; and between three and four in the afternoon he set out for Newmarket. His brother Stephen lost £11,000 two nights after; and Charles £10,000 on the thirteenth: so that, in three nights, the two brothers, the eldest not twenty-five, lost £32,000.'

Fox got by only by borrowing shamelessly from his friends, many of whom never saw their money again.

'The capital sufferer,' notes Walpole, 'was the young Earl of Carlisle, who tho' possessed of a very ample estate, was encumbered with his own and his father's debts. Yet had he borrowed of the Jews for Charles £14,000, for which he had bound himself to pay annually to those extortioners the amazing sum of £2,500 a year, a revenue he was so little able to furnish that he saw an execution in his house, and was obliged to retire into Yorkshire with his wife and children.'

When Fox's debts were finally added up, they amounted to the incredible sum of £147,000.

But while Fox was bailed out by his father and friends, and went on to have a distinguished political career, others were not so lucky, often with tragic results. Sir John Bland of Kippax Park, for example, ruined himself at the game of Hazard. He once lost £32,000 at a single sitting to a certain Captain Scott. In the end he shot himself on the road from Calais to Paris. Lord Montfort, of whom it was said by Walpole, that he 'would have betted any man in England against himself for self-murder,' also took his life after gambling away his entire fortune, and leaving his estates in a ruinous condition. It was not unusual for whole properties to change hands at the tables. Shelley Hall in Suffolk was lost at play by Thomas Kerridge, the last Squire, who died in 1743. According to tradition he gambled away the house room by room, and, when all the contents were gone and the house gutted, he pulled down certain portions and gambled away the bricks.

This passion was in no way confined to men. 'The surest road into the graces of a fine lady,' wrote Sir George Trevelyan in his *Early History of Charles James Fox*, 'was to be known as one who betted freely and lost handsomely ... It was next to impossible for a lad still in his teens to keep himself from the clutch of these elegant harpies.' Walpole complained that 'The ladies game too deep for me. The last time I was in town Lady Hertford wanted one, and I lost fifty-six guineas before I could say an Ave Maria. I do not know a teaspoonful of news. I could tell you what was trumps, but that was all I heard!'

In the latter part of the eighteenth century many ladies opened their town houses as private gambling clubs. Of these the most notorious were those of Lady Archer and Lady Buckingham-shire, who is said to have slept with a blunderbuss and a pair of pistols by her bedside to protect her Faro bank. From *The Times* of 13 March 1797, comes this account of her household:

'On Saturday came to be heard information against Lady Buckinghamshire, Lady Elizabeth Luttrell, Mrs. Sturt, and Mrs. Concannon for having on the night of the thirtieth of last January played at Faro at Lady Buckinghamshire's house in St. James's Square, and Mr. Martindale was charged with being the proprietor of the table. The evidence went to prove that the defendants had gaming parties at their different houses in

12. The Gaming Table at Devonshire House (Rowlandson)

rotation; and that when they met at Lady Buckinghamshire's, the witnesses used to wait upon them in the gambling room, and that they played at E.O., Rouge et Noir etc from about eleven or twelve till about three or four o'clock in the morning...'

The Lady Elizabeth Luttrell who is mentioned in this account was herself something of a black ewe, and she came to an extraordinary and tragic end. She was the sister-in-law of George III's brother, the Duke of Cumberland, and was described in a memoir by Lady Louisa Stuart as having been 'more precisely what the Regent Orléans entitled a Roué than one would have thought it practicable that anyone in petticoats could be.' Sir Robert Heron records that she 'resided with her sister the Duchess of Cumberland, played high and cheated much. She was commonly called the Princess Elizabeth. On the death of her sister she was thrown into gaol. There she gave a hairdresser £50 to marry her: her debts then becoming his, she was discharged. She went abroad where she descended lower and lower; till, being convicted of picking pockets at Augsburgh, she was condemned to clean the streets, chained to a wheelbarrow: in that miserable situation she terminated her existence by poison.' It would be hard to imagine a greater fall from grace.

A leading member of Lady Archer's circle who was hopelessly addicted to play was Georgiana Spencer, 5th Duchess of Devonshire. Though at the age of sixteen, when she married, her allowance of £2,000 a year might have seemed an inexhaustible fortune, she was soon losing hundreds of pounds a night, and was in the clutches of moneylenders like Henry Martindale. When her debts had risen to over £6,000, her friend the banker Thomas Coutts made a desperate, though unsuccessful, effort to persuade her to change her ways.

'It shocks me to think,' he wrote to her, 'what your Grace puts into Hazard by indulging a passion for play. There is nothing your Grace can acquire; you have already titles, character, friends, fortune, power, beauty, *everything* superior to the rest of the world ... all these you risk to gratify this destructive passion. I should be happy beyond expression if I could think that I had even the smallest share in saving your Grace from the dreadful consequences I foresee...'

13. LADY ELIZABETH LUTTRELL (Gainsborough)

But consequences are the last thing that the gambler considers. Had Thomas Lyttelton done so he might have kept his promises of reform to his uncle. Instead a letter written from Dijon in February 1765 shows that he had been forced to borrow a further £500 to discharge debts of honour, as well as £250 for expenses at Marseilles and Aix. His excuse for his behaviour was predictable:

'I have only one reflection to make in order to vindicate the enormity of my conduct from the charge of folly or downright absurdity. A man of violent and sensible desires who quits involuntarily a woman he loves with fury, cannot so recompose his passions as not to fall into some excess. The inebriation produced by high play is delicious to a mind that hates tranquility, and to a heart that is impressed with the image of a woman it cannot enjoy.'

He was careful to point out that this was not a reference to Miss Warburton, 'but to an Italian Lady.' It is scarcely surprising that when he finally returned home, it was to find that his engagement had been called off. His father received him back into the fold, declaring in a letter to his brother William his belief that Thomas would never game again:

'I hope his return into England, and cool reflection on the mischiefs of his past follies will enable his reason to get the better of any recent ill habits contracted by him abroad.'

It was a vain hope.

Thomas's reunion with his family did not last long, and he was soon an outcast again, returning abroad at the end of 1765. Whatever his bad behaviour was, and doubtless the gaming tables were involved, it was evidently too much for his father to bear. In a letter to Dr. Humphrey Owen, Librarian of Bodley College, Oxford, of 26 June 1766, he wrote:

'This is only to tell you that my graceless son refused to come over, and says he can live independent upon me. Never was anything so mad or so insolent as his letter...'

The letter referred to read as follows:

'My Lord, it is full time to give a definite answer to the proposals transmitted to me by your Lordship near a year ago, and on the acceptance of which you say the honour of my family, and future happiness depends. My Lord, I certainly have had leisure enough to reflect on the contents of these proposals, and after the most mature deliberation think it necessary to inform your Lordship that I think it the most monstrous and absurd proposition that ever was made by one man to another, and I do assure your Lordship as a certain and unalterable truth that I never will assent to all or any part of them.'

Though history does not relate exactly what were these 'proposals' that Lord Lyttelton had put to his son, one can surmise that they were to do with coming to live at Hagley, settling down, giving up gambling, finding a wife, and so on and it is a tribute to Lord Lyttelton that, in spite of the insolence of Thomas's reaction to them, he never gave up trying to bring his son to his senses, and to effect a reconciliation, much to the despair of many of his friends. When, for example, he wrote to Elizabeth Montagu in the autumn of 1766 to tell her that he had once again asked Thomas to come to Hagley, she replied strongly:

'I cannot say I relish the scheme of Mr. Lyttelton's being at Hagley. His mind is too much dissipated and shattered for study. He will bully your steward, debauch your tenants, and perhaps introduce a profligacy into your neighbourhood, which will be very detrimental to your Lordship as a landlord, and grievous to you as a Christian ... Yet I own anything may be better than his being in London.'

Thomas himself was only too aware of his own weaknesses. 'It is a great misfortune,' he wrote, 'that Vice, be what it may, will find someone or other to flatter it ... It requires a most gigantic resolution to suffer pain, when passion quickens every sense, and every enticing object beckons to enjoyment. I was not born a Stoic, nor am I made to be a martyr!'

In 1767 the family tried to halt Thomas's descent down the road to ruin by getting him a seat in Parliament. This, commented his uncle Charles, Bishop of Carlisle, would 'throw him into business and company proper for a young gentleman.' They chose for this purpose the neighbouring 'Pocket Borough' of Bewdley, a seat closely connected with the Lyttelton family, and in March 1768 he was returned as its Member, though with a majority of only three. He at once showed promise. His maiden speech, on 18 May, on the subject of the troubles in the American Colonies, was very well received. 'Mr. Burke,' wrote Elizabeth Montagu, 'told me the performance was in every respect such as to do him honour and give pleasure to his father, he not only having spoken with sense and eloquence, but with modesty and discretion...' Had Thomas kept his seat it may well have saved him. Unfortunately this was not to be. His opponents in the election disputed the result. They petitioned against him, and the committee which sat to consider this petition reported in their favour. In January 1769 his seat was transferred to his opponent.

The inevitable relapse took place. In June, at a Masquerade given by the Duke of Bolton, he 'terribly abused' Maria Waldegrave, the beautiful widowed Countess, who in 1766 had secretly married the Duke of Gloucester, a brother of George III. Though the marriage was not made public till 1771, everyone knew of it socially. 'Mr. Lyttelton,' wrote Lady Mary Coke in her journal, 'in the character of a Methodist preacher, reproved her conduct ... talking so much that he was at last desired to withdraw.'

A second incident combined to create the resentment of society against him further. Walpole relates how, at a supper at Almack's Club, Lady Archer, 'a young peeress remarkable for her tawdry dress and a prodigious quantity of rouge,' reproved Thomas for too much familiarity; upon which he retorted 'What! Do you pretend to talk, you drunken peacock?' and flung a glass of wine in her face. Her neighbour, William Combe, a boon companion of Thomas's, took the insult as intended for himself, unable to believe that his friend could be so brutal as to aim it at a woman. He challenged him to a duel, but Thomas, pursuing his usual means of avoiding the consequences of his mad behaviour, fled to France. With him went a certain Captain Ayscough, his cousin, and a man, according to Nicoll's *Literary Anecdotes of the Eighteenth Century*, also notorious for his debaucheries.

Thomas spent the next two years rambling about the Continent. Lady Mary Coke, in her journal of January 1770, wrote of him being at Marseilles, among the 'great number' of English there. 'Mr. Lyttelton is going on in his usual way. I saw a letter yesterday that mentioned his having put five-hundred Louis d'or on a card.' A few days later she says that she had heard he had lost

The finishing Touch.

14. LADY ARCHER (Gillray)

'£1,200 more than he had credit to pay, and has given a bill upon some banker in London. How I pity Lord Lyttelton!' The novelist Tobias Smollett ran into him in Venice early in 1771, and told of how 'He ventured in play like a madman: he lost one thousand sequins in cash and two-thousand eight-hundred upon credit, which in point of honour ought to have been paid within twenty-four hours, but which still remains unpaid.'

The result was a stream of begging letters to his father for more money. When his pleas failed, he threatened to sell his right to the succession of the estate.

'I had a most melancholy letter from Lord Lyttelton last post,' wrote Elizabeth Montagu to her husband. 'He has reason to entertain some apprehensions that his son has sold the reversion of the Estate and, as he says, sign'd and seal'd his ruin . . . Poor Lord Lyttelton will never again take pleasure in Hagley, doom'd and destin'd to fall to some usurer. What pity he built his fine house!

Happily this was a threat that Thomas never carried out.

In the Autumn of 1771 Thomas returned to England in the utmost secrecy in order that he might avoid the many creditors from whom he had escaped on his last visit. Early the following year, having remained in hiding 'till the hell-hounds which were in pursuit of me had relaxed their search,' he journeyed once again to Hagley, the prodigal son in search of reconciliation. His father seemed convinced that this time his mood of contrition was genuine. In reply to a letter from Lord Chatham, he wrote:

'I give you a thousand thanks for your very kind felicitations on the return of my son, who appears to be returned, not only to me, but to a natural way of thinking, and a dutiful conduct, in which if he perseveres, it will gild with joy the evening of my life . . .'

It never occurred to Lord Lyttelton for a single moment that he might have been in any way to blame for the way his son had turned out. Thomas was a highly intelligent young man, but with a wild and restless nature, and a weakness of character that led him always to take the easy way. Had he had a strong hand to guide him in the right direction, and encouragement not to give up at the first hurdle, there is every reason to believe that he might have turned out a brilliant success, rather than a wastrel. Thomas himself blamed his own shortcomings directly on 'the want of that kind of parental discernment which sees to the character of his child, watches over its growing dispositions, quietly moulds him to his will, and completes the whole by placing him into a situation suitable to him ... There is a great deal of difference between a good man and a good father; I have known bad men who excelled my father as much in parental care as he was superior to them in real virtue.'

Thomas had not been at Hagley long before he set about the ruthless conquest of an attractive widow, Mrs. Apphia Peach, who lived at the Leasowes, once the residence of the poet Shenstone, on the Hagley estate. His reasons were purely commercial. She had a fortune of £20,000 a year. 'Assiduity without love,' he wrote, 'tenderness without sincerity, and dalliance without desire afford the miserable, the hopeless, but the faithful picture of my sluggish journey to the temple of Hymen.' But in view of the fact that one of the issues of the match would be a 'separate maintenance and perhaps a titled dowry,' he considered the romantic aspect of little importance. He pursued her relentlessly, throwing himself at her feet, and protesting that she alone could be his salvation and help him to achieve the greatness which he knew was his desert. He had little difficulty in fooling his father into believing that this time he was genuinely in love. 'My dearest little woman is everything to me,' he wrote, 'the sweetest companion, the most sensible friend...' They were married in June. Mrs. Delany, writing to Lady Gower, expressed the sentiments of one and all on the subject:

> 'The adventurous widow, I am afraid at Hagley, will fail in her hopes of reforming a rake, and dearly pay for her presumption. Everybody is sorry, as she is well spoken of and much liked: but it is manifest that his whole scheme was to cheat her of her fortune. He prevailed with her to marry him before the writings were completed, which Lord Lyttelton was endeavouring to get finished as soon as possible; but now the wretch refuses to ratify them, so that he is now master of her fortune, and she unprovided for.'

Apphia's happiness was indeed short-lived. In February 1773 Mrs. Hood, a cousin of Thomas's, wrote that 'Domestic concerns in Hill Street have now come to their head, Mrs. Lyttelton and Lord Lyttelton being determined on a separation...' She went on to relate how Thomas 'has lived for the last two months with only laying at home now and then, at the gaming table, at the savoir vivre, and with women. His treatment of his wife on many occasions has been harsh and brutal...' Spring found him in Paris, in the company of a barmaid, a Miss Sarah Harris of Bolton's Inn at Hockerell.

In the Summer, back in England, the family name was once more dragged into a blaze of public notoriety when Thomas was involved in a brawl in Vauxhall Gardens, the most famous of the London pleasure gardens of the period. He was strolling there one evening with two friends, a Captain Croftes, and George Fitzgerald, whose love of duelling had already made him infamous as 'Fighting Fitzgerald,' when they came across the celebrated actress, Mrs. Hartley. Each time they passed her they insulted her by staring rudely into her face. Eventually her companion, the Reverend Mr. Bate, editor of the *Morning Post* and a noted pugilist, remonstrated with them and blows were exchanged. Bate then wrote an account of the affair and published it in the *Post*, causing a great stir. 'For the month past,' wrote Mrs. Boscawen to the Duchess of Argyll on 16 August, 'the town has talked of nothing but the fray at Vauxhall.'

Once again Thomas fled the country. 'Mr. Lyttelton,' wrote William Hickey, 'finding himself in such disgrace as to be nearly sent to Coventry by all respectable friends, went to the Continent, passing several months at the German Spa until he imagined the indignation his conduct excited had subsided.' Meanwhile his long-suffering father confided to Mrs. Montagu, with tear-filled eyes, that he was convinced his son was mad, and that, dreadful as the thought was, it was his only comfort. It was a comfort, however, that came too late. For some months he had been intermittently ill with an inflamation of the bowels, and on 22 August 1773, while Thomas was still abroad, he died. When the news reached Thomas he was in Paris.

'And I awoke, and behold I was a Lord!' he wrote. 'It was no unpleasant transition from an infernal and an uneasy pillow, from insignificance and dereliction, to be a Peer of Great Britain with all the privileges attendant upon that character, and some little estate into the bargain ... My natural genius will now have a full scope for exertion in the line of political duty, and I am disposed to flatter myself that the application necessary to make a respectable figure in that career will leave me but little time for those miserable pursuits which of late have been my only resource. But I must desire you not to expect an instant conversion.'

Reform for Thomas was made that much harder by the high moral esteem in which his father had been held. By contrast his own career, though no worse than those of Rochester, Killigrew or Spencer, was held to be influenced by the Devil, and his title of 'the Wicked Lord' was hard to shake off. He once wrote of how the parson at Hagley 'is in no small disgrace with his parishioners for entertaining so great a sinner as I am, and that one of them, who has seen me at Kidderminster, declares throughout the neighbourhood that I have a cloven foot.' Even when, after he had taken his seat, he succeeded in making a name for himself as a considerable orator in Parliament, the Mr. Hyde in his nature constantly lured him back to the gambling dens, and into the company of what a friend of his described as the 'outcasts of society.' 'There are moments', he reflected, 'when the full lustre of virtue beams upon me. I try to seize it, but the gleam escapes me, and I am reinvolved in darkness. The conflict of reason and passion is but the conflict of a moment, and the latter never fails to bear me off in triumph.'

It was not until another three years had passed that Thomas finally made a serious attempt to abandon his libertine ways. This was probably due to the deep impression made on him by the suicide of a close friend of his, John Damer, an event which created a profound sensation throughout society:

'it impressed the instances of pleasure, and all the gay world of fashion and frivolity, with a feeling which caused the event to be spoken of with bated breath and paled cheeks.'

The Honourable John Damer was the eldest son of Lord Milton, later created Earl of Dorchester, a peer reputed to have a fortune of £30,000 a year. John was educated at Eton, where he made friends with Thomas, and afterwards went with his younger brother George to Italy, where the latter was involved in a 'drunken riot' in Rome in which a coachman was killed. Soon after his return from Italy John married, in June 1767, Anne Seymour Conway, daughter of Field Marshal the Honourable Henry Seymour Conway, who brought with her £10,000. As far

15. The Hon. JOHN DAMER

as her father was concerned, he had made an excellent match for his daughter.

But John, along with his two brothers, George and Lionel, seemed bent on squandering his father's fortune before it came to him. In August 1776 Horace Walpole reported that the General had suffered from a stroke brought upon by his worries about his daughter's marriage.

'He is uneasy . . . with reason,' he wrote. 'Her husband, and his two brothers, have contracted a debt one can scarce expect to be believed out of England – of £70,000. Who but must think himself happy to marry a daughter with only £10,000 to a young man with £5,000 a year rent charge in present, and £22,000 a year settled? – and yet this daughter at present is ruined! . . . The young men of this age seem to have made a law amongst themselves for declaring their fathers superannuated at fifty, and then dispose of the estates as if already their own. How culpable to society was Lord Holland for setting an example of paying such enormous, such gigantic debts!'

But Lord Milton was a hard man. When John came to him to beg on bended knees for him to pay his debts, he refused to see him or his brothers. He had no intention of paying up. He let it be known that he expected the two elder boys to retire abroad to avoid disgrace. This was too much for John. On 15 August 1776, at three o'clock in the morning, after taking supper 'with four common women, a blind fiddler, and no other man,' he shot himself at the Bedford Arms in Covent Garden. 'What a catastrophe,' wrote Walpole, 'for a man at thirty-two, heir to two and twenty thousand a year ... Can the walls of Almack's help moralising when £5,000 a year in present, and £22,000 in reversion are not sufficient for happiness, and cannot check a pistol.'

Thomas himself lived for only another three years, and his death was as gossiped about as his life was. According to the account of his uncle Lord Westcote, which was drawn up and signed by him some ten weeks after the actual events, on 25 November 1779 Thomas recounted to a number of friends, the three Miss Amphletts and a Mrs. Flood, an extraordinary dream he had had the previous night. He was in a room when a bird flew in through the window, which suddenly changed into a woman dressed all in white who told him he was going to die in three days.

'In the evening of the following day, being Friday, he told the eldest Miss Amphlett, that she looked melancholy: but, said he, "You are foolish and fearful, I have lived two days and God willing I will live out the third." On the morning of Saturday he told the same ladies that he was very well, and believ'd he shou'd bilk the ghost. Some hours afterwards he went with them, Mr. Fortescue and Captain Wolsley, to Pitt Place at Epsom; withdrew to his bedchamber soon after eleven o'clock at night, talked cheerfully to his servant, and particularly inquir'd of him what care had been taken to provide good rolls for his breakfast the next morning; step'd into bed with his waistcoat on, and as his servant was pulling it off, put his hand to his side, sank back, and immediately expired without a groan.'

5

THE DEVIL'S DOING

'No study of the English landed family makes any sense unless the principle and practice of primogeniture is constantly borne in mind. It is something which went far to determine the behaviour and characteristics of both parents and children . . . Under such a system, both the elder and the younger children suffered. The latter normally inherited neither title nor estate, unless one of them happened to be heir to his mother's property, and they were therefore inevitably downwardly mobile . . .'

(LAWRENCE STONE, Family, Sex and Marriage in England, 1500–1800)

WILLIAM PARSONS was the second son of a Nottinghamshire Baronet, Sir William Parsons of Stanton-le-Wolds, and his wife Frances, a sister of the Duchess of Northumberland. He was born in London in 1717. That he was a difficult child is evident from the fact that on one occasion he barely failed to set on fire the family seat at Boveney, while on another he almost succeeded in killing one of his father's footmen with a blunderbuss. At the age of fourteen he was packed off to Eton where it was hoped by the family that a touch of severe discipline would set him on the straight and narrow. They were to be sorely disappointed for it was not long before William had gained a reputation amongst his schoolfellows for petty theft. He was caught out when he played a particularly mean trick on his elder brother. Their aunt, Mary, Duchess of Northumberland, had given each of them a five-guinea piece, which they were to show to her when she next met them. William immediately spent his, and then stole his brother's which he showed triumphantly to their aunt as his own. She, however, believing the older boy's story that his coin had been stolen from his pocket during the night, asked the Headmaster, Mr. Bland, to conduct an enquiry. There not being too many five-guinea pieces in circulation in the small town of Eton, it was hardly difficult to track down the shop at which William had changed his. For this offence, and for having stolen several

16. WILLIAM PARSONS

books, including a copy of Pope's *Homer*, from a high-street bookseller, William was, says the *Chronicle*, 'whipped till the skin was flayed off his back, and afterwards rubbed with pickle; but all the punishments he suffered, tho' ever so severe, could ever reclaim this unhappy man, or eradicate that natural propensity for wickedness.'

Soon afterwards Sir William removed his son from the school, and sent him to live with his wife's brother, Captain Dutton at Epsom. It was not destined to be a successful arrangement. He was not long there before he took a fancy to a young serving girl who worked for his uncle, and whom he seduced by first promising to marry her. He carried on this affair with her in secret for several months, until she became pregnant. William then abandoned her and she, in desperation, confessed all to Captain Dutton, who without hesitation sent his nephew back to his father;

'nor did he (so excessively he was irritated) ever forgive him it: and for that, and his other tricks, when Captain Dutton died (some years after) he cut Parsons out of all the large fortune he designated him...'

Sir William's next step was to send his son to sea, 'the general resource for such sort of sparks.' He obtained for him a commission as a midshipman on board H.M.S. *Drake*, sailing from Spithead to the West Indies, where it was due to be stationed for three years. William, however, was too easily bored to stay away for so long, and deserted before his time was up, managing to ship himself on board a Sheerness Man-of-War which was preparing to sail on her return home. When he arrived back in England, instead of risking the wrath of his father, he turned for help to his maternal aunt, the Duchess, throwing himself on her mercy. This kind-hearted but naïve woman received the prodigal with open arms, unquestioningly accepting his promises of repentance, and presenting him with a handsome cheque. He repaid her unkindly. On her watch chain she always carried a beautiful and favourite miniature set in gold. One night William stole it from her dressing-room and, unable to claim the large reward which she subsequently offered for it without arousing suspicion, sold it for a quarter of its value. He then had the effrontery to commiserate with the Duchess on her loss with the words, 'London is full of bad characters.'

The sight of gold, it seems, was too much for William to resist. Soon afterwards he stole a pair of gold shoe-buckles from a Mr. Graham in the Assembly rooms at Buxton. These he broke up and sold to a goldsmith in Nottingham. Unfortunately for him, the goldsmith had already learned of the theft and, identifying the pieces as belonging to Mr. Graham, reported back that they had been offered to him by Parsons. William was only saved from public disgrace by the intervention of his father who, desperate to save the family name from dishonour, made up the matter with Mr. Graham in private.

With the help of Captain Dutton Sir William now got his son back into the Navy, as midshipman on board H.M.S *Romney*, en route for Newfoundland. He appears to have spent most of the journey playing cards or dice, that is until his fellow officers discovered that he was playing with marked cards and weighted dice. When the ship finally reached its destination, and he was on shore, foolish were those ladies who sought his company, 'his figure being pleasing, and his manner of address easy and polite.' He had little regard for them, other than for gain. One of his favourite tricks was to feign admiration of ladies' jewellery, snuff-boxes, rings, etc which 'he had no sooner in his hand than, with a genteel air, he put them in his pocket, saying they were mighty pretty things, and he would keep them for their sakes, and so laughing the ladies out of them, he used afterwards to convert them into cash.'

Life in the Navy held little joy for William and on his discharge he was soon back enjoying a dissolute, extravagant life in London. But being a younger son with no fortune it was not long before money began to run short, and less and less was he able to find the wherewithal to gratify his expensive tastes. As his debts mounted he failed in all his efforts to persuade any member of his family, be it his father, his elder brother John, now a curate, his sister Grace, or his aunt Mary, to pay up for him. Accordingly, in despair, being 'pretty near exhausted as to cash' and threatened with arrest for debt, he accepted a position on the staff of the West Africa Company, and left the country. Sierra Leone, however, which was where he found himself, was hardly to William's liking, being short both on pretty women and gambling dens, and he soon made his way to Jamaica. It was while he was here that he committed an act, the consequences of which were to be responsible for his final downfall. He forged a letter in the name of his aunt in which she agreed to be answerable for any sum he raised up to £70. He then obtained the whole amount from a merchant in Kingston and, with the cash in his pocket, returned to England on the next available ship. Unfortunately for him the promissory note had arrived before him, and had been rejected by the Duchess. So incensed was she by her nephew's fraud that she disinherited him of the considerable sum of £25,000 which she had intended leaving him, settling it instead on his sister Grace.

William, however, was not finished yet. He now followed a path well trodden over the years by younger sons, for whom a good marriage, though often difficult to make without any land to their name, was the easiest way to independence. Heiresses had to be for ever on their guard against unscrupulous suitors. William managed to persuade Miss Mary Frampton, the daughter of an official in the Exchequer department, 'whose merit, as well as fortune, was deserving of a much better husband,' to marry him in February 1740, and he immediately received one-third of her £12,000 in cash. 'With the remaining £8,000 her relations purchased Exchequer-Tallies: and Parsons was annually to receive the interest of them. This was done by her friends as a precaution against her husband's extravagancies.' The marriage turned out to be a disaster for poor Miss Frampton, for though to begin with she lived relatively happily with her husband in a house in Poland Street, and bore him a son, it was not long before he was back at the gaming tables, and had run through his £4,000. He then induced her to sign a document authorising him to sell all of her holding in the funds. When this was done, and with no further use for her, he callously abandoned both her and his child.

In spite of his appalling record in the Navy, it seems that William had little difficulty in getting himself a commission in the Army, and as an ensign in the 34th Regiment of Foot, served for three years in Flanders. They were, commented an early biographer, 'three years of fraud and general wrong-doing.' One of these frauds was to obtain for himself the contract to provide the clothing for his whole regiment. As soon as he had fixed this, he absconded to England, uniforms and all, and sold the lot. Thus ended his Army career. The Duke of Cumberland ordered his commission to be sold, and the money raised upon it was distributed among the people he had cheated.

William now set himself up in a fine house in Panton Square which he furnished 'in a very genteel manner,' acquiring the finest silver and gold plate, and other goods from various tradesmen whom he ordered to bring him all their bills on one day, when they should dine with him, and he would pay them. On the appointed day they arrived only to find that the house had all the appearance of being empty. The doors were bolted, the shutters closed, the blinds drawn. Here William lived in darkness for nearly a year, slipping in and out through a stable yard at the back. When, by order of the suspicious landlord, the house was finally broken into, it was too late. The rooms were dismantled and the bird had flown.

Having run out of money once again, William now played his lowest trick by trying to cheat his sister out of the fortune, originally intended for him, that she had been left by the Duchess of Northumberland. He hired a footman acquaintance to help him carry out his scheme, which was to kidnap Grace at her home, and frighten her into marrying the footman. Her maid was bribed to help for £500. The plan that as soon as her 'husband' had his hands on her money, he would pay a handsome commission to William misfired, however, when the footman proved indiscreet. He

'appeared publickly in gay cloaths (with which he was supplied by Parsons), went to a milliners near where the young lady lodg'd, and bespoke some fine Dresden ruffled shirts etc, and was so impudent as to tell the milliner he was going to be married to Miss Parsons, niece and heiress of the Duchess of Northumberland.'

Unfortunately for him, while he was thus boasting, a lady he knew came into the shop, and on seeing her, he left, seemingly in some confusion.

'When the lady questioning the milliner who that gentleman was, she said he was a stranger to her, but was going to be married to Miss Parsons: "Married to Miss Parsons!" (returned the lady) "why he was once my footman."'

The beginning of the end for William Parsons came in February 1748 when, after a spree of fraud and swindling, he was finally arrested for forging a banknote in the name of a Mr. William Knight, which was directed to be paid at Honeywood and Fullers, bankers in Lombard Street. It was a clumsy affair, and he was caught and thrown into gaol. In August, at Rochester Assizes, he was convicted of the forgery and sentenced to death, 'but as great interest was made for him, particularly by his sister's husband, a gentleman in Kent of great fortune and reputation (Thomas Lambert Esq. of Sevenoaks) and in the commission of the peace, he obtained a reprieve for transportation for life.' He was taken to Maidstone gaol from where, while awaiting transportation, he wrote the following letter to his father, dated 27 August:

'Honoured Sir,
    After so profligate and infamous a life as I have led, I hardly dare to put pen to paper to intercede with you for forgiveness, but by being sincerely penitent of my many and enormous crimes, which I am, from the bottom of my heart, I hope to obtain of my Heavenly Father in the world to come: so by the same repentance here on earth, I hope to obtain forgiveness of my terrestrial parents, and my much injured wife. Certain it is, I am undeserving of the minutest charity from any of my relations, and in a more especial manner from you, whom I have so greatly and so oft offended. Notwithstanding my past misspent life, your goodness is so manifest to me in the letter and support you sent me by M. B_____, that during the short time the law allows me in this world (through a long and severe imprisonment) I shall, in the most grateful and humblest manner, be truly thankful for your tenderness and compassion towards me. I am,
    Sir, (tho' heretofore a profligate) now your sincerely
                                        penitent,
            and unhappy son,
                William Parsons

P.S. I beg forgiveness of my much injured wife and brother,
        and humbly beg their prayers to obtain pardon for me in
        the world to come.'

His subsequent career shows these words to have had a hollow ring.

Through the kindness of his father, it was arranged that on the voyage out to the American Colonies, William should be allowed to mess with the second mate, rather than being thrown in with the other convicts. As far as William was concerned, however, this was not good enough. He was 'highly offended with the Captain for refusing to let him eat at his table; and being very scurrilous to him for this act of civility, he was used like the other transports till they arrived in Putuxen River, in Maryland.' On his arrival in Maryland, the Governor, Lord Fairfax, for some reason, took pity on him and invited him to stay in his own house: 'He used him like his son and let him have a horse to ride at his pleasure.' William repaid this kindness by stealing the horse and riding off towards Virginia, on the borders of which county he robbed a gentleman of 'five pistoles, a moidore and ten dollars'. A few days later he committed another robbery on a lady and gentleman in a chaise, attended by a negro servant, stealing from them eleven guineas and some silver. Eventually he reached the Potomac river where, with money raised on yet another forged note, he persuaded a merchant to give him passage on a ship to England, explaining that he was on his way to take possession of an estate, after the recent death of his father.

On reaching England, William successfully continued the deception of his father's death, and his imminent possession of the family estate. In this way he managed to swindle several money-lenders, using the proceeds to set himself up in handsome lodgings with a carriage and pair and half a dozen servants. But the gratification of his expensive tastes required more capital than he could lay his hands on, and it was not long before the supply of foolish tradesmen and gullible women began to run out. As he dared not appear at the gaming tables for fear of being recognised, William decided there was only one course left open to him: 'he thought it more safe to rob on the highway, which project he put into execution.'

To begin with he was successful, committing several robberies at night on the road between Turnham Green and Hounslow Heath, and on each occasion getting away scot-free. He became over-confident, and hearing that a large sum of money was to be carried to London along this familiar road, he decided to lay in wait for it. While he was thus engaged there came by two gentlemen in a post-chaise and, out of boredom, William approached them. It was his bad luck that one of the men happened to be Mr. Fuller, who had originally prosecuted him at Rochester Assizes and who recognised him at once. Instead of making good his escape William followed these two men to their hotel, the Rose and Crown at Hounslow, where he handed over his pistols to them, and pleaded with them that they should let him go. This they might have agreed to had it not been for the untimely interruption of the landlord of the Rose and Crown, Mr. Day, who identified William as the notorious highwayman who had infested the area for many weeks. On examining him they found in his pocket a quantity of powder and ball, and the following day he was committed to Newgate.

On 21 January 1750, William Parsons was sentenced to death for having returned from transportation before the expiry of his term. In spite of appeals from his father to the Duke of Devonshire and the Duke of Newcastle to intercede with the King on his son's behalf, 'he was thought too deserving death to merit a reprieve.' Sentence was duly carried out on 11 February. Shortly before his death he told a friend:

'that he pleads it not as an excuse, by what is absolutely fact, that necessity and the neglect of his relations obliged him to commit almost every ill act of his life, contrary to his natural inclinations: for I ever had, says he, the utmost remorse and shock on me when doing ill: but starve I could not, to beg I was ashamed.'

The story of John Knatchbull is similar to that of William Parsons in that, not only did he leave an indelible stain on the family name, but he too blamed much of his downfall on his circumstances. The Knatchbulls were a typical family of respected landed gentry. John, born in 1789 at Provender, Kent, was the fourth son of Sir Edward Knatchbull, 8th Baronet, and his second wife Frances Graham. Of Sir Edward's other sons, the eldest Edward, later ninth Baronet, was destined for a great political career as a Cabinet Minister under Peel. His second son, Norton, went into the Navy and died serving as a midshipman in 1801, aged seventeen. Wyndham, the third, entered the Church, becoming Rector of Smeeth, Aldington, and Westbere in Kent, as well as Laudian Professor of Arabic at Oxford, where he was a fellow of All Souls College. Two other sons, Charles and Thomas, had respectable careers in the Army. Of the girls in the family, two of them, Frances-Anne and Mary, married Curates, respectively the Reverend Charles Hughes-Hallet of Higham and the Reverend W. W. Dickens of Wollaston House, Northants, while a third, Harriet, married an Admiral, G. H. D'Aeth of Knowlton Court. All in all they were a family who might have stepped straight out of a novel by Jane Austen.

The Knatchbulls were in fact well known to Jane Austen, who often referred to them in her letters, and whose niece, Fanny

17. JOHN KNATCHBULL

Catherine, daughter of her brother Edward, was eventually to marry Sir Edward Knatchbull, the ninth Baronet. On 23 September 1813 in a letter to her sister Cassandra, she writes of a visit paid by two of the boys, Wyndham and Charles (Mr. K's) and Wyndham's son Wadham, to her brother's house, Godmersham Park.

'Now what have we been doing since I wrote last? The Mr. K's came a little before dinner on Monday, and Edward went to the Church with the two seniors ... They are very good natured you know, and civil, and all that, but are not particularly superfine; however, they ate their dinner and drank their tea, and went away, leaving their lovely Wadham in our arms, and I wish you had seen Fanny and me running backwards and forwards with his breeches from the little chintz to the white room before we went to bed, in the greatest of frights lest he should come upon us before we had done it all. There had been a mistake in the housemaid's preparation, and they were gone to bed. He seems a very harmless sort of young man, nothing to like or dislike in him – goes out shooting or hunting with the two others all the morning, and plays at whist and makes queer faces in the evening.'

John Knatchbull was Wyndham's young brother. His father had ear-marked him at birth for a Naval career and, with this in mind, he was sent at an early age to Greenwich, to the school of Dr. Charles Burney, 'a very hostile man, proud in the extreme, and very severe in his discipline.' When he was fourteen, in 1804, he entered the service as a 'volunteer'. An extract from the *Naval Chronicle* of August of that year shows this to have been a customary manner of joining the Navy for the younger sons of gentlemen:

'*Le Tigre*, of 84 guns, Capt. Hallowell, is quite ready for sea: her quarter-deck will be very brilliant, as several young gentlemen of rank are going to make their first debut in the Royal Navy, on board *Le Tigre*. The Right Honourable Earl Spencer has brought down from Althorp, his seat, one of his sons, who is going as a volunteer with Capt. Hallowell, with several other of the younger branches of the nobility...'

Like that of William Paget, John's early career seems to have shown some promise. He was appointed midshipman in 1806, Lieutenant in 1810, and Commander in 1813, and he saw service in several theatres of War – Boulogne in 1804, the Azores in 1807, the Mediterranean, where he was wounded, and invalided for a year, from 1808 to 1812, and North Africa from 1814 to 1815. On the reduction of the Navy in 1815 he was retired and put on half-pay, a situation which hit him severely. In 1817 Thomas Parkin, then British Vice-Consul at Fayal in the Azores, wrote to the Admiralty to say that Captain Knatchbull was in debt to him for £355.5.5d since May 1815, and that he wished it to be regarded as an official debt to be paid by the Admiralty. They were furious and ordered John to explain 'a charge of so discreditable a nature against an officer of his rank in the Navy.' When the debt remained unpaid, the Navy Board was ordered to 'stop Captain Knatchbull's half-pay until his original debt to the Vice-Consul shall be discharged.' John protested, and the Admiralty reconsidered the matter, coming to the conclusion that his 'conduct was unbecoming the character of an officer,' and that 'his subsequent refusal to discharge the debt aggravated his original conduct.' They therefore directed the removal of his name from the list of the Royal Navy.

John now found himself without the only kind of work for which he had been trained, as well as with very little money. Nor did his father's death, in the Autumn of 1819, lead to great expectations. He was left £300 in the Will. Time hung heavily on his hands, and his existence soon became dissolute. One summer's night, 30 June 1824, found him at Vauxhall Gardens, with a friend named Steward, enjoying the 'Grand Concert of Vocal and Instrumental Music,' displays on the tightrope, fantoccini, fireworks, jugglers, pantomimes and vaudeville turns. He was elegantly dressed in a blue coat, white waistcoat, black pantaloons and black silk stockings. A gentleman named Lovett 'was admiring the performance of the fantoccini' when 'all of a sudden he felt his coat skirts agitated,' and he heard his companion call out 'Take care of your pockets.' Lovett immediately buttoned up his coat but 'soon afterwards he felt another curious movement of his coat' and, on turning round, saw John edging away, 'but from the respectability of his appearance, he had not the slightest idea that he could be a pickpocket.' In another part of the Gardens somebody reported to a member of the Watch that they had seen John picking pockets, and he was at once arrested on suspicion of having stolen a pocket book containing two sovereigns and a blank cheque from another complainant, one Henry Frederick de Dompière. These were found on his person when he was searched.

John was sent for trial in August, and found guilty of the charges against him. Mr. Justice Borough, acting on the Jury's recommendation for mercy rather than the death sentence, sentenced him to transportation for fourteen years. After three months in the Hulks, during which time he received a bad report for his rebellious nature, he was shipped to Australia, in December 1824. His arrival there was noted thus, the The Australian of 12 May 1825, under the heading 'Fashionables and Shewings up. Arrival Extraordinary':

'Captain Knatchbull, brother of the Baronet of that name, has become a visitant to this far-famed land. He arrived in the Asia. He quitted the Hall of his forefathers and the shores of his native land, at the pressing request of certain Lords of the Old Bailey ... The Captain is about to seek retirement in the varied Plains of Bathurst, where in all probability he will fix his residence for the next seven years – the period of his intended stay in Australasia.'

In his first few years in New South Wales, John behaved well. He worked firstly in a Government establishment at Bathurst. After this he was appointed as a Constable, and served as a police runner carrying the mail on foot once a week between Bathurst and Mount York, during which time he captured eight runaways, thereby earning remission on the time that had to elapse before he could apply for a ticket of leave. This he received in August 1829. Over the next two years he worked first in the district of Liverpool, and then as an overseer in the Department of Roads and Bridges in the district of Sydney. But just when things seemed to be going well for him, and he appeared to be serving his sentence in an honourable way, he was charged with forging the signature of a Mr. Justice James Dowling to a cheque for £6 10s. In February 1832 he was tried, found guilty and sentenced to transportation for seven years to Norfolk Island.

Norfolk Island, a penal station specially set apart for the worst and most desperate convicts, was a hell on earth, administered by a series of cruel and tyrannical governors, where the prisoners were crushed and beaten into submission. John served every day of that seven years, a nightmare existence that must have hardened him out of all recognition. In the light of this it is not surprising that four years after his release from Norfolk Island he was arrested for a brutal murder. At midnight on 6 January 1844, neighbours broke down the back door of a small chandler's shop at the North-East corner of Margaret Place and Kent Street, Sydney, which was kept by a widow named Ellen Jamieson. Inside they found her lying insensible in a pool of blood, her head almost battered to bits by a tomahawk. There, cowering behind the front door, his clothes covered in blood, was John Knatchbull. He ultimately confessed to the murder, although he always steadfastly denied that it was premeditated. 'The Devil instigated me to do the deed,' he said, 'and I did it.' Ten thousand people attended his execution on Darlinghurst Hill on 13 February 1844. It was a far cry from the genteel country life being led by his brothers and sisters back in England, from whose recollection his memory was forever banished. In a posthumously published memoir John wrote his own epitaph. Of his life, he said: 'For some part I may be blamed: for the rest I am to be pitied.'

6

A RESTLESS SPIRIT

*'I think it is my duty to put you in mind that, in so near a
relation as that of father and son, there is no medium between a
thorough displeasure and a thorough reconciliation.'*

(LADY MARY WORTLEY-MONTAGU to her husband)

IN the *Gentleman's Magazine* of January 1805, there is an account
by Mr. J. G. Pleydell of his meeting with an extraordinary
person while travelling through Venice in the Autumn of 1775.

'In his appearance and manners,' he related, 'he seemed a
complete Turk. He wore the yellow turban as a Prince of the
Turkish Empire, and shewed me his diploma of dignity,
signed by the Grand Signior, with the imperial seal affixed by a
ribbon. On visiting him I always found him sitting upon a
carpet in the manner of the Turks, generally with a long pipe in
one hand, and with the other stroking down his long beard
which reached to his girdle. There was a certain brilliancy in
his eyes, for which he was partly indebted to the Eastern
custom of tinging the edges of his eyelids with black ... In
person he was rather low, thin, and swarthy, but had the mien
of a man of fashion. A mute constantly attended him, standing
in the corner of the room with his hands across his breast ... I
frequently found him with a very handsome Negro youth,
about sixteen years of age, dressed very elegantly as a Turk. He
said he was his son, and he intended making his heir ...'

This remarkable figure was an Englishman, Edward
Wortley-Montagu, whose rebellious nature had long since made
him an outcast from his family. Edward was the son of that
celebrated woman of letters, Lady Mary Wortley-Montagu, a
daughter of the Marquess of Dorchester, who had disobeyed her
father's wishes that she should marry the Honourable Clotwor-
thy Skeffington, heir to a great estate, and had instead run off in
October 1712 with a millionaire diplomat Edward Wortley
(Montagu). This failed to bring her the happiness she had hoped

153

18. EDWARD WORTLEY MONTAGU (Romney)

for. She was a witty and intelligent woman, fond of town life and society, and her husband turned out to be a miser who confined her to the country, where she lived in almost continuous solitude for the first years of her marriage. Her son Edward was born in May 1713, and was a weak and sickly child. From the start his father seemed totally indifferent to his existence.

When Wortley was appointed British Ambassador in Constantinople at the end of 1716, his family moved there for a couple of years, and on their return they set up house in London. This enabled Lady Mary to resume the kind of life she had enjoyed before marriage ('Monday, at the drawing-room – Tuesday, Lady Mohun's – Wednesday, the Opera – Thursday, the Play – Friday, Mrs. Chetwynd, was how she had once described her life to Alexander Pope'). Having previously had almost no company other than her son, she now saw relatively little of him. As for little Edward, his foreign travels at such an early age had given him a precociousness and independence beyond his years, and he proceeded to run rings round the various keepers who were hired for him. It was to his mother's relief that, in 1720, he was finally packed off to Westminster School.

Edward ran away several times from Westminster, no doubt to escape the cruelties inflicted upon him by his Latin master.

> 'This tormentor,' he later wrote, 'grinned with a fiend's delight as he laid the lash across my naked flesh. Every morning my spine and buttocks were exposed, I was hoisted onto the back of an older boy and flogged until my shrieks echoed through the long room.'

He returned home only to more punishment. He was beaten in the evening, locked up in a large cupboard without food, beaten in the morning, and concentrated on escaping elsewhere, working variously as a linkboy, and a sweep, but on each occasion ending up back at Westminster. There seemed to be no quelling his rebellious spirit. In July 1726, his mother wrote to her sister, Frances:

> 'That young rake, my son, took to his heels t'other day, and transported his person to Oxford; being in his own opinion thoroughly qualified for the University. After a good deal of search we found and reduced him, much against his will, to the humble condition of a schoolboy.'

It transpired that at Oxford he had enrolled himself in a course in Oriental languages, and had taken up with a mistress, seven years his senior.

Being reduced to the humble condition of a schoolboy did little to tame Edward, however. It was too late for such measures, and the following July Lady Mary was once again complaining: 'My young rogue of a son is the most ungovernable little rake that ever played truant.' In August he disappeared completely.

'I am vexed to the blood by my young rogue of a son,' she confided to her sister. 'He has contrived at his age to make himself the talk of the whole nation. He has gone knight-erranting, God knows where; and hitherto 'tis impossible to find him . . . Nothing that ever happened to me has trouble me so much.'

His father offered twenty pounds as a reward for news of his whereabouts.

'The purlieus of Covent Garden,' wrote one of Edward's tutors, the Reverend John Forster, 'were searched in vain. Even the circuit of St. Giles's was paced by the friends and relatives of the family. Advertisements, handbills, all proved inefficacious.

It was a year before he was finally discovered, working for a fishmonger in Blackwall, and the Reverend Forster made it quite clear with what contempt he thought of 'a Duke's grandson stooping, in so depraved a manner, to the calling of a common fishseller.'

Four months later Edward was off again, this time making his way to Portugal where he got a job working on a vineyard. He eluded capture for two years, and when he was returned to England the Reverend Forster managed to persuade his father to give him one more chance. His faith in his charge was, however, sadly misplaced, for shortly after this Edward made a third attempt at escape. This time his father was unyielding in his wrath. 'I disclaim a son I fear I can never reclaim,' he told Forster who was once again pleading on Edward's behalf. Eventually he agreed to receive his son back into the fold only on the condition that he underwent a preliminary period of banishment. He was sent out to the West Indies.

Edward returned to England in 1730. He was still quite unrepentant, and in defiance of his parents he almost immediately married a woman called Sally, variously described as a 'laundress' or 'washerwoman.' He also gambled and drank heavily, and kept the worst company. It was not long before the creditors were hammering at the door. His father now as good as disowned him. The only communication he would have with him was through his agent, John Gibson of Soho, whom he instructed to appoint a new tutor who was to take his son abroad.

The next six years Edward spent in Europe, at first in the company of the new tutor, John Anderson, and then on his own, his wife Sally having been long since abandoned. In later life he was to give his own, highly coloured, version of events to a friend:

'I have been making some trials that have not a little contributed to the improvement of my organic system. I have conversed with the nobles in Germany, and served my apprenticeship in horsemanship at their country seats. I have been a labourer in the fields of Switzerland and Holland, and have not disdained the humble professions of postillion and ploughman. I assumed at Paris the ridiculous character of a petit-maître. I was an abbé at Rome. I put on at Hamburg the Lutheran ruff, and with a triple chin and a formal countenance, I dealt about me the word of God, so as to excite the envy of the clergy. I acted successively all the parts that Fielding has described in Julian. My fate was similar to that of a guinea, which at one time was in the hand of a Queen, and at another is in the fob of a greasy Israelite.'

It was finally decided by Edward's parents that their son should take up permanent residence abroad. Ysselstein, in Holland, was chosen as a suitable place, Anderson and Gibson were appointed as his moral guardians, and Edward was given an allowance of £300 a year. Wortley was still determined to have no direct dealings with his son, and he thus instructed Lady Mary, who in July 1739 had left England to live in Italy, that she was to be responsible for keeping an eye on him, and paying his allowance. Needless to say it was not long before she was listening to pleas for more money and a change of scene.

'He desires to leave the town where he now is,' wrote Lady

Mary to her husband, 'because he says there is no temptation to riot, and he would show how able he is to resist it.'

Such humbug did not carry any weight with her. She was only too aware of the real reason.

'I can perceive by his letters,' she continued, 'he is in the same folly of thinking he can make a figure, and imagines that your immense riches will finish him off with all the fine things he has a fancy for.'

From her home in Venice Lady Mary wrote on 17 June having heard that he had 'considerable debts in Italy, particularly at this place, but as he kept himself altogether in low company he did not pass for my son.' This must have been a relief to Lady Mary who was fêted in Venice as a great English lady, and spent much of her time in the company of sovereign princes. She had no scruples whatsoever about denying that Edward was her son.

'The Procurator Grimani asked me once,' she told her husband, 'if a young man who was here was of your family, bearing the same name. I said slightly I knew nothing of him, and he replied he always supposed, from his behaviour, that he was some sharper who had assumed the name to get credit.'

She added with some relief, 'I was glad to have it pass over in this manner, to avoid being daily dunned by his creditors.' She still worried continually that he might descend on her. 'If he should come where I am,' she complained, 'I know no remedy but running away myself. To undertake to confine him would bring me into a great deal of trouble and unavoidable scandal.'

Little did his mother realise just how close Edward was to doing exactly what she so feared. It had occurred to him that the best way to safeguard himself against his creditors, whom he was nowhere near to being able to pay, in spite of the fact that his father had recently raised his allowance by fifty pounds a year, was to put himself under the protection of his mother. Then, not only would the creditors think twice before dunning him, her position in Venetian society being so high, but she might also pay up for him in order to avoid scandal. Having formulated his plan, he put it to her in sycophantic terms:

'I should be infinitely obliged to you if you would permit me to have the honour of accompanying you whilst abroad. You would then be a witness to my whole conduct and I should have no occasion for any allowance at all, since everything would be at you La'ship's disposal. I could not express with how deep a sense of gratitude I should be touched if you would be pleased to grant me this favour; you would by it put into my own power to convince you of my sincerity and my attachment to you by obeying the least of your orders, and it would be out of the power of my enemies to misrepresent my behaviour or misinterpret my actions. I should have the happiness of being so continuously near so tender a mother, and the satisfaction of having it in my power (by searching with the greatest zeal everything that could give your La'ship the least pleasure) to show you with how much tenderness I am, Madam, your La'ship's most dutiful son and humble servant, Ed. Wortley.'

Sadly, Lady Mary's reply to these outpouring of filial affection does not survive, but the fact that Edward never did descend on her suggests that she disregarded them.

As soon as he saw that he was not going to prevail on his mother, Edward came up with two new schemes. He first of all suggested that he should become an M.P., his reason being that, by law, the persons of M.P.'s were sacrosanct from their creditors. He would thus have been able to move about safely, and even possibly return to England. Lady Mary laughed the idea off as 'very absurd'. Secondly he suggested that he should immediately divorce his abandoned wife, and marry an heiress.

'I am sorry to trouble you,' wrote Lady Mary to her husband on 15 August 1741, 'on so disagreeable a subject as our son, but I received a letter from him last post, in which he solicits your dissolving his marriage, as if it was wholly in your power, and the reason he gives for it is so that he may marry more to your satisfaction. It is very vexatious (though no more than I expected) that time has no effect, and that it is impossible to convince him of his true situation.'

Lady Mary was convinced that on no account should Edward be allowed any easy way out of his troubles, which she believed would be a licence for him to behave even worse. On 8 September, she made her feelings quite clear to her husband:

'This is a very nice subject for me to write on, but I think it is my duty to put you in mind that in so near a relation as that of father and son, there is no medium between a thorough displeasure and a thorough reconciliation. If you take the latter part, I am persuaded that there is nothing you can do for him, and that he will find people to be of his own mind. I very well know him; he is capable of making up a fine story to move pity, and can behave himself so, to the eye of a stranger, as to make a tolerable figure even to a man of sense...'

Early in 1742, still as anxious as ever to lay his hands on more of the Montagu money than a mere £350 a year, Edward tried a new ploy. Temporarily abandoning his plans to become an M.P. or to remarry, he instructed Gibson to ask his father to buy him a commission in the Army. His mother's reaction to this news was as cynical as ever. 'I am fully persuaded myself that he can never make a tolerable figure in any station in life.' His father, on the other hand, was delighted and decided that, rather than resort to the usual letters through Gibson, he would ask Lady Mary to see Edward. She was in France at the time, staying in Lyons, and agreed to the plan, albeit reluctantly, insisting that Edward should travel incognito lest anybody should suspect that he was her son. That she had every reason to distrust him is evident from a story which she related to her husband on 6 May:

'I saw a Savoyard man of quality at Chambery, who knew him at Venice, and afterwards at Genoa, who asked me (not suspecting him for my son) if he was related to my family. I made answer he was some relation. He told me several tricks of his. He said that at Genoa he had told him that an uncle of his was dead, and had left him five thousand pounds, or six thousand pounds per annum, and that he was returning to England to take possession of his estate; in the meantime he wanted money; and would have borrowed some of him, which he refused. I made answer that he did very well. I have heard this sort of conduct in other places...'

The meeting between mother and son took place in Orange early in June. Edward, she reported, had changed so much that she scarcely recognised him. He had lost his beauty, had grown fat, and looked at least seven years older than his true age of twenty-nine: 'and the wildness that he always had in his eyes is so much increased it is downright shocking, and I am afraid will end fatally.' She found him perfectly civil, but noted how submissive he was, and how flattering and insinuating his manner.

> 'He began to talk to me in the usual silly cant I have so often heard from him, which I shortened by telling him that I desired not to be troubled with it; that professions were of no use where actions were expected; and that the only thing could give me hopes of a good conduct was regularity and truth. He very readily agreed to all I said...'

When she upbraided him for his extravagance, he made the lame excuse that Mr. Gibson had told him, 'it became Mr. Wortley's son to live handsomely.' She finished by telling him that

> 'the most becoming he could now act would be owning the ill use he had made of his father's indulgence, and professing to endeavour to be no further expense to him, instead of scandalous complaints, and being always at the last shirt and last guinea, which any man of spirit would be ashamed to own.'

Edward then enquired whether or not his father had made his Will, begging his mother to exert all the pressure she could to see that the Will was not changed out of his favour. 'I plainly tell you, she replied, 'that I will never persuade your father to do anything for you till I think you deserve it.' He answered, 'by great promises of future good behaviour and economy.' On this note Edward and his mother parted, much to her relief. They were never to see each other again.

On 20 September 1743, Edward realised his new ambition, and received his commission in the Army, as a Cornet in the Seventh Hussars, under Sir John Cope. It was not long before he was writing rhapsodies to his mother of his new life, and naturally of the great success he was achieving. Nor did it take him long to complain that his allowance of three hundred and fifty pounds was hardly adequate, considering he needed a 'handsome equipage'. Lady Mary was not taken in by his claims, and remarked that 'he should have no distinction in equipage from any other Cornet, and everything of that sort will only serve to blow his vanity, and consequently heighten his folly.'

In fact, Edward managed not to disgrace himself in his Army career. Early in 1745 he served as A.D.C. to General Sinclair in the First Regiment of Foot, and fought at the Battle of Fontenoy.

General Sinclair bothered to write to Mr. Wortley to tell him that his son had acquitted himself to his satisfaction. On 29 May 1745, he was promoted to Captain-Lieutenant in the Royal Scots. He was eventually captured by the French early in 1746 when the British Garrison at Brussels surrendered, and he remained a prisoner until September when he was set free in an exchange of prisoners. On his release he was sent to Army headquarters at Breda in North Brabant, where he made the acquaintanceship of a cousin of his, a man of great influence, John Montagu, Earl of Sandwich, who was Second Sea Lord. The two became firm friends, and Sandwich used his influence to get Edward a seat in Parliament. On 18 July 1747, he was returned as member for the county of Huntingdonshire. He thus gained both immunity from his creditors, and the ability to return to England.

Lady Mary remained sceptical of her son's success with Lord Sandwich.

'I should be extremely pleased,' she wrote to her husband on 24 April 1748, 'if I could entirely depend on Lord Sandwich's account of our son. As I am wholly unacquainted with him, I cannot judge how far he may be either deceived or interested. I know my son (if not much altered) is capable of giving bonds for more than he will ever be worth in view of any present advantage.'

In April 1748 Sandwich, now First Lord of the Admiralty, was appointed as the King's plenipotentiary at the Congress of Aix-la-Chapelle. He chose Edward as his secretary. This close association with Sandwich encouraged Edward to write once again to his mother asking for his allowance to be increased. His new position would after all, he argued, involve him in much extra expense. Lady Mary remained unmoved.

'I am very sorry,' she replied, 'to find you still continue in the vain way of thinking that has been your ruin. I will not ask your father to increase your allowance; it is amply sufficient for all the show you ought to make. Your past extravagances are known to all that know your name; a modest behaviour and a frugal expense are necessary to persuade the world you are convinced of the folly of your former conduct. The very reasons you give for desiring a larger income prove you do not want it, since Lord Sandwich's presenting you as his relation entitles you to more respect than an embroidered coat or a rich livery, which gains no esteem, but among the weakest of both sexes, and only serves to draw the eyes of the mob, and even by them is oftener ridiculed than admired ... Prudence and decency will recommend you to the thinking part of mankind, and make you a blessing, as you have been hitherto a misfortune to your affectionate mother.'

This was advice that Edward patently failed to heed. When he returned to London at the end of 1750 from the protracted conferences at Aix-la-Chapelle, he was a sight to behold.

'Our greatest miracle,' wrote Horace Walpole to Sir Horace Mann on 9 February 1751, 'is Lady Mary Wortley's son, whose adventures have made so much noise: his parts are not proportionate, but his expense is incredible. His father scarce allows him anything: yet he plays, dresses, diamonds himself, even to distinct shoe-buckles for a frock, and had more snuff-boxes than would suffice a Chinese idol with an hundred noses. But the most curious part of his dress, which he has brought from Paris is an iron wig; you literally would not know it from hair...'

This was something that Edward's father could not bring himself to describe to his wife, as is clear from a letter she wrote to him on 24 May 1751:

'I can no longer resist the desire I have to know what is become of my son. I have long suppressed it, from a belief that if there was anything good to be told, you would not fail to give me the pleasure of hearing it. I find it now grows so much upon me that, whatever I am to know, I think it would be easier for me to support than the anxiety I suffer from my doubts. I beg to be informed, and prepare myself for the worst, with all the philosophy I have.'

There was far worse to come. First, in July, Edward made a bigamous marriage to a Miss Elizabeth Ashe, whom he had met while visiting one of his less respectable acquaintances, the high-wayman James Maclean, who was in prison awaiting execution. Miss Ashe was the inseparable companion of Lady Petersham, a woman whom Walpole described as being of very bad character. To Edward they were 'two of London's wildest and most wonderful women.' The marriage took place on 21 July 1751, and the couple left to honeymoon in Paris. 'Young Wortley,' recorded Mrs. Edward Montagu, wife of a first cousin of Edward's father, 'has gone to France with Miss Ashe. He is certainly a gentleman of infinite vivacity; but methinks he might well have deferred this exploit till the death of his father.' The newly-weds did not travel alone; with them went two cronies of Edward's, Lord Southwell and a Mr. Theobald Taffe M.P. Taffe was an Irish adventurer of doubtful repute who, according to Walpole, divided his time between the Duke of Newcastle and Madame de Pompadour, 'travelling with turtles and pineapples in post-chaises to the latter, flying back to the former for Lewes races, and smuggling Burgundy at the same time.' During the Spring of 1751 Taffe and Edward had spent many an evening together gambling at the French Embassy in London, where they acted as 'faro bankers' to Madame de Mirepoix, wife of the ambassador. Their plan was to continue their sport in Paris. It ended in disaster.

'It is supposed they cheated a Jew,' recorded Walpole in November, 'who would afterwards have cheated them of the money he owed, and that to secure payment, they broke open his lodgings and bureau, and seized jewels and other effects; that he accused them; that they were taken out of their beds at two o'clock in the morning, kept in different prisons without fire or candles for six and thirty hours; have since been released on excessive bail; are still to be tried, may be sent to the galleys, or dismissed home, where they will be reduced to keep the worst company, for I suppose nobody else will converse with them.'

The Jew was one Abraham Payba, alias James Roberts, a London insurance broker, who had fled to France with his mistress after a fraudulent bankruptcy. He accused the two men of having got him drunk and cheated him out of eight hundred and seventy Louis d'or at Hazard with loaded dice. They had then extorted out of him notes for that amount, payment of which he had stopped, as a result of which they had forced entry into his lodgings at the Hotel D'Orléans, and stolen all his money and jewels. They were both arrested and dragged off to prison. Taffe was taken to the Fort L'Eveque and 'a little cell, hardly room to turn about, without any fire or candlelight'; Edward to the

Châtelet and 'the dungeon of the prison, where all the furniture was a wretched mattress and a crazy chair.'

News of the scandal reached Lady Mary in November, and much to the shame of Edward's father, the story was soon the gossip of London. For once Wortley decided to heed Gibson's pleas for money for Edward: 'considering the situation he is now in,' he wrote, 'it is absolutely necessary that something should be done.' He paid up, hoping thereby to keep his son out of further trouble.

The trial of Edward and Taffe took place on 20 January 1752, and ended on 25 January with a verdict of not guilty, a verdict that was reversed on appeal by Payba. By then, however, Edward was already home in England. As for his new wife, Miss Ashe, she had returned to London early in the New Year, to be once again reconciled with Lady Petersham.

During the next few years Edward divided his time between two houses, one in London and another, Barham House, at Boreham Wood, and is known to have kept various mistresses by whom he had three children, Neddy, George and Mary. He gave up his seat for Huntingdon in 1754, exchanging it for one of Lord Sandwich's pocket boroughs, Boissney in Cornwall, but between that year and 1762, when he ceased to be an M.P., he never once visited his constituency, or even made his maiden speech. His only achievement of any kind in this period was the publication in 1759 of a book entitled *Reflections on the Rise and Fall of the Ancient Republics, adapted to the Present State of Great Britain.* He sent a copy to his mother who gave it short shrift.

'I received from an unknown hand,' she wrote to her daughter, Lady Bute, 'without any letter of advice a very nonsensical book, printed with your brother's name to it, which only serves to prove to me that . . . he is still a knavish fool. This is no news to me; I have long wept the misfortune of being mother to such an animal.'

She wrote him a long letter on his shortcomings as an author. The very fact that she showed some interest seemed to delight Edward, who in his reply spoke of 'the joy I must feel on receipt of your letter. It was a joy too big for utterance, and was I to inform your Ladyship of the effects it produced, they would appear extravagant.' Referring to 'the deep sense I have of my past ill-conduct, for which I have long felt and ever shall feel the most painful self-abhorrence,' he then embarked upon a canticle of repentance.

'I have some years since,' he said, 'bid a final adieu to the hurry and dissipation of a town life. My thoughts have been entirely turned upon the past, and I now labour to make all the atonement in my power for my former follies, and to form such a character as I would wish to die with...'

But it was too late for words such as these to soften the hearts of his parents. When his father died, on New Year's Day, 1761, he left his entire fortune of £1,340,000 to his daughter, Mary, Countess of Bute. He was able to do this because, having eloped with Lady Mary, there had been no marriage settlement, and consequently no entailing of his estate onto any son his wife might bear. Edward was left £1,000 a year, to be raised to £2,000 on the death of his mother, but the will specified that the money bequeathed to him was 'not to descend to any children he may have by his many wives.' 'I think your brother has far more than he deserves' Lady Mary told her daughter.

Edward was furious at the will and resorted to the lowest trickery in a desperate attempt to improve his position. He secretly inserted a false proviso in it, and threatened to circulate a scandalous story concerning his mother and his own legitimacy if the Butes did not agree to give him half his father's fortune. This was to the effect that while his father was Ambassador in Constantinople, Lady Mary had one day smuggled herself into the harem of Sultan Mustapha, the Grand Signior, in the disguise of a eunuch, and had consequently ended up in his bed. It was Edward's claim that he was the result of this union, and that this was the reason why his father hated him. He also tried to involve his mother in a plan to get more money from the will.

She wrote scathingly to him:

'Son, I know not how to write to you, and scarcely what to say. Your present conduct is far more infamous than the past: it is a small sign of reformation of manners when you durst attempt to disturb an indulgent (too indulgent) father's dying pangs for mercenary considerations; and are now defaming a too fond mother by the most impudent forgery. I think no single man deserved bread that cannot live decently and honourably on

£1,600 per annum rent-charge: I lived on half that sum with your worthy father when you was born and sometime after, without ever borrowing or raising money on contingencies, or even on certainties, which was in some measure our case. I can add no more; you have shortened your father's days, and will perhaps have the glory to break your mother's heart. I will not curse you – God give you a real, not an affected repentance. M. W. Montagu.'

Having been, in his opinion, as good as cut out of his father's Will, Edward decided to leave England once and for all. His intention was to make a grand tour of the East. He entrusted his two sons to the care of his solicitor and his banker. His daughter Mary he decided to take on the first leg of his tour, which was to be to Venice, where he intended to place her in a convent. Six servants were also to accompany him, and a mysterious figure known only as Miss Cast, but variously described as Mary's governess, his cousin or his sister-in-law.

'I am setting out at last to explore the Orient,' he wrote. 'I shake the dust of an ungrateful country from my heels perhaps, it will appear, for the last time. I shall journey in splendour to Constantinople; and hope to be receive by the Sultan...'

To John Gibson he wrote, 'London shall know me no more.'

He arrived in Venice early in 1762. Elizabeth Montagu's brother, the Reverend William Robinson, saw him there, and wrote of the meeting to his sister. He had found him hard at work studying Arabic, in preparation for his great tour:

'He really studies very hard. He rises before daylight, and has let grow his whiskers – this, and with the addition of a turban, which he wears in the house, makes him a very odd figure ... He has a sister-in-law with him – as he calls her, a Miss Cast – you will see a good name for one of his females. He has too a young girl of twelve years old he proposes to make a nun of: he has lodged her with a priest of St. Peter's, with a view of instructing her in the Roman Catholic religion. I forgot to tell you she is his daughter.'

He went on to tell how, when told that his daughter could not take the vows as she was a Protestant, Edward replied that this was no obstacle as to him all religions were the same. 'He purposes being in the East eight or ten years,' he concluded, 'which is a considerable time for a man turned fifty, and from which indeed he will probably never return.'

Edward was in Pisa in September 1762 when news arrived that his mother had died. Edward had never stopped trying to involve her in plots to get more of his father's money, but in her Will she managed to have the last word on her unscrupulous son. Its final clause read: 'I give to my son Edward Wortley, one guinea, his father having amply provided for him.'

In April 1763 Edward sailed to Egypt in the company of one Nathaniel Davison, a young man whom he had engaged as a secretary-companion before he left England. They arrived in Alexandria on the nineteenth. Among the letters of introduction he had was one to a Monsieur Joseph Varsy, a French merchant from Marseilles, with whom he soon became firm friends. In the Spring of 1764 Varsy invited Edward to stay at his father's house in Rosetta, thirty miles west of Alexandria. The other house guests were Madame Varsy, formerly a Miss Dormer, and her sister Caroline, wife of the Danish Consul, Herr Feroe, who was at the time absent in Europe. She was twenty-one, very beautiful and was soon quite fascinated by the extraordinary Edward, who now dressed in the full Oriental manner, and called himself the Chevalier de Montagu. He started giving her lessons in Arabic, and did his utmost to seduce her. His chance came at the end of May when there came news of a terrible tragedy. A letter arrived from some official source in the Netherlands to say that her husband had been drowned in a storm at sea. Edward lost no time in proposing to her, and in July they were married at Rosetta.

But Herr Feroe was not dead at all. The whole story of his 'drowning' had been dreamed up by Edward in order to help him in his seduction of the man's wife. It was not long before news came that Herr Feroe was on his way back to Egypt. Edward immediately told his 'wife' of the dreadful 'mistake' which had occurred. As it turned out Caroline far preferred being La Comtesse de Montagu to being the wife of the dull old Danish Consul. Realising that her husband, now fully awake to what had happened, would be bent on revenge, the couple fled from Cairo in the middle of the night. 'Like Moses pursued by Pharaoh's host,' Edward later wrote, 'I guided my steps towards the wilderness . . . I set out for Cairo by the road known by the name of Tauriche beni Israel, the road of the Children of Israel.'

They travelled first to Sinai, and thence to Jerusalem where Edward, fulfilling a promise he had made before his wedding, was received into the Catholic Church at the Monastery of St. Salvator. As Caroline was, however, still worried about her married status in the eyes of God, Edward arranged for proceedings to go forward before the Ecclesiastical Tribunals in Rome and Tuscany to declare her marriage to Feroe null and void on the grounds that he was a Protestant, while she was a Catholic. This was to take a great deal longer than he expected.

September 1765 found Edward in Venice again where he was seen by the famous surgeon Dr. Samuel Sharp, who recalled the meeting in his *Letters from Italy*.

'One of the most curious sights we saw amid these curiosities was the famous Mr. Montagu... All the English made a point of paying him their compliments in that place, and he seemed not a little pleased with their attention... His beard reached down to his breast, being of two and a half year's growth, and the dress of his head was Armenian.'

Edward made it clear to Dr. Sharp that he was now completely taken up with the ways of the Arabs, and that his intention was to abandon all Western habits.

'He was in the most enthusiastic raptures with Arabia, and the Arabs: like theirs his bed was the ground, his food, rice, his beverage water, his luxury a pipe and coffee. His purpose was to return once more amongst that virtuous people...'

After a series of long wanderings, to Egypt, back to Italy, then to Turkey, a restless spirit continually in search of fulfilment, the year 1769 found Edward living in the Turkish manner at Smyrna, where he perfected the Turkish language to such a degree that he complained that he had forgotten how to speak English, and was in danger of 'losing his Arabick.' By 1771 he was in Syria when the news finally reached him that the nullity of Caroline's previous marriage had been declared, and that therefore they were once again married, this time according to the rites of Rome. He returned at once to Rosetta to resume his life with her, a life that was to be lived in the Turkish manner, as had become his custom. Thus their house was divided into the

'Selamik', the men's quarters, and the 'Haremlik', the women's quarters.

It was not long before Edward's restless spirit drove him to take up a mistress. She was a black woman called Ayesha who had worked in his household when he had first come to live in Egypt. He had her brought from Alexandria, where she was living, and set her up in a small house less than a mile from his own. He spoke of his passion for her to a friend, Sir William Watson, of the Royal Society, with whom he had a regular correspondence.

> 'I am now so smitten with a beautiful Arabian that she wholly takes up my time; she only is the object of my every attention; she, though not in blooming youth, has more charms for me than all the younger beauties.'

She brought with her to Rosetta a young black boy called Massoud, whom Edward sometimes claimed as his son, others as his adopted son. When in 1772 he proposed making Massoud his heir, it was too much for Caroline, and soon after she left him. Ayesha then moved into his house, and there were rumours that he accepted the Mohammedan faith, and went through a Moslem marriage ceremony with her.

The following year Edward abandoned Ayesha, just as he had so many others, and taking Massoud with him, travelled to Italy and back to Venice, where he was to spend the rest of his life.

During the years which he spent in Venice, Edward became, in his own words, 'a part of the polite education of any noble youth who comes to this place on the Grand Tour,' and as such he is mentioned in many memoirs and diaries of the time. To visit him was obviously an extraordinary and fascinating experience.

> 'There were no chairs,' observed Dr. John Moore, tutor to the young Duke of Hamilton, who visited him in 1775, 'but we were desired to seat ourselves on a sopha, while Mr. Montagu placed himself on a cushion on the carpet, with his legs crossed in the Turkish fashion.'

After they had drunk some sweet Turkish coffee, and eaten some dried figs and Turkish Delight,

> 'some aromatic gums were brought and burned in a small silver tray. Mr. Montagu held his nose over the steam for some

minutes, and sniffed up the perfume with peculiar satisfaction;
he afterwards endeavoured to collect the smoke with his
hands, spreading and rubbing it carefully along his beard
which hung in hoary ringlets to his girdle.'

A hubble-bubble was brought which Edward smoked while
regaling his guests with tales of the Orient. All the while two
huge black mutes, wearing nothing but small, square 'modesty
nets of metallic mesh,' and silver bracelets and ankle rings, fanned
their master with peacock plumes.

Fortunately for posterity, George Romney, recuperating in
Venice after an illness, painted a portrait of Edward in full Turkish dress, which was completed only shortly before his death.
Early in April 1776, while staying at an inn at Padua, he got the
tiny, sharp, wing-bone of a Becca-fica, or Ortolan, stuck in his
throat. Although he managed to dislodge this by choking himself
with bread pellets, it left some kind of wound. This developed
into an infection which proved fatal. He died on 29 April. He had
already prepared his own epitaph:

> 'Eduardus Vorthleyus a Monte Acuto, an English Nobleman,
> formerly an arbitrator for peace on behalf of his King at
> Aix-la-Chapelle, distinguished for learning and for the writing
> and publication books, outstanding in his knowledge of East-
> ern affairs, customs and languages, well travelled in Egypt,
> Arabia and Ethiopia after various adventures and vicissitudes
> has found rest here.'

He was cremated and his ashes placed in the English cloister of
the Eremetari at Padua.

Perhaps a more suitable epitaph was provided by his cousin,
Mrs. Edward Montagu:

> 'One had read that the believers in the transmigration of souls
> suppose a man who has been rapacious and cunning does a
> penance in the shape of a fox; another, cruel and bloody, enters
> the body of a wolf; but I believe my poor cousin, in his
> pre-existent state, having broken all moral laws, has been
> sentenced to suffer in all the various characters of human life.
> He has run through them all unsuccessfully enough.'

7

HEIRS AND DISGRACES

Wealth, my lad, was made to wander,
Let it wander as it will;
Call the jockey, call the pander,
Bid them come and take their fill.

When the bonny blade carouses,
Pockets full and spirits high,
What are acres? What are houses?
Only dirt, wet or dry!

(From a poem by DR. SAMUEL JOHNSON, on the coming of age of Sir John Lade, a reckless young spendthrift.)

WHEN Edward Wortley made it known to the Earl of Dorchester that he wished to marry his daughter, the Earl emphasised that he would only agree to the match on the condition that he be willing to settle his estate on any son that his daughter might bear him. This, Wortley was extremely reluctant to do, telling Lady Mary that 'if I marry I must have more liberty over my estate than your father seems willing I should.' His refusal to conform to the Earl's wishes, and his subsequent elopement with Lady Mary turned out to be a sensible move, for it allowed him in the end to protect his estates against the undoubted ravages of an heir of whom he strongly disapproved. Primogeniture is a custom, rather than a law, and in breaking the custom Edward Wortley was very much the exception. This is why, through countless generations, the estates and collections of many families have so often suffered at the hands of their descendants.

On 30 August 1773, Horace Walpole wrote to Henry Seymour Conway:

'I returned last night from Houghton . . . where I found a scene infinitely more mortifying than I expected; though I certainly did not go with the prospect of finding a land flowing with milk and honey. Except the pictures, which are in the finest preservation, and the woods, which are become forests, all the rest is ruin, desolation, confusion, disorder, debts, mortgages, sales, pillage, villainy, waste, folly and madness. I do not believe that £5,000 would put the house and buildings into good repair.'

Two days later he shared more painful details with the Countess of Upper Ossory:

'The two great staircases exposed to all weathers, every room in the wings rotting with wet, the ceiling of the gallery in danger, the chancel of the church unroofed, the waterhouse built by Lord Pembroke tumbling down, the garden a common, the park half-covered with nettles and weeds, the walls and pales in ruin, perpetuities of livings at the very gates sold, the interest of Lynn gone, mortgages swallowing the estate, and a debt of above £40,000 heaped on those of my father and brother. A crew of banditti were harboured in the house, stables, town, and every adjacent tenement...'

To Walpole, lover of all things beautiful, a sight such as this was too much to bear.

'I sat down by the waters of Babylon,' he confessed, 'and wept over our Jerusalem – I might almost say over my father's ashes, on whose gravestone the rain pours!'

Houghton, the subject of this terrible desolation, was one of the most magnificent houses in England. Built by Sir Robert Walpole between 1722 and 1735, with little regard to cost, it was the wonder and envy of all who saw it. The exterior was designed, in the grandest and most elegant Palladian style, by Colin Campbell, whilst the interior contained the work of the most outstanding craftsmen of the day; plasterwork by Artari, marble chimney-pieces by Rysbrack, and, above all, extraordinarily beautiful furniture by William Kent. In every detail of construction and decoration Walpole took the keenest interest. A contemporary, Sir Thomas Robinson, for example, writing to Lord Carlisle in 1731, expressed his astonishment at 'the vast quantity of mahogany, all of the doors, window-shutters, best staircase etc being entirely of that wood.'

But Houghton was planned as more than just a palatial tribute to the greatness and riches of Sir Robert Walpole. It was built also to house his collection of works of art, perhaps the finest in Europe. After politics, paintings and sculpture were Walpole's passion, and from 1720 onwards he indulged it to the full. From all over Europe old masters were gathered up and sent home, works by Titian, Raphael, Rubens, Rembrandt, Poussin and Domenichino. These were bought not only by Walpole himself, but on his behalf by his children, relations and friends. While on the Grand Tour, for example, his sons Robert and Edward both spent a good deal of time acquiring suitable sculpture.

'I have seen every statue,' wrote Edward from Naples on 15 August 1730, 'and piece of that kind of antiquity that is worth seeing at Rome, among which there is nothing to be had that could possibly serve your purpose. Those that are valuable and most entire are either entail'd or in the hands of people that won't part with them. I have desired Mr. Swinny, whom I believe you must know, to procure two such if he can meet with them...'

By 1736 Walpole had in his possession four hundred and twenty-one paintings, as well as numerous masterpieces of sculpture. They were the glory of Houghton, and would have remained so, had it not been for the wanton folly and extravagance of one man.

George Walpole, third Earl of Orford, was the grandson of Sir Robert, being the only son and heir of his eldest son Robert, the second Earl. He was the offspring of a marriage so disastrous that his paternity was seriously in doubt. His mother, Margaret Rolle, a substantially rich heiress from Devon, had, much against her will, been forced into marriage with Lord Walpole at the age of sixteen, and by the time George was born in 1730 rumours of her infidelity were rife. Certainly George's uncle Horace is reported in the Farrington Diary as saying of him: 'I am well convinced that he was not the son of my brother.' Contemporary gossip attributed paternity to Sir George Oxenden, that 'proud, conceited, lewd man,' wrote the first Earl of Egmont, who 'got the lady of my Lord Walpole with child, and this unlawful issue will inherit the estate.' According to Lord Hervey, however, 'from the extreme aversion' that his mother showed to this 'poor little animal from the very hours of its birth' the judicious believed that the child really was that of her husband whom she detested. Whatever the truth may have been, Lady Mary Wortley

19. LORD ORFORD (GEORGE WALPOLE)
and his mistress, 'PATTY' TURK

Montagu described her as a woman whose character was held 'in universal horror'.

Soon after George's birth Lady Walpole, who considered she had fulfilled her task of providing Houghton with an heir, as well as with the benefits of her dowry, ran off with a lover, Thomas Sturgess, a fellow of King's, and probably one of the 'collection of free thinkers' who, according to Lady Mary Wortley Montagu, 'met weekly at her house, to the scandal of all good Christians.' They fled to Italy, where she was to have a succession of lovers, and was to spend the majority of her life.

George, therefore, grew up an only son, alone, brought up mostly by a succession of tutors and indulgent relations. Almost all that is known of him comes from Horace Walpole's letters. At the age of twelve he was considered to be 'a most charming boy, but grown excessively like his mother in the face.' The next we hear of him, six years later in 1748, he is described as 'a wild boy of nineteen.' whose bad companions and the courses into which they were leading him were to be deplored. Walpole had good reason to be worried. When Sir Robert Walpole died in 1745 he was discovered to be £40,000 in debt. His son Robert, the new Earl, managed to keep on at Houghton only with the help of a considerable income from various patent places which his father had procured for him. The office of Auditor of the Exchequer alone brought him £7,000 a year. Were he to die these would revert to the Crown, and since he was incurring new debts all the time, the situation would be fairly serious. 'There would soon be an end to the glory of Houghton,' wrote Walpole.

His fears were well justified when, in March 1751, his brother died. It was not just the loss of income from all the rich places and sinecures that the estate suffered from. There also appeared on the scene Lady Orford who, on hearing of the death of her husband, had immediately married one of her old lovers, Sewallis Shirley, who came to claim from the estate every penny to which she was entitled, and as much else as she could get her hands on. When all was said and done Walpole pronounced his nephew to be 'the most ruined young man in England.'

There was a solution to the problem. This was for George to marry Margaret Nicoll, a considerable heiress who had been introduced to the family by John Chute, a close friend of Horace Walpole's. But in spite of all Walpole's efforts to persuade his nephew to take this step, George refused to do so, even though

Miss Nicoll had herself agreed to the plan.

'It is impossible to answer you,' wrote Walpole to Sir Horace
Mann in July 1751, 'why my Lord Orford would not marry
Miss Nicoll. I don't believe there was any particular reason or
attachment anywhere else: but unfortunately for himself and
for us, he is totally insensible to his situation, and talks of
selling Houghton with a coolness that wants nothing but being
intended for philosophy to be the greatest that ever was ...'

Apart from the odd disparaging remark about the young
man's 'indolence' and 'inattention', and the suggestion that his
own dissipation was involving him in many more debts, Walpole
referred very little to his nephew in the next few years, until, in
1755, he drew an unsparing portrait of his character for Sir
Horace Mann.

'His figure is charming,' he wrote; 'he has more of the easy,
genuine air of a man of quality than you ever saw; though he
has a little hesitation in his speech, his address and manner are
the most engaging imaginable; he has a good breeding and
attention when he is with you that is even flattering; you think
he not only means to please, but designs to do everything one
can wish – but this is all: the instant he leaves you, you, all the
world, are nothing to him – he would not give himself the least
trouble in the world to give anybody the greatest satisfaction:
yet this is mere indolence of mind, not of body – his whole
pleasure is outrageous exercise. Everything he promises to
please you, is to cheat the present moment, and hush any
complaint – I mean of words; letters he never answers, not of
business, not even of his own business; engagements of no sort
he ever keeps. He is the most selfish man in the world, without
being the least interested; he loves nobody but himself, yet
neglects every view of future and ambition ... You will ask me
what passions he has – none but of parade; he drinks without
inclination; has women, not without inclination, but without
having them, for he brags as much as an old man; games
without attention; is immeasurably obstinate, yet, like obstinate people, governed as a child. In short it is impossible not to
love him when one sees him; impossible to esteem him when
one thinks on him.'

It was no wonder, he declared in despair, 'I am forced to give
him up.' Little did Horace realise, when he wrote these words,

just how much time and energy he was to spend in the future on sorting out his nephew's affairs.

George's greatest weakness, and therefore that which involved him in the most considerable expense, was his passion for sport, in both a practical and a speculative sense. His love of coursing was famous. He is recorded as having kept at one time as many as fifty pairs of greyhounds, and it was his fixed rule never to part with a single puppy until he had made a fair trial of its speed. He also kept a large string of racehorses, and with the horses and the dogs there naturally went the rather motley crew of shady characters who were inclined to inhabit that world, the jockeys, grooms, bookies etc, none of whom were likely to curb his spending. According to Burke,

> 'The Prince of Wales, when occasionally visiting at Houghton used to say he saw at no other place such a profusion of game of every description, such a display of attendant game-keepers, such a noble though plain hospitality; and a park so curiously and infinitely stocked with every original beast and fowl of almost all countries, from the African Bull to the Pelican of the wilderness.'

There was also an eccentric side to his sporting activities. On 1 October 1756, in a letter to Sir Horace Mann, Walpole wrote:

> 'If folly and extravagance are symptoms of a nation's being at the height of their glory, as after-observers pretend that they are the forerunner of its ruin, we never were in a more flourishing situation. My Lord Rockingham and my nephew Lord Orford have made a match of five-hundred pounds, between five turkeys and five geese, to run from Norwich to London.'

The wager was that the geese and turkeys should be walked from Norwich to Mile End Turnpike, 'that person to win who first brings in most cattle alive to the turnpike.' Sadly history does not relate the outcome of this fantastic bet. It was also said that George was frequently to be seen driving a carriage drawn by four red deer, which on one celebrated occasion were pursued by a pack of hounds which they had met on the road to Newmarket.

Apart from a visit to Houghton in 1761, which depressed him because of the decline he noticed had taken place since his last visit, Walpole's first real understanding of the destruction being wreaked there by George and his friends came in 1773, when his nephew was taken seriously ill. The circumstances, as related to Sir Horace Mann, were as follows:

'I have a melancholy tale to tell you of . . . my Lord Orford. He had a cutaneous eruption. By advice of his *groom* he rubbed his body all over with an ointment of sulphur and hellebore. This poison struck in the disease. By as bad advice as his groom's, I mean his own, he took a violent, antimonial medecine, which sweated him immoderately; and then he came to town, went to Court, took James's pills without telling him of the quack drops, sat up late and, though ordered by James to keep at home, returned into the country the next day. The cold struck all his nostrums and ails into his head, and the consequence is insanity.'

Lady Orford was in Florence when she heard of her son's illness, and was reluctant to come over to England. She claimed that her age and ill-health would not permit such a journey, nor could she be of any use to her son in his condition. She inveigled Sir Horace Mann to write to Walpole begging him that he and his brother Edward should take care of their nephew and his affairs. Though they were loath to do this, for fear of their motives appearing suspect, the two brothers realised they had little choice if they wished to avoid George being subjected to a Commission of Lunacy. As Edward was something of an 'indolent recluse', most of the business devolved upon Horace.

Walpole found that things at Houghton were far worse than he had imagined and, as we have seen from his letters to Seymour Conway and Lady Ossory, he was deeply upset by the picture of desolation and disrepair which presented itself. But, in spite of the fact that, on his admittance, he knew little of money and accounts, the memory of his father and of the former glories of Houghton strengthened his determination to do all he could to improve the situation. It was to be an uphill struggle.

'My Lord has contracted debts of every kind,' he wrote in September to his cousin Thomas Walpole, 'and when the bills are all come in, I think they will exceed £40,000, independent of the debts of his father and grandfather, which leaves him infinitely poorer than a beggar . . . He has been plundered in the grossest manner by every species of dependant, and some of his "friends" I doubt have not spared him ever since his fortune began ... I have got rid of his dogs and most of his horses: the rest will be sold in the beginning of October.'

By the end of the Autumn Walpole had in fact achieved some degree of success in putting his nephew's affairs on a sounder basis than they had been for some time. But in late December, as suddenly as he had fallen ill, George made a complete recovery and it was not long before his uncle was writing of how all his good work was being fast undone: 'he is dispensing already by handfuls and pocketfuls the savings of a whole year.' During the remainder of his life George suffered from intermittent bouts of insanity, but on each subsequent occasion his uncle's care of him went no further than that of his physical well-being. Walpole could never forget the ingratitude with which he had been treated after the first illness, and refused to interfere any more in his nephew's finances, particularly since all the old cronies were soon back again exerting their unhealthy influence.

'Some of his old conductors,' he told Sir Horace, 'have furnished him with a new attorney, who is indecently eager to riot in what I had gleaned from the ruin. This is the present situation and the future prospect.'

On 1 October 1778, soon after recovering from his second attack, George wrote to his uncle that he was intending, once and for all, to settle the affairs of the family and pay off the creditors of his grandfather. Under the terms of their father's Will both Horace and Edward Walpole stood to inherit a certain amount of money, only a fraction of which they had yet received. George suggested that if they were both to agree to renounce their right to the inheritance of Houghton, he would see that the money which was due to them should be paid at once. With the improvement of their nephew's finances in mind, both men readily agreed to this plan.

'We are both old men now,' wrote Horace, 'and without sons to inspire us with future visions. We wish to leave your Lordship in as happy and respectable situation as you was born to; and we both have given you all the proof in our power by acquiescing in your proposal immediately.'

Subsequent events show them to have been extraordinarily naïve to have put such faith in a man who had already shown himself to have been notoriously lacking in judgement.

Two months after they had so generously agreed to the breaking of the entail of Houghton, the two uncles were horrified to learn that their rascally nephew was arranging to sell their father's collection of pictures, the supreme glory of Houghton, to the Empress Catherine of Russia. Apart from family considerations, this collection was regarded as being of national importance. In April 1777 John Wilkes, in a debate in the Commons on an intended application to Parliament to secure the Houghton pictures for Britain, had referred to it as

'of acknowledged superiority to most in Italy, and scarcely inferior even to the Duke of Orleans in the Palais Royal at Paris ... a noble gallery ought to be built in the spacious garden of the British Museum for ... that invaluable treasure.'

The sum agreed upon with the Empress for the sale was £40,000, but since they had heard that George had apparently compounded his grandfather's debts for £15,000, the uncles quite rightly saw the sale as being unnecessary. Horace had his own suspicions as to who was behind the plan.

'I am persuaded that the villainous crew about him, knowing that they could not make away clandestinely with the collection in case of his death, prefer money, which they can easily appropriate to themselves.'

But they were powerless to stop it.

'It is the most single mortification to my idolatry for my father's memory that I could receive,' lamented Horace. 'It is stripping the temple of his glory and of his affection. A madman excited by rascals has burnt his Ephesus. I must never cast a thought towards Norfolk more, nor will I hear my nephew's name if I can avoid it.'

The sale went ahead, and the walls of Houghton were stripped bare. The pictures were shipped to Russia, where many of them still hang in the Hermitage. They were replaced, much to Horace Walpole's horror, with paintings by, among others, Cipriani, whom he sarcastically described as 'that flimsy scene painter,' and with other elaborate commissions.

'He has now bespoken another piece,' he wrote to Sir Horace Mann in 1781 'frantic enough; for the subject is both indecent and shocking. Perhaps you have forgotten the story: it is that of Theodore and Honoris, from Dryden's *Fables*, where the naked ghost of a scornful mistress is pursued by demons and worried by bloodhounds. The subject, were it endurable, could only be executed by Salvator or Spagnolet. Imagine it attempted by modern artists, who are too feeble to paint anything but fan-mounts!'

It was too much for Horace.

'Well, adieu to Houghton!' he wrote. 'About its mad master I shall never trouble myself more. From the moment he came into possession he has undermined every act of my father that was within his reach, but having none of that great man's sense or virtues, he could only lay wild hands on lands or houses: and since he has stripped it of its glory, I do not care a straw what he does with the stone or the acres.'

The reference to stone alludes to the fact that George had not stopped at selling the pictures. He had also sold the great steps outside the West Front to one of his gang, Lord Clermont. Had Horace had any idea that he might one day inherit Houghton when he wrote these words, then he might have written differently. As it was he was taken completely by surprise when, on the death of his nephew in 1791, after another bout of illness, he learned that he had been bequeathed the whole of the Norfolk estates. He later confided to Lady Ossory that this had come as a terrible shock to the 'vile set of miscreants' who had surrounded George, and who believed that, under their influence, his will had been changed to pass on nothing but the title to his uncle. Horace's own feelings were mixed.

'I am not vain of being the poorest Earl in England: not delighted to have outlived all my family, its estate and Hough-ton, which, while it was complete, would have given me so much pleasure – now it will only be a mortifying ruin, which I will never see.'

20. Strawberry Hill, Middlesex

Horace never did return to Houghton; he was by then too old and infirm. He spent the remaining few years of his life at Strawberry Hill, his house at Twickenham, and from here dealt with all the business of his new estates. He had bought Strawberry Hill in 1749, having fallen in love with it at first sight, two years previously:

> 'A little plaything house,' was how he described it then to a friend, Marshal Conway, 'and is the prettiest baubel you ever saw. It is set in enamelled meadows with filagree hedges;
> A small Euphrates through the piece is rolled,
> And little fishes wave their fins in gold.
> Two delightful roads, that you would call dusty, supply me continually with coaches and chaises; barges as solemn as Barons of the Exchequer move under my window – Richmond Hill and Ham walks bound my prospects . . . Dowagers as plenty as flounders inhabit all around, and Pope's ghost is just now stirring under my window by a most poetical moonlight.'

Over the years he transformed it into a Gothic castle. Strawberry Hill was the first great love of Horace Walpole's life, and when in March 1761 he wrote to George Montagu, lamenting the fate of Houghton, he reassured himself that at least 'Poor little Strawberry . . . will not be stripped to pieces by a descendant.'

It is ironical that this is exactly what did happen to his beloved home. On Walpole's death in 1797 Strawberry Hill passed to his cousin Anne Seymour Damer, widow of the suicide John Damer. She finding it too expensive to keep up, eventually relinquished it to the ultimate heirs, the Earls of Waldegrave, of whom it would be hard to imagine two people less well suited to being its inheritors than the sixth and seventh Earls.

John James, sixth Earl Waldegrave, was Horace Walpole's great nephew through his descent from Maria Countess of Waldegrave, the second daughter of Sir Edward Walpole. He succeeded to the title in 1794 when his elder brother George was drowned in a bathing accident at Eton, and is described by the present Lady Waldegrave in her history of the family as having been 'Not so much bad as hopeless'. He was backward at school and remained semi-literate all his life.

After school and a tour abroad with a tutor, John James entered the Army, in which his career was distinguished only by the fact that he kept his mistress in the field.

'When the British Army was about to enter France,' wrote
Captain Gronow, 'I was struck with the beauty and attain-
ments of the chivalrous Lady Waldegrave who accompanied
her Lord throughout the war. Her conduct was the theme of
the army and she won universal praise and admiration. She
was the perfect heroine . . . she had a splendid figure and was
one of the best riders I ever saw. She was not at all masculine in
her style; her voice and manner of speaking were remarkable
for sweetness and grace. I cannot hope to see her like again.'

These were sentiments that were not shared by John James's
family, least of all his mother, Elizabeth Laura, Countess of
Waldegrave, who saw her only as a harpy who was leading her
son into ruin. In a letter to her youngest son William in June 1814,
despairing of his older brother, she wrote:

'his vile companion is spending faster than ever – and he keeps
an open table at Antwerp for all officers who her attention –
she hints that she is privately married but that is not owned –
Waldegrave only calls her Annette. Her marriage is *not*
believed and Officer's wives do not visit her.'

That at this point she was not married to Lord Waldegrave is
without doubt. Her real name was Annette King, and she was the
daughter of William King, a carpenter from Hastings. From the
moment she ran off with John James, however, who met her
when she was living as the wife of a Mr. Stanley, a commissary,
she referred to herself as 'Lady Waldegrave'. John James himself
made it quite clear to his family that his intention was to marry
her.

'What a contrast,' wrote his brother William, 'instead of a
woman whom we would be delighted to acknowledge as a
daughter and sister – to have attached to us, one who has been
the lowest most disgraceful rank of life – one whom we have
every reason to suppose to possess a corrupted heart, a vicious
understanding and who has gained her ascendancy in the most
profligate manner, it is dreadful to think of it for a moment . . .'

In October 1814 Annette gave birth to a son who was named
John James Henry, but it was not until she became pregnant a
second time, in May 1815, that a marriage did finally take place,

21. GEORGE WALDEGRAVE, 7th Earl

on 3 October in the Hotel Sebastiani, Rue St. Honoré in Paris. The witnesses were a Major J. Clark and a Lieutenant John Picton of John James's regiment. On 8 February 1816 Lady Waldegrave gave birth to another son, George Edward.

Early in May John James and his new wife returned to England. His mother's death earlier in the year had at least spared her the embarrassment of ever having to meet the woman she disliked so much. On 11 June, George Edward was christened Viscount Chewton in Twickenham Church. One of the more curious entries to be found in English parish registers also records that on the following day, 'John James, Earl of Waldegrave, married Anne, Countess of Waldegrave.'

From the start the young heir's position was an extremely shaky one, none the less so for the fact that his parents' remarriage had raised a considerable amount of doubt about the truth of the story of the Paris wedding. His upbringing, which was unfortunate to say the least, surely goes a long way to explaining his behaviour in later life. His father was throughout his life extraordinarily hesitant about treating him as his heir, and did not like to address him, or allow other people to address him, by his courtesy title of Lord Chewton. Indeed, he seems to have resented the 'cruel injustice' which debarred his eldest son, John James Henry, from the family honours, and he may have objected to the second, and perhaps less-loved, son being preferred before the first. Whatever the reason, it cannot have done any good to George Edward's confidence. Also, his education was highly erratic. Owing to his mother's dubious reputation, his parents were not received by 'polite society', and spent most of their time abroad, almost always on the move, and more often than not pursued by creditors. In later years George Edward spoke of his mother with bitterness and hatred.

When his father died, after two crippling strokes, in 1835, the Waldegrave properties were split up between George Edward, now the seventh Earl, and his illegitimate older brother. John James Henry, now a dashingly good-looking though heavy-drinking young man, inherited the Eastern estates, while the rest of the property, comprising Strawberry Hill, its contents and the surrounding lands, as well as a large estate and House, Harptree Court, in Somerset went to George Edward, who was by now beginning to establish himself as something of a hell-raiser. He was part of a set of young rowdies, much akin to the rakes of earlier days, who were constantly in search of trouble. The leader of the gang was Henry de la Poer Beresford, 3rd Marquis of Waterford. Notorious as 'Wild Lord Waterford', this equivalent of a latter-day 'Hooray Henry' spent most of his time frequenting the sporting hostelries of London, such as Limmer's hotel, where he conceived his riotous pranks, many of which ended in the police courts.

In July 1838, for example. Waterford was twice in court. On the first he was accused of being drunk and disorderly in Piccadilly at five o'clock one morning, after having been seen by a policeman 'committing the insane freak of making the foot pavement his road.' When asked by the magistrate if he had any witnesses who could contradict the charge of furious driving he answered:

'The best witness would be my horse. I'll call my horse if your worship thinks proper.'

He was found guilty and fined.

'The Marquis paid the money,' noted *The Times* correspondent, 'and turning to the policeman, made some unhandsome remarks on his evidence ... The Marquis took his friend the Earl of Waldegrave's arm, and left the office.'

The second occasion was more serious and found him in the Crown Court at Derby before the Lord Chief Justice, charged with a number of friends, including Sir Frederick Johnstone Bart, the Honourable Charles Hyde Villiers, and a Captain Reynard, of 'having committed a riot at Melton Mowbray, of assault upon certain constables and watchmen, and of common assault.' It was a 'frolic' that Rochester and his friends would have been proud of. The group were in the town of Melton for Croxton Park Races. At half past two in the morning they were rowdying about in the streets of the town, when they came upon some watchmen. After failing in their best endeavours to start a fight they moved on, attempting next to capsize a caravan, with a man inside it, which was standing in the street. The watchmen managed to prevent this. They then came across a woman drawing water for brewing, and upset her pails as fast as she filled them. Next some flower pots decorating the window of a tradesman's house inspired Waterford to stand upon the shoulders of one of his friends and hurl them all to the ground. The owner, having been woken up by the fearful racket outside, called a watchman who attempted to stop their fun. This unfortunate man was immediately set upon, thrown to the ground, and kicked and trampled. When he was almost unconscious, Waterford painted his face and throat thickly with red paint. By this time the constables had been aroused, and they soon arrested the gang, who were then in the process of painting bright red everything they could find. Eventually the constables took Captain Reynard, who seems to have been identified as the main culprit, off to gaol.

He did not stay there for long. Fourteen of his friends turned up at the prison, and demanded that he should be set free. On being told by the constables that this could not be done without the order of a magistrate there were numerous cries of 'I'm a magistrate,' 'So am I,' etc. When the constables still refused to give in, they were knocked down and overpowered by the mob, who then seized the prison keys and carried off Captain Reynard in triumph on their shoulders. On the following day, after having been positively identified as having taken part in the riot, Waterford and three of his friends were arrested. They were all found guilty and fined. 'The Court,' noted *The Times* correspondent 'was crowded to suffocation during the trial.'

In May 1839, at Holy Trinity Church, Brompton, John James Henry was married to Frances Elizabeth Anne Braham, daughter of the distinguished tenor John Braham. On their return from their honeymoon the couple decided to pay a visit to George Edward at Strawberry Hill, where they found that the servants had been instructed to treat them as if they were the master and mistress of the house. A few days later the new Mrs. Waldegrave was writing to her mother:

'I would not have imagined anyone could have been so kind or so like a brother as my new dear relation ... George seems to have made up his mind that we are never to leave him. I am quite mistress here, at least so they please to say.'

It was the beginning of an extraordinary 'ménage à trois', a period that was described by Frances's father as being filled with 'singing, drinking, and yelling'. It ended, however, abruptly, in April 1840 when, after a prolonged fit of delirium tremens, John James Henry died, a victim of his own excesses.

George Edward lost no time in moving to console the widow, to whom he had become close during the months of her husband's deteriorating health. With almost indecent haste he made his intentions quite clear. He told her that he wished to marry her, that he had always wished to marry her since the first time he had set eyes upon her, at a dinner given by his mother at Strawberry Hill. Unfortunately for him his brother had proposed first. He assured her that, though the Marriage Act of 1835 strictly forbade a wedding between a wife and her deceased husband's brother, this case was an exception since, as John James Henry had been illegitimate, he was therefore not a true brother. He added that, according to his lawyer, they could anyway marry quite legally if the ceremony were to take place in Scotland where the Marriage Act was not valid. Though at first Frances hesitated, being anxious not to flout public opinion too blatantly, it was not long before she gave in. They were married in Edinburgh in September, in St. George's Chapel, York Place.

When news of the wedding filtered south, society was scandalised. The whole affair deeply offended Victorian morality, and many doubted the validity of the means by which the marriage had been achieved. George Edward's reputation was anyway at its lowest ebb owing to the notoriety he had achieved from his involvement in a disgraceful incident which had taken place the previous June, and which had come close to murder. He was returning to Strawberry Hill, along with a number of his cronies, including Lord Waterford, and a certain Captain Duff, after a day at the Derby and an evening at Kingston Fair. He had, in his own words, 'been getting bloody drunk all day on account of losing so much money at the Derby.' Outside the Swan Inn in Hampton Wick they all became involved in a fracas. A policeman, Constable Charles Wheatley, who tried to intervene, was repeatedly beaten about the head with a stout stick, and then kicked to the ground, whereupon a cab was 'driven over the constable while they held him down, whereby he was rendered unfit for duty.' According to George Edward's Aunt, Elizabeth Waldegrave, writing to her husband at the time, there was at first doubt whether or not the constable would survive. He recovered, however, and George Edward and Captain Duff, being the only two who were caught in the act, the others having escaped, were committed on bail to the Assizes. The public, who were beginning to be more than a little irritated by the hooliganism of the

Waterford set, hoped to see an example made of them. The news of the wedding on top of this made George Edward an outcast.

After lying low in Edinburgh for three months the newly-weds returned to England in May 1841 for George Edward to stand trial. Both he and Captain Duff pleaded guilty and were fined, £20 for Duff, £200 for George Edward, and sentenced to six months' imprisonment in the Queen's Bench. The leniency of the sentence caused an outcry, the Queen's Bench being an almost luxurious penalty. Certainly George Edward seemed little affected by it.

> 'My own darling,' he wrote to Frances from the court, continuing nonchalantly, 'six months' Queen's Bench. I shall send Beavan to tell you when we have arranged our apartments. For God's sake take care. Be under no fear that I will do anything or look at anybody.'

Their apartments were comfortable rooms over the lobby of the prison which had formerly been inhabited in 1820 by Sir Francis Burdett, who was incarcerated there after Peterloo. From Strawberry Hill came servants, carriage, silver and china, and a huge brass bed, draped in crimson velvet, all of which were followed by Frances herself, and together the Waldegraves passed the prison sentence in some style.

During the six months he spent in the Queen's Bench, George Edward had ample time to brood on what he considered were the injustices of the Twickenham magistrates who had committed him to the Assizes in the first place. When he came out in early September he had formulated a plan which he believed would serve as a perfect revenge both upon them and upon their borough which he now hated. A ruined, empty Strawberry Hill, he felt, would disgrace and injure them, and he thus set about the sale of its entire contents. When his uncle William heard about the sale, he wrote to his wife:

> 'So the trinkets at Strawberry Hill are to be sold. O perpetuity! O fame! and family pride! Those acquisitions of Horace Walpole fall into the hands of a Jewess and are sold.'

The sale of the contents of Strawberry Hill, which lasted twenty-four days, and began on 25 April 1842, was perhaps the most written about auction ever held in England. The catalogue of it went through eight editions and was available in places as far apart as Paris and Leipzig. The auctioneer George Robins, 'The King of Puffery', generated spectacular publicity, and the private view attracted thousands of fashionable people. Not everyone was impressed. *The Times* commented on the dirty and neglected appearance of the poor little villa and its grounds:

'It would almost appear that not a shilling had been expended upon it, or upon anything in it, for half a century ... its brilliancy is now entirely gone, its gilding rubbed off, and little remains that would lead anybody to suppose that he by whom it was planned was remarkable in his generation for refinement of taste.'

It went on to describe much of what was being sold as 'rubbish'. Others produced parodies of the catalogue, offering for sale items as divers as

'a lock of hair from the tail of Whittington's cat; the nozzle of the identical pair of bellows with which Alfred the Great ought to have blown the fire when he suffered the cakes to burn; the bridge of the fiddle on which Nero played while Rome was burning; and a pimple from Oliver Cromwell's nose.'

Apart from one or two family portraits, such as Reynolds' famous 'Three Ladies Waldegrave,' and the odd piece of furniture, which were bought in, almost everything in Strawberry Hill was sold. The total realised by the sale was £33,450. George Edward and Frances did not themselves stay till the end. Halfway through they left to go abroad, first to Germany and then to Switzerland. This was the start of a scheme, dreamed up by the family lawyer Pearson, to make absolutely certain, once and for all, of the validity of their marriage. He had discovered that in Prussia marriage with a deceased husband's brother was perfectly legal. His plan was simply that they should become Prussian citizens, and then remarry. It was expensive, but effective. They rented an estate called Boisrond in the Swiss canton of Neuchâtel, then still subject to the King of Prussia, and here spent the two years necessary for them to become Prussian citizens. They appeared to live on an incredibly grand scale.

'We have sent to England for the phaeton,' wrote Frances to her brother Ward, 'and one of the English grooms and three horses. We are also going to have Faithful the large dog, two very handsome setters for Waldegrave to shoot with, and a rough terrier for me. George [a valet] is now made Steward, and we shall have an English under Butler and head Footman, also an English cook and kitchen maid, Housemaid, Lady's Maid, and perhaps two laundry maids and another groom who is Swiss . . . Our courier travels before us in a carriage and pair of post horses – in one place we had six horses, they are dressed in scarlet and gold and when we enter any town, or a carriage is before us, they blow their horns for the people to know we are coming.'

As soon as the two years were up, in June 1844, George Edward and Frances were remarried yet again at the village of Dombresson near Neuchâtel. There was now no longer any reason why they should not return home, particularly since George Edward was beginning to get restless. He wrote, for example, to his brother-in-law describing the 'horror of abroad.' They sailed to England in August, and took up residence at Harptree Court in Somerset. Here they might have lived very happily, had not George Edward's health begun to fail. The doctors diagnosed cirrhosis of the liver, a direct result, no doubt, of the excesses of his youth. This caused him to become increasingly lethargic, and even eccentric. He began to insist, for example, that Frances drove in her carriage only if the curtains were fully drawn, so that no stranger might ever set eyes upon her. No remedy proved effective, and Frances soon realised that his case was hopeless. Dr. Symonds of Bristol, who looked after him in his last days, later wrote that he could never forget the contrast between the radiant beauty of the young countess, and the ghastly pallor of her dying husband. The end mercifully came for George Edward on 28 September 1846. He was thirty years old.

8

MELTING FORTUNES

*'He seems only to have existed for the purpose of giving a
melancholy and unneeded illustration that a man with the finest
prospects may, by the wildest folly and extravagance, "foully
miscarry in the advantage of humanity, play away an uniterable
life, and have lived in vain."'*

(VICARY GIBBS, *The Complete Peerage*)

'IF riches were the solid foundations of human happiness,
Mrs. Long-Wellesley's felicity would have been durable, for
her possessions were princely. Of a noble descent herself, on
her mother's side, she had to bestow on the object of her choice
an estate of £50,000 a year – a palace in Essex for a residence –
an extensive park surrounding it – a similar domain and residence in Wiltshire – lands situated in other counties – another
residence in Hampshire, Tylney Hall ... These extensive possessions have been overwhelmed by a debt which drove her
from her native soil ... to extricate her husband from the
embarrassments of his situation and the clamours of his
creditors ... Her splendid mansion, Wanstead, is no more –
dismantled and sold in lots, it has passed like a shadow from the
land ... Tylney Hall has likewise been dismembered. The next
presentation to her livings in Essex have all passed under the
hammer – her park is yielding to the plough share – her woods
are bowing to the axe – Draycot, the venerable seat of her
ancestors, where she was born and reared ... alike deserted ...
All this reverse of fortune she lived to experience in a few
years.'

The rich heiress, the destruction of whose estates are referred
to in this contemporary memoir, was Catherine Tylney-Long,
the sister and co-heir of Sir James Tylney-Long, the eighth and
last Baronet of Draycot in Wiltshire. When he died in 1805, she
had inherited, as well as vast amounts of land, the income from
which was £25,000 a year, a personal fortune of £300,000. This
laid her open to siege by numerous fortune-hunters, and it is said
that when she drove in the park her suitors rode round her
carriage as the Guards surrounded the King's. She was no easy
game, however, and turned down many offers of marriage

which she suspected were made for the wrong reasons, including one from the Duke of Clarence. It was unfortunate for her that when she finally made her choice she picked the rottenest apple in the basket.

William Wellesley-Pole was the only son and heir of Lord Maryborough the elder brother of Arthur Wellesley, later Duke of Wellington. In 1809, aged twenty-one, he had been taken by his uncle out to the Peninsular on his staff. When he showed little predilection for anything other than drink, gambling, horses, and women he was quickly returned home, where he idled his time away and soon got into debt. One day, according to the diarist George Elers,

> 'A sudden thought struck him. His mother was on terms of great intimacy with Lady Catherine Long, the mother of the rich heiress. He wrote to his mamma, and conjured her to do all in her power of putting him in Miss Long's company. He proposed six times and was refused. He proposed a seventh time and was accepted.'

She appears to have been foolish enough to accept him after he had fought a duel on her behalf.

One of the first things William did after the wedding, which took place in 1812, was to take his wife's name, Tylney-Long, and insert it before his own surname, thus becoming William Pole Tylney-Long Wellesley, a name which was commemorated in the 'Loyal Effusion by W. T. Fitzgerald', in the brother's Smith's 'Rejected Addresses':

> 'Bless every man possessed of aught to give;
> Long may Long-Tylney Wellesley Long Pole live.'

Having long since spent his own inheritance, he then set about squandering hers. 'In Wellesley's dissolute hands even so great a fortune as his wife's melted away like newly-fallen snow.'

Wanstead, which stood in an extensive park, was a large and magnificent house. Designed by Colin Campbell for the first Earl of Tylney in 1715, the front was two hundred and sixty feet long, while inside were to be found the finest pictures and furniture, and ceilings painted by Kent. For ten years, under the rule of its new master, it was the scene of every conceivable luxury, and William became a well-known figure about town, famous, for example, for his night parties to the theatre, followed by extravagant suppers back at Wanstead, a six-mile drive. Night after night, day after day, he lived as if there were no tomorrow. The inevitable result was financial ruin.

'Where's Brummell? Dished.
Where's Long Pole Wellesley? Diddled!'

wrote Byron in 1822, and in the Spring of that year the sale of the contents of Wanstead House was announced:

'Monday, June 10, and thirty-one following days. Magnificent furniture, collection of fine paintings and sculpture, massive silver and gilt plate, splendid library of choice books, splendid and costly china, the valuable cellars of fine-flavoured old wines, ales, etc.'

The following year the great house itself, the building of which had cost more than £360,000 was sold. It fetched only £10,000.

William fled to Italy in disgrace. If Catherine ever entertained any notion that past events, together with the fact that his allowance was now only £4,000 a year, might have sobered him up, she was to be sadly mistaken. William had not been in Italy for more than a few months when, in 1823, he seduced Helena Bligh, the wife of a Coldstream Guards officer, Captain Thomas Bligh and eloped with her. In the Wellington archives there are several scruffy letters from William to his uncle, the Duke, attempting to justify his action. He claimed that Mrs. Bligh had been driven out of her house by the repeated cruelty of her husband and his brother.

'I found her one morning,' he wrote, 'in a flood of tears, and she asked me the meaning of an expression her husband had used towards her of being like a bitch at heat who is followed by all the men. She then, in as delicate terms as she could use, said he had called her a whore, that the Duke of Wellington was a rascal and had ruined his prospects in life and much other conversation of the same tenor.'

So far as William's father was concerned, the fact that his son had not only ruined his wife, but now cruelly abandoned her was the last straw. He disowned him. The Duke of Wellington on the other hand, probably for the sake of William's three children,

22. Wanstead House (J. Gendall)

William, James, and Victoria, did his utmost to mend his nephew's marriage, and effect a reconciliation. He entered into a lengthy correspondence with all the families involved; he sent Helena's father a cheque for £100 to fetch her home from Italy, and he again and again begged William to pay his debts and to return separately. By 1824, however, it was clear that he was fighting a losing battle. Helena became pregnant, and Captain Bligh instituted proceedings against William full of exotic evidence provided by Italian servants. He claimed that his wife had been seduced on the slopes of Mount Vesuvius during a midnight excursion of fifty persons in carriages, and that Mr. Long-Wellesley had rented a villa next door from which he could climb into her bedroom window, having hired one of the late King Murat's gigantic bodyguards to bar his own door. All hopes of any reconciliation effectively disappeared when, on 22 August 1825, Helena Bligh gave birth to a son, William Wellesley-Bligh.

Catherine, in the meantime, was living with her two unmarried sisters, the Misses Long, in Hampshire, and planning to divorce William and make her children wards in Chancery. Before she could achieve any of this, however, she died, on 12 September 1825, of a heart-attack, brought on, so the family claimed, by a violent letter which she had received from William only a few hours previously in which he demanded the return of his children. The story, when it got out, aroused public opinion to such an extent that Lady Maryborough had to warn the Duke and Duchess of Wellington not to attend the funeral as a mob was preparing to insult anyone with the name of Wellesley.

In accordance with their sister's deathbed wishes, the Misses Long now themselves made the Long-Wellesley children wards in Chancery. They appointed the Duke of Wellington as guardian who, in accepting, promised to execute his guardianship of the children 'zealously ... for their benefit and welfare, and in opposition to all mankind.' William was furious. 'A man and his children ought to be allowed to go to the Devil in his own way,' he told the children's tutor, but in spite of strenuous efforts and appeals he officially lost custody on 1 February 1827.

The crisis point in this affair was reached in the summer of 1827 when, after appealing and losing once again against the custody order, William made a threat on his uncle's life, swearing that he would shoot him and 'expiate the crime on the scaffold.' He did not in fact attempt to carry out the threat but instead tried another approach. He believed that, if he could prove that all members of the Wellesley and Long families were more vicious and immoral than he was, the Court of Chancery would have no choice but to grant him custody of his children.

He began by issuing a pamphlet against his uncle. The Duke of Wellington, he asserted, had only one motive in wishing to be guardian of his nephew's children, and that was to lay hands on the money of his eldest ward, William, which was due to him under a family trust. He went on to attack his morals, alleging that it was common knowledge that Mrs. Arbuthnot was living with him at Apsley House as his mistress. And what of his intrigues with the present Marchioness Wellesley before they were married, and with her sister Lady Hervey which had killed 'poor Sir Felton Hervey'; with Lady Charlotte Greville, and with Mrs. Freese, 'whose son he educated with his own.' 'This is the man who wants to be the guardian of Mr. Wellesley's children,' thundered the pamphlet, 'and who pretends to be a more MORAL man than their father.' When the Duke became Prime Minister, this pamphlet was prominently displayed in the shop window of a publisher off Drury Lane, as part of No. 18 of *The Rambler's Magazine* or *Frolicsome Companion*.

He next issued an affidavit against the Misses Long in which it was contended that his children had 'been suffered to associate with low menials who had been discharged from their Deponent's service . . . and with persons of loose and profligate habits and have thus acquired or are in danger of acquiring low and abominable practices alike injurious to their health and morals.' In what was a masterpiece of scandalous invention laid before the Lord Chancellor, he claimed, among other things, that the Misses Long 'from whose interference with the education of his said children he had always been most averse from a fear of the evil example they would set his children from a knowledge of . . . the gross improprieties, licentiousness and indelicacies of behaviour of which they had been frequently guilty,' had picked a playfellow for the nephews who was having intercourse with his aunt; that their niece's governess and her sister were prostitutes both living with the Misses Long's uncle; that the younger Miss Long had committed incest with this same uncle, that all the rest of the Long family were drunken blasphemers, and that the children's two aunts had 'a libidinous relationship' with each other.

Nobody took the affidavit seriously and William once again lost his appeal. He also lost the protection of the Duke who, until this moment, had never ceased trying to reconcile him with his father. But this time he had gone too far. In August 1829 the Duke wrote to him explaining that the threat to shoot him, followed by the libellous pamphlet, put him in an awkward position. If the libels were to appear in a newspaper with a wider circulation than the *Frolicsome Companion*, then he might have to prosecute. He ended his letter:

'It is not desirable that there should be much intercourse between us. Believe me ever yours most affectionately Wellington.'

It is hard to believe that the Duke could still have had any affection for his nephew.

William's children were now placed under the permanent guardianship of the Duchess of Wellington and Sir William Courtney, a family friend. They did their best to protect and educate them. Unfortunately with James, the younger brother, they failed. At the age of fourteen he was enticed away from Eton by his father, who took him to London. The Duchess was horrified:

'Ill as I have been, weak as I am,' she wrote, 'violent as are the wretched boy's threats, I would rather take my ward home this moment, than leave him to the certain ruin of the house in which I fear he now remains. Good God, I think of this with horror.'

After several unsuccessful attempts to get the boy back, Sir William realised that, short of kidnapping him, they were powerless.

William now made unscrupulous use of his young son, employing him as a decoy for his elder, monied, brother. Together they did their utmost to lure the boy to join them. If he came to London, James wrote, their father had promised to give them cigars and jewellery. He taunted young William that he would be considered 'an old school girl' rather than an Old Etonian if he consented to be 'a toad-eater to the Duchess of Wellington, the Duke and his sons.' He reminded him that the Duke was their father's 'most inveterate enemy.' But it was all to no avail. Although young William was essentially a weak character who would slip off to an ale-house or cock-pit as soon as her eyes were off him, he had become attached to the Duchess and she felt there was hope for his future. 'I have read somewhere,' she told his tutor, 'never to despair of any human creature while you can discover as much heart as you can rest the point of a pin on.'

If the Duchess had survived to keep a constant eye on her charge he might have been saved from ruin. Unfortunately, on 24 April 1831, she died, and the stage was set for his downfall. In the summer of 1831, William made an unsuccessful attempt to kidnap his daughter Victoria, the failure of which landed him in the Fleet Prison. On his release he somehow persuaded young William to join him, and fled abroad.

In February 1834, the Duke of Wellington received an anonymous letter, postmarked Calais, which turned out to be a plea that he should intervene and save his young great-nephew from the fate which awaited him if he were to be left with his father. It also brought him up to date on certain events which had taken place since William and his son had left England.

'Your Grace is probably aware that for some time past Mr. Wellesley (father) has been residing with his son at Calais – the Royal State apartments of Deakins Hotel! – a train of 12 to 15 of his own servants!! – dinner-parties etc on a scale of reckless extravagance, at once dishonest and indescribable; ... all this has been carrying on without means, save those realised amongst Jews, or procured from money-lenders upon the strength of the embryo inheritance in Oct next of his son Mr. Wellesley Junior... After a Calais career of 8 or 10 months Mr. Wellesley was at length arrested and lodged in the Boulogne jail ... To extricate this gentleman from prison it became necessary to lodge the amount £4,500 about; – and to enable Mr. Wellesley to raise this sum or rather £6,000 his son, as he told me himself, was obliged to sign a bond of £29,000!!! ... Released from durances the first use Mr. Wellesley made of his regained liberty was to return to Calais, and at nine of the same evening decamp for Bruxelles taking with him an English officer's daughter whom he had debauched prior to his imprisonment... During Mr. Wellesley's detention in jail his son's visits were frequent and his attentions unremitting – but even in the prison chamber was preserved that ostentatious display of state for which Mr. Wellesley has been so much celebrated, the very best living, dinner, company, etc, etc – Mr. Wellesley (son) at length fell ill, but his indisposition was considered slight, altho' his disorders, for they were plural, were discovered to be of that order modestly described by Lord Byron as "A general subscription of the ladies," the consequence of unrestrained passion at an unguarded moment after leaving his father's prison banquet flushed with wine and high in fever...'

The letter went on to say that a notorious money-lender had just arrived from London, and was asking the whereabouts of Mr. Wellesley, leaving no doubt in the writer's mind that 'the son is wanted to complete some new contract besides perhaps to become collaterall security for a house or rather a palace which it is said Mr. Wellesley is in treaty for at Bruxelles, not omitting the Duke of Orleans' stud of horses which in his moments of madness Mr. Wellesley talks of purchasing ...' the writer signed himself 'An Old Soldier', adding that he would send the Duke his real name if an advertisement were put in a Brussels paper signed 'Waterloo'.

It was quite clear to the Duke from reading this letter that William had every intention, and was indeed on the point of, of robbing his son of every penny he could get his hands on. 'Old Soldier' was immediately contacted, and turned out to be a Monsieur Rochefort. On his advice they dispatched an eminent legal adviser to Brussels to sort out young William's affairs. Before he could achieve anything, however, William wrecked his chances, causing a scandal by publicly accusing him of having seduced his son. This was all too much for the Duke who, there and then, washed his hands of the whole affair.

The story of the family from here on is not a happy one. Helena Bligh had married William in August 1828, and on the death of his father, then the Earl of Mornington, became fourth Countess of Mornington. By then William had long since abandoned her. She survived until 1869, but her obituary in the *Gentleman's Magazine* described her as having been 'wasted with care, involved in debt, living in garrets, and even occasionally applying to a police magistrate or parish for assistance as Countess of Mornington – an honoured name borne before her by the mother of Wellington and Wellesley.' The last the Duke heard of her she was living in the Wanstead workhouse. Her son William Wellesley Bligh lived to be only twenty-six.

Young William lived to be fifty; James thirty-six. Their father, then on an allowance of ten pounds a week from the Duke, died suddenly in poverty on 1 July 1857, at lodgings in Thayer Street, Marylebone. An obituary in the *Morning Chronicle* commented somewhat acidly:

'Redeemed by no single virtue, adorned by no single grace, his life has gone out without even a single flicker of repentance; his "retirement" was that of one who was deservedly avoided by all men.'

As an example of 'overshadowing ruin' William's life does not stand 'unparalelled in the records of British Prodigality', as a certain contemporary once wrote.

There were many equally great spendthrifts who seem to have existed solely for the purpose of demonstrating that the greater the fortune, the faster it can be blown. The fourth Marquis of Ailesbury, when he was only twenty-eight, had liabilities of £345,462. George William Thomas Brudenell-Bruce, more generally known as Willie, was the grandson of the third Marquis of Ailesbury, and a descendant of James Brudenell, seventh Earl of Cardigan who had, with such gallantry, led the Charge of the Light Brigade at Balaklava. This courageous blood, however, had long since disappeared. His father George, nicknamed 'the Duffer' died in Corsica aged twenty-nine, in May 1866, recuperating after a lifetime's devotion to the pleasures of the flesh and the bottle. Willie was then only five, and as his mother, Evelyn, showed little inclination to look after her children on her own, he and his sister Mabel were brought up mostly by their grandparents. When his grandfather, Lord Ernest, became third Marquis in 1878, on the death of his brother, Willie was given the courtesy title of Lord Savernake, and introduced to the Savernake tenantry as the official heir. His inheritance was considerable. The Savernake estate, situated in Wiltshire, and on the borders of Hampshire and Berkshire, consisted of forty-thousand acres. This included the famous Savernake Forest, of which the Brudenell-Bruces were the hereditary Wardens, and which was then at its zenith as a woodland.

'All the trees planted by those two great Wardens, the last Bruce and the first Brudenell, were in their prime. The avenues were perfect. The great beeches, mile upon mile of them, stood

23. GEORGE WILLIAM THOMAS BRUDENELL-
BRUCE, 4th Marquis of Ailesbury

in their serried ranks, with never a dying tree nor yet a half-grown one among them.'

Altogether it was one of the finest properties in the south of England. As well as at Savernake there were also great estates in Yorkshire, at Jervaulx, Whorlton, and Tanfield, which had been held in the family for three hundred years.

The high hopes entertained by the third Marquis for his grandson were to be sorely disappointed. Willie was sent to Eton which he left under a cloud, after having refused to be birched for impertinence to the Headmaster. Finding himself out in the world with a generous allowance and little to occupy his time, he took to attending race meetings. This was the beginning of the rot, for his genial nature and future inheritance made him prey to a set of undesirable spongers who saw him as a soft touch.

'The fourth Marquis was by no means a bad-hearted fellow,' wrote a first cousin of Willie's in later years. 'He had plenty of pluck, would, and did, fight anybody who cared to tackle him, was always ready to share his last fiver with a pal . . . drink and bad company ruined my cousin. He would have vigorously denied being a snob but he was a snob because he chose deliberately to mix with blackguards having found that in that class alone he was treated with deference.'

When he was not betting, and losing, heavily, Willie was idling around London in the company of these 'friends', supporting both himself and them in an orgy of wine and women.

Throughout his short life, and much to the disgust of his family, Willie continued to prefer the company of jockeys and grooms, cabbies and costermongers to that of his own class. He was usually dressed in a heavy box coat, similar to those worn by coachmen in the early part of the century, and he wore a hard black hat with a low flat crown. On this extraordinary coat were real half-crowns instead of buttons. He loved to speak in rhyming slang, and his command of the vernacular earned him the nickname 'Billy Stomachache.' Willie also loved actresses, in particular Miss Dolly Tester of the Theatre Royal, Brighton.

'In her early days at least,' wrote C. B. Cochran in his autobiography, 'poor Dolly had not altogether an easy life, but then no-one who was in close association with that extraordinary set of young men who, in the Jubilee decade, painted the town red, could reasonably expect a bed of roses. Socially it was a curious period. A group of young fellows of varying social origins found themselves in possession of large fortunes and inbred with the desire to throw those fortunes away. Some succeeded; others, through no fault of theirs, had something left at the end of their efforts.'

On 6 May 1864, at a Registry Office in Hanover Square, Dolly married one who succeeded. She became Lady Savernake.

By this time rumours had reached the third Marquis of his grandson's wild behaviour. He sent his lawyer to investigate and discovered to his horror that Willie had run up debts of more than £175,000, most of them to money-lenders like Sam Lewis, who in return for a signature at the foot of some document would advance large amounts of cash to hard-up young men at outrageous interest rates. Knowing that the entail on Savernake happened to end with Willie, he was faced with the dreadful possibility that should his grandson be declared bankrupt, then the Savernake estate, which he and his predecessors held so dear, might have to be sold to raise money. There was only one answer to the problem. This was to sacrifice the Yorkshire properties, in return for a renewal of the entail by Willie, so that at least the estate might be saved for another three generations. With a heavy heart he thus gave orders that Jervaulx, Tanfield, and adjacent properties should forthwith be put on the market. In September 1886 he paid one last visit to his beloved Yorkshire:

'Sept. 3rd. Went up to Jervaulx Abbey; very lovely. Alas, am very sad and melancholy...
Sept. 7th. Went (again) over the dear old Abbey.
Sept. 15th ... drove over to Tanfield Rectory, Woods, Lodge and church all most lovely and beautiful. Alas! for the last time ... Sept. 16th. Took a drive in new carriage made low and comfortable for me to get in and out of ... Went to see old Maugham who revealed to me that Tanfield Woods Hall River and all were sold. Another nail in my coffin and one of the last it must be.'

Within two months the old Marquis was dead, shortly after telling his son Henry that Jervaulx 'would always be written across his heart.'

With the death of his grandfather, 'poor, unfortunate Willie,' as the old man had once described him, became the fourth Marquis. With his debts paid off from the proceeds of the York-shire sales, he now had the chance to salvage something of his life. This he chose not to do. He simply continued with his old life-style, and went back to Sam Lewis when he needed cash. Unfortunately, he also turned to dishonest methods of raising money. On 30 September 1887 he was expelled from the Jockey Club for fraud in connection with the running of his horse Everitt. It transpired from the enquiry that he had ordered the jockey to pull up the horse during the Harewood Handicap at the August meeting at York. The stewards were also satisfied that he had ordered horses to be stopped on several other occasions. How seriously this was regarded at the time can be judged by this extract from *The Times*:

'He who violates them [the rules], and is condemned by the Stewards of the Jockey Club for so doing, incurs the penalty of social extinction. To come under the censure of the Stewards in its gravest form is worse for a man than to be declared a defaulter on the Stock Exchange, or to be requested to resign by the committee of a leading club. For what it implies is that most unpardonable of all offences – that a man has proved himself unworthy to associate with his equals in that as to which they are most sensitive, their pleasures. We regret that this is the fate which has befallen the bearer of an honoured name, ... The best that can be said for Lord Ailesbury is that he is very young.'

The piece ended on a note of moral indignation, deploring the fact that, not only had Willie disgraced his own family, he had brought into disrepute the whole peerage. 'The world can toler-age a Gracchus leading the mob, or a Lord Nelson violating the ties of family. It cannot tolerate a Marquis who is warned off Newmarket Heath...'

Ruined both socially and financially, Willie found himself in a quandary. There was no more money forthcoming from the estate, and he was under considerable pressure from the money-lenders to pay up his debts having mounted again to some £230,000. They impressed upon him that although he was only tenant of Savernake for life there was nothing to stop him from selling so long as he had the consent of the trustees. He would not himself be able to touch the capital from such a sale, but it would be put into the hands of the trustees to invest as they thought fit, and out of the revenue they would have to provide him with an adequate income. Surely, suggested the money-lenders, this would be preferable to being declared bankrupt? After consulting with his personal solicitor, Mr. Newburn-Walker, who was also a trustee and who, being primarily a business man, considered the idea a sound one, Willie discreetly let it be known that under the right circumstances he would be willing to sell. It was not long before he was approached by the brewery millionaire, Sir Edward Guinness, who had for some time been looking for a country estate and who put in a bid for three quarters of a million pounds.

When news of the intended sale reached Lord Frederick Brudenell-Bruce, Willie's uncle, and the other trustee, he was deeply shocked. His priorities were quite different from those of Mr. Newburn-Walker. He looked at it from the family point of view, that their ancestors had lived at Savernake since Domesday, and that it was therefore quite wrong to sell. Even more furious was Lord Henry Brudenell-Bruce who was the senior uncle and, Willie being childless, the next heir. He also had three children, including a son, whose interests were naturally near to his heart. But instead of directing his wrath at Willie, he reserved it for Sir Edward Guinness whom he bitterly attacked as 'a mere upstart merchant, a nouveau-riche Irishman' who was cashing in on Willie's misfortune. He devoted himself to placing every possible barrier in the way of the proposed sale. Thus faced with the determined opposition of the entire family, there was only one course left for 'dear Willie,' as the family were wont to call him, to take. In 1891 Lord Henry was served with a document entitled 'The Humble Petition of the Most Honourable George William Thomas Brudenell-Bruce, Marquis of Ailesbury.' It was a petition for leave to sell the entire Savernake estate. The battle now entered the law courts.

From the first moment that Willie stepped into the witness-box, on 7 August 1891, to be cross-examined by Sir Horace Davey, appearing for Lord Henry Brudenell-Bruce, the hearing went against him. He made no concession to the solemnity of the proceedings, behaving more as if he were on the stage than in a court of law. Moreover his cross-examination clearly proved the truth of Sir Horace's premise that there was only one reason for the sale: 'in order to pay off the money-lenders who had preyed upon the extravagance of this youthful tenant for life.'

Sir H: 'And are you 28?'

Lord A: 'They reckon me twenty years older than I am.'

Sir H: 'Is it not a fact that Mr. Lewis makes you an allowance?'

Lord A: 'No, but if I want money I go to Mr. Lewis for it – that is if he likes to lend it to me.'

Sir H: 'And he lets you have what you want?'

Lord A (laughing): 'He does not always let me have what I want. I go to him for money and he lets me have some.'

Sir H: 'Is it not a fact that you are living upon money received from Mr. Lewis, and that you depend upon him for your daily maintenance?'

Lord A: 'Partly, certain.'

Sir H: 'Mainly?'

Lord A: 'Yes, I will say that.'

Sir H: 'Is not Mr. Lewis very anxious that this contract should be carried into effect?'

Lord A: 'Yes, I don't want to be rude, but if a man owed you £200,000, you would want to get it, wouldn't you?' (*laughter*)

Sir H: 'I did not ask for that. He is very anxious to receive it, is he not?'

Lord A: 'Certainly.'

After hearing all the evidence Mr. Justice Stirling judged that the sale was not in the interest of the family at large, and dismissed Willie's petition.

This decision was reversed on appeal, the judgement being that, even though the Court had little reason to sympathise with Willie:

'I do not think he can be more compendiously described than as a spendthrift who has ruined himself by his own extravagance and folly and who has brought disgrace upon the family name, and exposed the family estate to destruction for the rest of his life.'

The effect of the sale not taking place would be disastrous. The tenant for life would be bankrupt, having already mortgaged his life interest, and the money-lenders would administer the estate with the purpose only of squeezing every possible penny out of the property, with the result that 'in all human probability everybody connected with it will be ruined unless it is sold.'

Months of litigation followed, with the uncles finally taking their appeal to the highest level, but here, in the House of Lords, the judgement also went against them. Even so the squabbling was still not over. There followed endless arguments about how the proceeds of such a sale should be split up, what was to be done with the family heirlooms etc. In the end Lord Iveagh, as Sir Edward Guinness had now become, who had been waiting patiently in the sidelines, became so disgusted with the way in which the family were carrying on that he withdrew his offer. Lord Henry had won.

After this failure to sell the family property, 'poor dear Willie', having not a penny to his name, went to live with his agent, Mr. Feltham, at a suburban villa in Brixton, where he eked out an existence on an allowance of £20 a week. 'It's hard times,' he used to complain. 'In the old days I used to give the dog a roast fowl. Now I can hardly afford a bird for myself!' He made one last attempt to wring a little more money out of Savernake. He discovered that, as tenant for life, he was entitled to cut timber. Savernake Forest suddenly took on a new and more cheerful significance. 'I'll make those damned squirrels jump further,' he cried, and gave orders that the Forest should be cut down and sold. Fortunately for posterity fate intervened. Early in 1894 he fell seriously ill. He died on 10 April. His body, weakened by years of over-indulgence, had no resistance. 'It has been said,' comments the *Complete Peerage*, 'that his death was only mourned by the Radical Party who thus lost for their speeches a most eligible example of hereditary legislators.'

If 'dear Willie' was no shining example of the greatness and wisdom of the British aristocracy, then nor was the fifth Marquis of Anglesey, immortalised in the family as 'Mad Uxbridge' whose passing the Radicals must have equally mourned. Henry Cyril Paget, fifth Marquis of Anglesey, was born in June 1875, and was officially the only son and heir of the fourth Marquis by his second wife, Blanche Mary Boyd, whom he married in Paris in 1874. According to family legend, however, he was in reality the illegitimate son of the French actor, Coquelin, a notorious womaniser, with whom his mother had had an affair soon after her marriage. Credence is given to this story by the fact that, after

24. HENRY CYRIL PAGET, 5th Marquis of Anglesey

his mother died young in 1877, he was brought up by Coquelin's sister. He thus spent most of his formative years abroad, and in the company of theatrical people, which may well account for much of his later eccentricity. He was a delicate, rather over-sensitive child who, having no brothers and sisters, used to lavish all his affection on a large collection of pets. He made up for any loneliness he might have felt by continually dressing up in the theatrical costumes that were always available and losing himself in a world of fantasy.

Henry Cyril, then the Earl of Uxbridge, first came to his father's estates at Plas Newydd, on the Isle of Anglesey, at the age of eight, where he was put into the hands of various tutors to prepare him for school. It must have been a strange and remote existence for a motherless boy who had been brought up among foreigners. A friend from those boyhood days was later to recall how he spoke fluent French and Russian, and that he spent very little time amongst boys of his own age.

'An aged Scottish nurse of pious life,' he reminisced, 'was the first person I remember to have been his companion, and often would they be seen walking or driving in a pony carriage in the neighbourhood of Llanfair.'

He eventually completed his education at Eton.

When the young Earl came of age in June 1896, great festivities were held at Plas Newydd to celebrate the occasion. Seventeen large marquees were erected in the grounds to accommodate the thousands of people who came to present their best wishes, and to attend a series of glittering banquets and entertainments. The celebrations lasted from Tuesday 16 June to the following Friday when fifteen hundred school-children from all the Anglesey villages 'held high carnival at Plas Newydd.' A local newspaper commented that 'much interest was evinced in, and many good wishes expressed for the future of the good-looking young man of 21, who was heir to so fair an inheritance and who seemed to have a future of promise before him.' This 'fair inheritance' consisted of ten thousand acres in Anglesey, seventeen thousand five hundred acres in Staffordshire, and fifteen hundred in Derbyshire, with a value of at least £110,000 a year. It is curious to note that both Henry Cyril and his father were conspicuous by their absence from these festivities.

MELTING FORTUNES

On 20 January 1898, Henry Cyril married his cousin Lilian Florence Maud Chetwyn, daughter of the notorious 'Pocket Venus', Lady Florence Paget, who was half-sister to the fourth Marquis. For Lily, a stunningly beautiful young girl, with pale green eyes and bright red-gold Titian hair, who might have stepped straight out of a painting by Rossetti, this marriage, which was forced upon her by her mother, turned out to be a disaster, a fact which is borne out by its annulment only two years later. The Earl of Uxbridge, whose slightly foreign appearance and tastes had earned him the reputation of being a trifle eccentric, turned out to be a great deal more than that. It was noted in a contemporary newspaper that on the day of their wedding the groom bestowed upon his bride 'magnificent gifts of jewellery.' The truth is that Henry Cyril did not just love jewellery, he was obsessed by it. It is said that on their honeymoon he took Lily to Paris, and that when she stopped to admire the window display of Van Cleef and Arpels he bought the entire display for her. He then, ignoring her tearful pleadings not to be turned into such a spectacle, made her wear the whole lot to the races.

When his father died in October 1898, the new Marquis threw all caution to the winds. With his newly acquired fortune, and with a total lack of regard for his responsibilities towards his estates, he began to let his fantasies run wild. Inspired by Lily's beauty he started on a new and extravagant craze. With the help of a travelling Polish jeweller, Morris Wartski, whom he established in a shop in Llandudno, he set about the creation of a remarkable collection of jewellery. His passion knew no bounds. Within two months of inheriting his estates he had mortgaged his life interest in them, as well as in certain policies of life insurance, to various bankers in order to raise £100,000 with which to buy more and more precious stones. Nothing escaped his notice. The cream of his collection was part of a magnificent emerald necklace which had once belonged to Marie Antoinette. There was soon not a jeweller in Europe who did not know that if he acquired some particularly rare and fine gem, he would almost certainly find a buyer in the Marquis of Anglesey.

Henry Cyril had a peculiar and favourite way of admiring his jewels, a way that horrified his young and inexperienced wife. Each night he made her undress, and he would then cover her naked body with precious stones until she stood before him dripping in emeralds, rubies and diamonds. He then forced her to sleep wearing those jewels. As far as is known, he never laid a finger on her. He just stared. When the marriage was annulled in 1900, the grounds were non-consummation.

After Lily had left him, driven out by the degrading treatment to which she was subjected, Henry Cyril immersed himself in a new folly – amateur theatricals, on a stupendous scale. He began by converting the chapel at Plas Newydd, by now grandly renamed Anglesey Castle, into a theatre. Called the Gaiety, it was modelled after that of Sarah Bernhardt in Paris, and was decorated throughout in white and blue. When closely packed it was capable of holding about 150 people. He turned the organ loft into a private box for his own use. Although the first performances took place before an audience consisting of the household and a few relatives, with various servants and stable-hands making up the cast, he very soon graduated to much greater things. At the end of 1900 he spent considerable sums on modernisation:

> 'Electric light plant was installed, special scenery painted, limelights on the most improved plan fixed, and the whole place rejuvenated in accordance with all the latest notions. The lighting alone must have cost some £600 to fit up.'

Then in 1901 he commissioned a London company, that of Mr. Alex Keith, to open the new improved theatre formally with a production of *Aladdin*. The Marquis himself played the role of Pekoe, 'the Vizier's son, a bit mooney on Yummy-yum,' in a series of costumes that left the audience gaping with astonishment. One was a tightly-fitting suit of white cloth, with a cloak lined with pale salmon-pink silk, and garters, necklaces, rings, and other ornaments ablaze with turquoises and diamonds. The jewels on one costume alone were estimated as being worth over £40,000, while the value of those used in the whole production was said to have amounted to over half a million.

At a given point during each show Henry Cyril would take over the stage for a performance of 'the Butterfly Dance', a solo of his own invention. As he fluttered about before an audience drawn largely from his tenants and local shopkeepers, he became immortalised as 'the Dancing Marquis'. The late Sir Clough Williams-Ellis, who was one of the survivors of that age to have seen him, remembered him thus:

MELTING FORTUNES

'As a sort of apparition he was quite unforgettable – a tall, elegant and bejewelled creature, with wavering, elegant gestures, reminding one rather of an Aubrey Beardsley illustration come to life... In these parts – strongly non-conformist Welsh – his frivolous antics were not approved, especially his conversion of the chapel at Plas Newydd into a theatre.'

Inspired by his own performances at the Gaiety, nothing could now hold back the Dancing Marquis. Firmly convinced that his talents should be shared with the world, he financed a series of tours for Mr. Keith and his company, which had been elaborately equipped for this purpose. They travelled with specially painted scenery and their own orchestra, and many of their props were exact copies of furniture from Anglesey Castle. For his own use, and that of his personal staff of four men, the Dancing Marquis had 'a handsomely-fitted motor car, to say nothing of a fabulous amount of luggage, and the case containing his jewels. The value of some of the individual stones is enormous; one pear-shaped pearl pin is estimated at £10,000, others are considered to be worth £4,000 and £13,000 respectively, while a diamond and turquoise ring is worth a mere paltry £1,500.' When the company was assembled it consisted of fifty people and five truckloads of baggage and scenery.

Although the Butterfly Dance was performed whenever possible, the programme on these tours was by no means restricted to *Aladdin*. Other favourites were *The Marriage of Kitty*, in which the Dancing Marquis 'was admitted by some capital critics to be distinctly good,' and *The Ideal Husband*, a part that 'might have been written for him he went through it so naturally.' He did not impress Sir Clough Williams-Ellis, however: 'The only time I saw him act was as the Marquis in the successful musical comedy "The Country Girl" – his voice was quite inadequate.' From time to time he would appear under a pseudonym, as when the company played the Central Theatre, Dresden:

'In the Central Theatre last Sunday, a new artist appeared under the name of "San Toi". In a dark house and on a dark stage he produced kaleidoscope pictures in lifesize. In quick succession San Toi appeared in the costumes of the different nationalities and in all sorts of fancy dress. The splendour and the brightness of the colours, the tasteful combination, and the constant change of the beautiful pictures thrown by electric

light on the slender form of the artist, clothed in white, glad-
dened the eyes. The likeness of the German Emperors. William
I, Frederick III, and William II, of the German heroes of the last
decades, and of the Sacon Royal couple were beautifully
rendered. The production was without any flaw, and was
received with great applause. The artist himself is a most
interesting personality. He is Lord Anglesey, an English Marquis, the head of a noble and well-known English family with a
seat and a vote in the House of Lords.'

At the end of each performance the Dancing Marquis distributed
photographs of himself amongst the audience.

The expense of these tours was colossal, and it was not long
before the Dancing Marquis found himself in a state of hopeless
insolvency. The crash came in June 1904 when his trustees took
over all his property in order to raise money with which to pay
off the growing list of creditors. The final liabilities involved
amounted to a staggering £544,000, a large proportion of which
was owed to jewellers: £26,651 to Morris Wartski, £40,200 to
Goudstikker and Son, £31,080 to Haardt Devos, Brussels,
£21,300 to Dobson and Sons, and £16,754 to Lacloche. The
results of these purchases were discovered by the trustees in large
trunks in the attics of Anglesey Castle. When opened, they
revealed a pirate's treasure of pearls, emeralds, and diamonds,
innumerable gold cigarette and cigar cases, many of them beautifully studded with the finest diamonds and rubies, two hundred
gold scarf pins, plain and jewelled, and what was perhaps the
most remarkable item of all, a magnificent twenty-two foot long
chain of gold and precious stones, to which, at intervals of about
an inch, were attached hundreds of charms in gold and antique
silver. Amongst diverse other discoveries were large amounts of
fine 'paste' jewellery, all set in solid gold and silver, and the
world's largest collection of walking-sticks.

There followed the great Anglesey Castle sales at which all
these jewels and the rest of the Dancing Marquis's belongings
were dispersed. So vast was his accumulation of possessions that
the sales lasted for over forty days, in the course of which
seventeen thousand lots were auctioned, including anything of
remotest value from motor cars to pedigree dogs. A detailed look
at some of what was sold gives an insight into exactly how the
Dancing Marquis squandered much of his fortune.

'Gentlemen, I am selling at a shilling dogs for which pounds have been paid,' were the opening words of the auctioneer Mr. Dew on the first day of the sale, 4 August 1904, as he set about the dispersal of the Marquis's kennels. There followed a motley procession of hounds onto the rostrum: Fox Terriers, Welsh Terriers, Skye Terriers, Collies, Chows, Borzois, Pugs, and Pomeranians. 'There was a spirited contest,' reported the correspondent of the *North Wales Chronicle* 'for Ireland's Bee Bee, a dainty blue toy which, used to nestling on scented laps and the petting of jewelled fingers, shivered with apprehension at the contact of deal boards, and would not show off before crude strangers.' At the end of the day, when the last of the dogs had been finally disposed of, the auctioneer moved on to 'the richly embroidered silken coats of the toy dogs, with the Marquis's crest in silver on them, and the elaborate little portmanteau, lined with quilted and padded silk and soft rugs, in which the pets accompanied their master on his travels.'

That their master liked to travel in style became quite evident over the next few days when under the hammer went the Marquis's considerable collection of carriages, horses, yachts, and numerous motor cars. The latter included a 28 H.P. Pullman 'Mors' which 'reproduced in motor car form the luxury of the Pullman Railway carriage... There was elegant accommodation for four passengers inside in the shape of a revolving armchair at each corner. Polished mahogany woodwork and dark red Morocco upholstery gave the inside furnishing an appearance of luxurious elegance. The decorations of the ceilings were in the Louis XV style, and there were blue plush curtains and bands, whilst a Wilton pile carpet was laid on the floor. It did not require the assurance of the auctioneer's catalogue that money had been no obstacle in the construction of this travelling drawing-room.'

The sale of his personal clothing took three days. 'It was the personal clothing of one man,' commented a reporter, 'but it might fairly be said that there was personal clothing enough for a regiment.' The details were fantastic.

'Boots! There were washleather boots, crocodile leather boots, and chamois leather boots – boots with skates fastened to them, and boots without, – snowboots and galoshes, patent court shoes and grey suede shoes, silk tapestry slippers and crimson leather slippers, printed leather slippers and Jaeger's wool slippers – even down to sandals – in fact there was a complete collection of everything that could by any chance be strapped, buckled or laced upon the foot of man...'

It might have been the entire men's department of a grand London store that was being sold. There were overcoats, cloaks, covert coats etc of every cut, cloth and variety. Of these the *pièce de résistance* was a full-length sable overcoat with twenty tails and ten heads hanging from it, which was reputed to have cost a thousand guineas, and had been his favourite coat.

'The Marquis's elaborate stock of night and underwear was brought to view. Such pyjamas! And such nightshirts! There were thirty suits of the finest silk pyjamas, some splendid black silk shirts – twenty-four suits of fancy silk pyjamas and jackets; and still the cry was – They come! The magnificent nightshirts, however, elicited something like a gasp from the audience. Some of them were bright crimson in colour and embroidered with Oriental splendour.'

A feature of the sale was 'the dazzling array of smoking and lounge suits of every conceivable colour . . . with rare exceptions, none of the articles had ever been worn,' and the 'wonderful Anglesey waistcoats,' which had achieved 'notoriety all over the world. Gentlemen from Melbourne and New York had come over specially to snap them up.' Two hundred and sixty pairs of white kid gloves, fifty-two dozen silk and linen handkerchiefs, eleven dozen collars, two hundred and eight pairs of socks, on and on went the auctioneer until every cupboard, wardrobe and chest of drawers in Anglesey Castle was stripped bare.

Amongst the more remarkable items that appeared in the sale were the walking-sticks.

'Many of them had round knob handles so thickly encrusted with diamonds, rubies, amethysts and emeralds that the setting was almost invisible, and several had gunmetal knobs with matched rose diamonds trailing over the dull surface in fanciful design, or set to exhibit the crest or initials of the owner. Some of the handles were made of chased or unchased gold, others of lustrous enamels, in which pearls and diamonds had been placed. The gem of the collection was a gold-mounted stick with round top set with diamonds, pearls, turquoise, sapphires, rubies, beryls etc... Of the eccentric and bizarre there was much. When the auctioneer set in motion a beautifully modelled cockatoo's head, which adorned the head of a stick, it lifted its crest of hackles, opened its mouth and blinked its eyes. By the same mechanical aid the yellow ivory head of a Chinaman leered and grinned most realistically, a donkey flapped its ears, and a duck opened and shut its bill . . .'

No object that was considered capable of raising even a shilling escaped the auctioneer's hammer. They even sold his Coronation robes, the most treasured possession of a Peer of the realm. 'Gentlemen, we really don't like to sell these things,' commented the auctioneer. 'There have been many painful things during this sale, and this is one of the most painful. The Trustees, if they could would have let Lord Anglesey have these things back, but they couldn't, and so the only thing to do was to put them up . . .'

'Up at the castle,' described a reporter 'the situation for the old retainers is almost a tragedy. There are a few servants left in the house, and there are several scattered over the grounds. A man nearly eighty was sweeping one of the drives yesterday. He swept wearily, with lethargic stroke. He has grown old in the Anglesey service. "I suppose," he said, "they'll put me up for sale with the things about the place. I'm one of 'em." . . . There are many beside him to whom the Anglesey estate is more than a home, and they hardly realise yet that they may have to say goodbye. A hard-featured woman, employed in the grounds, bit her lip yesterday as she admitted the possibility of departure of the old servants of the place.'

When the sales were over, the Dancing Marquis left for France, from where he was never to return. The following year, after suffering two bad attacks of pleurisy, he died at the Hotel Royale in Monte Carlo. He was thirty, and a bankrupt in the capital of extravagance. 'He seems only to have existed,' commented Vicary Gibbs in a memoir 'for the purpose of giving a melancholy and unneeded illustration that a man with the finest prospects, may by the wildest folly and extravagance, as Sir Thomas Browne says, "foully miscarry in the advantage of humanity, play away an uniterable life, and have lived in vain."'

9

MAD AND SINFUL PASSIONS

'The deed is done, I have chosen exile, solitude, seclusion, slander, in preference to living with him.'

(LADY LINCOLN, to her father, August 1848)

BEFORE the marriage of his daughter Elizabeth to Lord Chesterfield in 1692, George Savile, first Marquis of Halifax, published for her, as a New Year's gift, a tract entitled 'Advice to a Daughter'. It contained advice on Religion; Husband; House, Family and Children; Behaviour and Conversation; Friendships; Censure; Vanity and Affectation; Pride, and Diversions. The longest of these sections, and therefore that with which he appeared to be most concerned, was on how she might live as happily as possible with her husband. It expressed an almost medieval attitude to women, yet this was an attitude that was to be prevalent amongst a majority of men right through to the middle of the nineteenth century.

'It is one of the disadvantages belonging to your sex,' he wrote, 'that young women are seldom permitted to make their own choice; their friends care and experience are thought safer guides to them, than their own fancies; and their modesty often forbiddeth them to refuse when their parents recommend, though their inward consent may not entirely go along with it. In this case there remaineth nothing for them to do, but to endeavour to make that easie which falleth to their lot...'

He urged her to accept that

'there is inequality in the sexes, and that... the men, who were to be the law-givers, had the larger share of reason bestowed upon them, by which means your sex is the better prepar'd for the compliance that is necessary for the better performance of those duties which seem to be most properly assign'd to it.'

Although it might seem unfair that men could claim 'large

grains of allowance' for certain 'frailties' which in a woman
would be considered 'in the utmost degree criminal' but which
'in a man passeth under a much gentler censure,' there was, he
stressed, a good reason for this.

> 'The root and excuse of this injustice is the preservation of
> families from any mixture that may bring a blemish to them:
> and whilst the point of honour continues to be so plac'd it
> seems unavoidable to give your sex the greater share of the
> penalty. But if in this it lieth under any disadvantage, you are
> more than recompens'd by having the honour of families in
> your keeping.'

The reality of all that Halifax said to his daughter was that she,
or any woman, might be forced to marry a man she disliked for
reasons of family interest. In a society that was so acutely conscious of status and hierarchy one of the greatest fears of a parent
was social derogation in marriage, that a child of theirs, whether
male or female, should form an alliance with a family of lower
estate or degree than their own. Thus when in 1836 Lord Charles
Pelham-Clinton, a younger son of the fourth Duke of Newcastle,
announced his intention of marrying a Miss Madge Orde, his
father was outraged.

> 'My dear Charles,' he wrote on 19 November, 'various and
> numerous as have been the incidents in my life which have
> caused me astonishment, nothing I must plainly own has given
> me more inexpressible astonishment than the letter which I
> received from you last night. I have a most decided objection
> to such a union for almost innumerable reasons but for none
> more than the odious and intolerable connection which would
> thus be ... rivetted. What you can see in Miss Orde that is
> attractive in any way is what I am utterly at a loss to conceive.
> Here is an unfortunate girl, miserably and most objectionably
> connected in every way and quarter, with nothing I can see to
> recommend her either in appearance or in anything else, with-
> out money ... I should consider that such a rippish and wholly
> objectionable marriage would be a disgrace to my family and
> you may depend on it I would never admit her into any house.'

Daughters, being the lowest end of the family hierarchy, were,
on the whole, considered only useful to strengthen family ties,
and many parents settled marriages by treaty without any regard

to their daughter's wishes. This often led to great unhappiness. Mary Granville, better remembered as Mrs. Delany, the diarist, never forgot the misery she suffered when she was forced at the age of seventeen to marry Alexander Pendarves, a Cornish land-owner of nearly sixty, a man towards whom she had formed 'an invincible aversion'.

'Everything he said or did by way of obliging me,' she later wrote, 'increased that aversion. I thought him ugly and dis-agreeable: he was fat, much afflicted with gout, and often sat in a sullen mood, which I concluded was from the gloominess of his temper. I knew that of all men living, my uncle had the greatest opinion of, and esteem for him, and I dreaded his making a proposal of marriage as I knew it would be accepted. In order to prevent it, I did not in the least disguise my great dislike for him; I behaved myself not only with indifference but rudeness: when I dressed, I considered what would become me least: if he came into the room when I was alone, I instantly left it, and took care to let him see I quitted it because he came there. I was often chid by my two wise aunts for this behaviour. I told them plainly he was odious to me, in hopes they would have had good nature enough to have prevented what I foresaw; but Laura called me childish, ignorant and silly, and that if I did not know what was for my own interest, my friends must judge for me. I passed two months with dreadful apprehensions ... I assure you the recollection of this part of my life makes me tremble at this day ...'

Mary Granville was forced into this marriage by her uncle Lord Lansdowne who 'rejoiced at an opportunity of securing to his interest by such an alliance, one of some consequence in his country, whose services he at that time wanted,' and who thus 'readily embraced the offer and engaged for my compliance; he might have said obedience, for I was not entreated, but com-manded.' Although she loved someone else, and dreaded the prospect of the marriage, she had no choice but to agree to it:

'He took me by the hand, and after a very pathetic speech of his love and care for me, and of my father's unhappy circum-stances, my own want of future, and the little prospect I had of being happy if I disobliged those friends that were desirous of serving me, and his offer of settling his whole estate on me; he then, with great art and eloquence, told me all his good qualities and vast merit, and how despicable I should be if I could refuse him because he was not young and handsome…'

He also threatened that if her lover came near his house 'I will have him dragged through the horse-pond.'

'Such an expression,' she admitted, 'from a man of my uncle's politeness, made me tremble, for it plainly showed me how resolute and determined he was, and how vain it would be for me to urge any reasons against his resolution.'

When an aristocratic woman dared to marry outside landed society, it was considered quite unacceptable. 'I can't bear when women of quality marry one don't know whom!', exclaimed George II within the earshot of Lady Pembroke, who had just married Bernard North-Ludlow, an army captain of no birth or fortune. But at least she was a widow, who had been married to the Earl of Pembroke. If an unmarried girl did the same, the shock was far worse.

'A melancholy affair has happened to Lord Ilchester,' wrote Horace Walpole, 'his eldest daughter, Lady Susan (Fox-Strangeways), a very pleasing girl, married herself two days ago at Covent Garden to O'Brien, a handsome young actor. Lord Ilchester doted on her, and was the most indulgent of fathers. 'Tis a cruel blow.'

The Duchess of Argyll went into harangues when Lady Anne Paulett's daughter eloped with a country clergyman. When Lady Harriet Wentworth ran off with an Irish footman her relatives 'went into agonies of affliction,' were 'monstrously shocked,' and were blooded by their physicians.

If a woman wished to have a lover, she had to do so in absolute secrecy for, unlike men who often openly kept mistresses, if she were found out, she risked being socially ostracised. Thus Miss Sophia Howe, a Maid of Honour to Queen Caroline, when she was Princess of Wales, was ruined in reputation when it was found out that she had been seduced by Lord Lonsdale's brother, Anthony Lowther. An extract from Sir Charles Hanbury William's poem describing the Duchess of Manchester's 'Morning,' shows the curious effect the very mention of her name subsequently had on the assembled company:

'The general found a lucky minute now –
To speak – "Ah, Madam! had you known Miss Howe! –
I'll tell you all her history", he cried.
At this Charles Stanhope gaped extremely wide –
Poor Bateman sat on thorns – her grace turned pale –
And Lovel trembled at the impending tale.'

Poor Miss Howe died in 1726 'with a blemished reputation and a broken heart.' Another young woman who was equally condemned was Anne Vane, the sister of Lord Darlington, who in 1732 gave birth to an illegitimate son, the paternity of whom was claimed by Frederick, Prince of Wales, Lord Hervey and Lord Harrington.

As the eighteenth century moved towards its close, the situation for women grew even worse. This was due to the fact that, from about 1770, starting among the middle classes, there began a strong revival of moral reform, paternal authority, and sexual repression, the driving force behind which was the spread of the Evangelical movement. God was seen to direct day to day events within the household through his representative on earth, the Husband and Father. It was constantly emphasised that the will of the parent was the will of God. With this reassertion of patriarchal authority, the status of the woman inevitably declined. The new ideal of womanhood involved total abnegation, making the wife a slave to convention, propriety and her husband. Society turned its back on those who refused to conform to this ideal.

Just such a one was Jane Elizabeth Digby, Lady Ellenborough, a woman of the greatest courage and conviction, whose charm, wit, and individuality marked her apart from most of her generation, and who is the least deserving person in this book to be considered in any way 'black'. Yet this is exactly how she was judged by her contemporaries.

'One fine day,' wrote Edmund About, the French satirist, 'she climbed on the rooftops and shouted distinctly to the whole of the United Kingdom, "I am the mistress of Prince Schwarzenberg!" All the ladies who had lovers and did not say so were greatly shocked; English prudery reddened to the roots of its hair.'

Jane Digby was the daughter of Captain Digby, a son of the

25. JANE DIGBY, Lady Ellenborough

Dean of Durham by his marriage to Jane Coke, widow of Viscount Andover, and a daughter of Thomas Coke of Norfolk. Her loveliness was apparent by the time she was thirteen. 'Such dear pretty children,' wrote Harry Keppel in 1821 of her and her cousins the Ansons, with whom she shared lessons in the schoolroom at Holkham, her grandfather's home, 'and little Miss Digby, oh! so beautiful!' Three years later, in the Autumn of 1824, when she was barely seventeen, she was married to a man who was twice her age, Edward Law, Baron Ellenborough. This was a match which was actively encouraged by her parents, who considered it to be extremely advantageous, in spite of the fact that Lord Ellenborough was a very unpopular man, with a reputation for rakishness. 'Lady Anson will have it that he was a very good husband to his first wife,' recorded Thomas Creevy in his diary, 'but all my impressions are that he is a damned fellow.'

Once he had netted the 'sensation' of London society, as Jane had been ever since she arrived there, Lord Ellenborough installed her in his house at Roehampton and left her to twiddle her thumbs. This was the fate of many aristocratic young girls, who soon discovered that marriage did not live up to their romantic ideals. The houses to which they were brought were usually administered by a large staff, which left them little to do except spend the mornings deciding what to wear, and the afternoons indulging in endless rounds of visiting. There was also a common assumption amongst men that passion was reserved solely for mistresses or courtesans.

Jane, who was blessed with a wild and restless spirit, soon found this life unbearable, and it did not take her long to find consolation elsewhere. When the journals of Sir Frederick Madden were unsealed in 1920, they revealed that as early as the Spring of 1827 Jane was having a clandestine love affair. Madden, then a young scholar and official of the British Museum, was at that time working at Holkham in Norfolk, cataloguing the library. In his diary of 13 March 1827, he wrote:

'Lady Ellenborough, daughter of Lady Andover, arrived to dinner, and will stay a fortnight. She is not yet twenty, and one of the most lovely women I ever saw, quite fair, blue eyes that would move a saint, and lips that would tempt me to forswear Heaven to touch them.'

Eleven days later he had apparently achieved his desire.

'In Library till four. Then out,' he recorded on Saturday 24 March. 'In the evening drew pictures for Lady Anne Coke and Miss Anson. Also played whist and won. Lady E. lingered behind the rest of the party, and at midnight I escorted her to her room – fool that I was! – I will not add what passed. Gracious God! Was there ever such good fortune!'

Jane told no one of this little intrigue, which remained a secret for the better part of a century. This was not the case with her second affair. In April 1828, two months after she had given birth to her first child, a son and heir, she embarked upon a passionate

226

romance with a young attaché at the Austrian Embassy. Gossip had always hinted that Lord Ellenborough's only reason for marrying was to beget an heir, and his behaviour after the birth of his son certainly seemed to confirm this. He spent less and less time with his wife, and it later transpired that he had agreed to their having separate bedrooms. Jane was thus feeling frustrated and unloved when she met, at a ball at Almack's, Prince Felix Schwarzenberg, a dashingly good-looking womaniser, with a thick black moustache. She was the perfect target for his affections. 'Female society amongst the upper classes,' wrote Captain Gronow in his reminiscences 'was most notoriously neglected, except by romantic foreigners, who were the heroes of many a fashionable adventure that fed the clubs with ever-acceptable scandal.'

Schwarzenberg became her lover, a fact that London society was soon well aware of since Jane elected to appear quite openly on the arm of her handsome Prince. This was accepted so long as their association remained outwardly respectable. That her husband appeared not to object strengthened their position. They restricted their passion to what they imagined were secret afternoons spent at the Prince's lodgings at 73 Harley Street, and the occasional weekend in Brighton.

Early in 1829, however, the Austrian Ambassador in London, Prince Esterhazy, began to worry that if Lord Ellenborough did suddenly decide to take exception to his wife's behaviour a public scandal might ensue which, involving as it did an Embassy official and the wife of a cabinet minister, could do irreparable harm. He thus gave Schwarzenberg a severe warning about his conduct which frightened him enough to make him change his lodgings, and to give the appearance of having dropped Lady Ellenborough by starting a flirtation with another lady. But Schwarzenberg had completely underestimated Jane's fierce determination and passion. Her fury at being scorned drove her to state publicly that she had been cruelly abandoned by her lover. This was a grave mistake.

'The accusation of Lady Ellenborough,' wrote Count Apponyi in his journal of March 1829, 'shocks all of London society. In the meantime he is ardently courting the Countess of Hatzfeld. They say that Prince Esterhazy is furious with our attaché...'

Esterhazy was indeed furious and in April, alarmed by reports that Schwarzenberg and Lady Ellenborough were once again being seen in each other's company, he took a more serious step. He informed Prince Metternich in Vienna of his worries, who agreed that Schwarzenberg should be removed from London as soon as possible.

In May 1829, Jane was told by her lover that he had been recalled to Vienna. Her devastating reply was to tell him that she was three months pregnant, and that as she had not slept with her husband for over a year, she thought it unlikely that he would accept the child as his. She therefore suggested that she too should leave the country with him, a proposal he refused to agree to.

Jane decided therefore to confess her love for Prince Schwarzenberg to her husband, and to ask for a separation, all the while concealing her condition. She would then leave for Europe and join him before her pregnancy became known. What she actually said to Lord Ellenborough is not recorded but from a letter she wrote to him on 23 May, the day after her confession, it seems likely that she lied about her adultery. 'I again renew,' she wrote, 'all the assurances I gave you last night that in act I am innocent.' When her family learned of her desire for a separation, they were horrified. Both her mother, and her aunt, Lady Anson, rallied together to try and prevent the family name being dragged through the mud. But the more they tried to persuade Jane to beg her husband for forgiveness and to effect a reconciliation the more adamant she became in her determination to leave him. She remained quite unmoved by lurid descriptions of the horrors of life as a ruined woman. In despair they banished her, with her former governess Miss Margaret Steele to look after her, to a remote seaside cottage in Devon.

But Jane could hardly keep her pregnancy secret for long, and by the summer of 1829 both her family and her husband had discovered that she was carrying the Prince's child. This forced Lord Ellenborough's hand. However great the disgrace of such a proceeding, he had to divorce her in order to salvage his honour. In the meantime Jane had heard from her lover who assured her that, although he could never marry her, 'for the sake of his own future,' if she came to Europe and had the baby, he would look after her in a devoted manner. Her family too wanted her out of the country before the divorce proceedings got under way. It was therefore decided that she should take up residence in Basle, Switzerland, which was one of the places suggested by the Prince. She left England on the last day of August 1829.

When news of the impending divorce came out, the gossips went to town.

'Lord Ellenborough,' wrote Mrs. Harriet Arbuthnot in her diary, 'is now engaged in investigating his wife's conduct and certainly, if the stories she used to tell of herself are true, he will not have great difficulty in proving her guilt. It is quite melancholy that so beautiful a creature, only two and twenty, should be so depraved. She used to boast that she would go to Schwarzenberg's lodgings and find him in bed and go up to his rooms. She met him at all kinds of houses and places in the neighbourhood of London, and not satisfied with doing so, told her stories to anybody who would listen to her...'

The divorce itself, which needed a private act of Parliament to make it fully legal, caused a sensation. The Press had a field-day describing in detail the evidence of all the various witnesses – waiters, grooms, house-maids, coachmen etc – who were called to testify. As the woman, Jane bore the brunt of the disgrace. In his novel *Le Lys dans la Vallée* in which one of the characters, Lady Arabella Dudley, was partially drawn from Lady Ellenborough, Balzac wrote:

'Never did a nation more elaborately scheme for the hypocrisy of a married woman by placing her always between social life and death. For her there is no compromise between shame and honour; the fall is utter, or there is no fall; it is all or nothing – the To Be or Not to Be of Hamlet.'

The divorce was approved by Parliament on 6 April, by which time Jane's reputation was in tatters:

'The last crime against the marriage vow,' commented *The Times*, 'was (perhaps frequently) committed by that lost creature, scarcely more than just arrived at womanhood.'

Jane arrived in Basle late in September 1829. Prince Schwarzenberg arrived to see her on 10 November, and two days later she gave birth to a little girl, whom she named Mathilde. In February of the following year she left Switzerland and joined the Prince in

Paris where he was serving at the Austrian Embassy. He set her up in a house in the Faubourg St. Germain, and later in the Place du Palais opposite the Palais Bourbon. Her irregular status made it impossible for her to be received at the French Court, or at many of the functions which the Prince had to attend, and, although there is no doubt that to begin with he was delighted to see her again, the affair was doomed. The novelty and excitement of a clandestine romance had long since worn off. Jane hung on because she seriously hoped that, despite all he had said to the contrary, the Prince might one day marry her. She became pregnant again, but by the time she gave birth to a son, Felix, in December 1830, her lover was once again publicly carrying on with other women. Sadly the child died only a few weeks later, and with it any hope that the birth of a son might change the Prince's mind about marriage. In May 1831, Schwarzenberg left Paris and returned to his native country of Bohemia.

In the late summer of 1831 Jane moved to Munich, where she continued to create a sensation. King Ludwig I of Bavaria met and fell passionately in love with her, and she was thought by many to have become his mistress. Certainly they became close friends and confidantes, but in much of her correspondence with the King Jane spoke of how she was still in love with Prince Schwarzenberg. Another man who assiduously courted her, and whose mistress she became, was a German nobleman, Baron Karl Venningen, to whom in January 1833 she bore a son, Heribert. They were married in November, although popular opinion still had it that she was the King's mistress.

The Baron failed to tame the restless spirit of his beautiful English wife. In spite of the fact that she bore him a second child, a daughter, in the Autumn of 1834, only a year later she was involved in yet another liaison, this time with a Greek Count, Count Spiro Theotoky, from Corfu, who, at twenty-four, was four years her junior, and whom she met at a Carnival Ball in Munich. This affair with the Count kindled the same intense passion as she had felt for the Prince, and once it was aroused there was no subduing it. A letter she wrote to King Ludwig in July 1837, in reply to his enquiries about her marriage to the Baron, gives an extraordinary insight into Jane's hopelessly romantic nature:

'The Baron and I,' she wrote, 'go on what the world may call "well" together: the difference that exists in our characters cannot be changed. His *really* noble qualities are justly appreciated and esteemed by me. I am attached to him from affection and habit, but between ourselves, his want of demonstration and warmth of feeling stifle a passion I fain would feel, and which, once felt, and returned, would prevent my wandering in thought to other objects. The misfortune of my nature is to consider "Love" as All in All, without this feeling life is a dreary void – no earthly blessing can compensate its loss, and having at first setting out in life sacrificed all without regret to one great and absorbing passion, the necessity of loving and being loved is to me as the air I breathe and the sole cause of all I have to reproach myself with.'

In the spring of 1839 Jane abandoned the Baron and fled to Paris with Spiro, posing first of all as his niece, and later pretending that she was his wife. In March 1840 'Madame Theotoky' gave birth to a son, Leonidas. It is interesting to note, and surely a comment on what an extraordinary woman Jane must have been, that her husband completely forgave her for deserting him:

'My friendship and attachment to you,' he wrote to her in June 1840, 'will end only with my life . . . May I learn someday soon that you are completely happy. Think then, under that beautiful sky of the Orient, that in cold and sad Germany, a warm and faithful heart is beating for you, a heart which will never forget the happiness and the heavenly bliss you gave him during several years. If the Almighty should decide otherwise about our fate, remember me still – my house will be a secure haven for an unhappy Jane.'

Jane's family were not so forgiving. In their view this latest elopement was the last straw. In his biography of Jane, E. M. Oddie recounts a story that used to be told by the Hon. Henry Coke a son of Jane's grandfather by his second wife, who died at a great age in 1916.

'He had stayed as a boy at Minterne with Admiral Digby and Lady Andover. His attention was diverted one morning at breakfast to the picture of a beautiful woman, with tumbling ringlets and a sweet face. Being interested, he asked whose picture it was. When an old man he could still remember the horror of that moment – could remember the appalled silence after his innocent question had exploded like a bombshell. He was told to get on with his breakfast in a voice that precluded any possibility of pursuing the enquiry. He knew that unconsciously he had committed a major crime. The first thing he noticed when he came down to the dining-room for the next meal was that the picture had been removed. Afterwards he found it hanging, its face to the wall, in the Housekeeper's room.'

This incident took place in the summer of 1839, when Henry Coke was only twelve. It is quite clear from the fact that Henry had no idea who Jane was that her grandfather, for one, would allow no mention of her. Although Jane was eventually reconciled with her mother, her father never forgave her for her elopement with Theotoky, and never saw her again.

Jane and Spiro remained in Paris till the Spring of 1841, when they sailed for Greece. They stayed first on the island of Tinos, where Spiro's father was Governor. Then, early in 1842, they left for Corfu where Spiro was to manage the family estates. During the previous year Jane had obtained a divorce from the Baron and she now went through some kind of marriage ceremony with Spiro. Two blissful years followed. They lived in a villa at Dukades, the family estate, in grand feudal style. In Paris Jane had bought all kinds of treasures with which to decorate her house. The drawing-room was Parisian in style with gilt cornices, mirrors and chairs. Spiro loved to read, and his hobby was bookbinding, so she built for him a beautiful library modelled after the one she remembered at Holkham. The dining-room glittered with silver and crystal, and there was a magnificent dinner-service for one hundred which she had ordered from Paris, emblazoned with gold bands and the Theotoky crest. Corfu had a British High Commissioner, Lord Nugent, who lived in a grand regency Palace of St. Michael and St. George, and life on the island was gay. There were numerous balls, concerts and receptions, and the Theotokys kept lavish openhouse. It was a very eighteenth-century existence, quite unlike the moral atmosphere that prevailed in England.

In the summer the Theotokys moved to Athens, where Spiro had been appointed as an aide-de-camp to King Otto, son of Ludwig of Bavaria. Once again Jane turned heads wherever she went, and in particular she attracted the attention of the King.

This caused bitter jealousies. The Queen, Amalia, took a strong dislike to Jane because she commanded admiration which should by rights have been hers, while at the Court Balls people said she danced better than the Queen. Spiro played the resentful husband and, to spite Jane, began to flirt wildly with the women of the Court. This led to several affairs which Jane soon heard about. Their marriage was kept together only by their mutual love of their son. In the Summer of 1846, however, tragedy struck. While on a visit to the Italian Spa of Bagni di Lucca, Leonidas fell from the top-floor balcony of the house in which they were staying and was killed instantly on the marble floor of the hall at the feet of his mother. This terrible event marked the end of Jane and Spiro's life together.

Jane was inconsolable. She had loved Leonidas more than any of her other children, and she believed that his death must be a punishment for the way in which she had neglected the others. She did not return to Athens until 1849, and during this dark period of her life, which is unrecorded, legend has ascribed to her 'six Italian husbands', a story which she always vigorously denied.

Early in 1852 Jane embarked on her most romantic and adventurous love-affair to date. General Cristodoulos Hadji-Petros was the leader of the Palikari, 'the brave ones,' the fierce band of mountain freedom-fighters who had initiated the Greek War of Independence. In 1851 he was made aide-de-camp to the King, and Jane fell in love with him from the first moment she set eyes on him. The fact that he was nearly seventy meant nothing to her. He was a hero, the man who had inspired Byron and other supporters of the Greek cause. He also had a son, Eirini, a delicate boy whom she grew to love, and who filled the gap left by Leonidas. When Hadji-Petros was made governor of the mountain province of Lamia, Jane did not hesitate to sell her house in Athens, and accompany him to his rugged outpost in the mountains.

'The next day,' wrote Edmond About, 'she was reigning over Lamia. All the town was at her feet, and when she came out to go for a walk, the drums were beating in the fields. This delicate woman lived with drunkards, galloped on horseback in the mountains, ate literally standing up on the run, drank

233

retsina, slept in the open air next to a big fire, and found herself in excellent health.

Jane's life in Lamia lasted no more than a few months. When word filtered back to Athens that the Countess Theotoky was living openly in the mountains with a man who was little more than a brigand, society was horrified. Queen Amalia now saw her chance to take her revenge on Jane. She insisted that Hadji-Petros be instantly dismissed from government service for openly keeping a mistress. His reaction to his dismissal was far from gallant.

'Your Majesty had me removed,' he wrote to the Queen; 'this is without doubt because I lived with Countess T; but whatever my enemies have said to you, I declare upon my soldier's honour that if I am the lover of this woman, it is not for love but for profit. She is rich and I am poor. I have a rank to live up to, children to educate. I trust therefore...'

The Queen remained unmoved. To see Jane well and truly humiliated, she had the letter posted up publicly for all to read.

Jane had no difficulty in forgiving her lover. She believed that he would have said anything to keep his position, and that he had quite simply lied in order to do so. She returned with him from Lamia, and they once again set up home in Athens. Her forgiveness did not last long. Soon after their arrival in Athens, Jane's maid, Eugenie, complained of Hadji-Petros's constant attempts to seduce her. This left Jane distraught, especially since she had sacrificed what was left of her reputation in Athens for this man. It was a wrong she could not overlook, and, rather than risk being wooed back to him by a series of plausible excuses and promises of good behaviour, she made up her mind to leave him at once. She had anyway been planning a trip to Syria to buy horses, and she seized upon this journey as an opportunity to escape. On 6 April 1853, three days after her forty-sixth birthday, she sailed from Piraeus for the East.

One has a picture of this sad, middle-aged English aristocratic lady, thousands of miles from her native soil, an outcast from the society into which she was born, sitting alone on a sailing boat taking her to the wild Lebanese shore. 'I can hardly tell why it should be,' William Kinglake had written, 'but there is a longing for the East very commonly felt by proud people when goaded by sorrow.' When her ship arrived at Beirut, Jane engaged a string of horses to take her to Jerusalem, from which city she proposed to tour Palestine before making her way to Damascus, en route to Palmyra, where she intended to explore the classical ruins. Here her journey would have ended had it not been for an event that was to change the course of her life.

While riding down to the Jordan she met, and became totally infatuated with a young Arab Sheikh called Saleh. 'My heart warms towards these wild Arabs,' she wrote in a letter to her mother. An affair followed, the excitement of which was so great as to sweep away all thoughts of Hadji-Petros and to fill her with a determination to settle down and live in Syria, and to marry Saleh. When she returned to Athens late in 1853, and announced her plans to her friends, they were utterly scandalised; but true to form, the more they threw up their hands in horror, the more determined she became. She returned to Syria before the year was out, virtually cutting off all ties. Here her romantic nature failed her. It had never occurred to her for a moment that for Saleh his brief affair with the beautiful white lady was but a passing adventure. She hurried back to him only to find that in her absence he had taken another woman.

Jane was incapable of remaining without a man for long. While brooding alone and heart-broken in Damascus, she remembered the kindness that had been shown to her by another Arab, Medjuel el Mezrab, son of a great Sheikh, who had escorted her on a dangerous journey across the desert during her previous visit. He had admired her and at the end of the journey had even proposed to her. At that time, however, she had had thoughts for no one but Saleh. She joined a caravan to Baghdad to give herself time to think things over, and on the return journey she made up her mind to accept Medjuel's proposal, if it was still open. He had in fact never forgotten her. As the caravan approached Damascus he rode out to meet it, bringing Jane the gift of a valuable Arab mare. A few months later they were married at Homs.

If the scandal of her divorce and her elopement with Prince Schwarzenberg in 1830 had shocked the comparatively gay and rakish England of George IV, that of her marriage to an Arab when her three previous husbands were still living was too much for her family to accept. Rakishness had all but gone from Old England. They now lived in a society in which sobriety and gravity of demeanour were the order of the day. Poor old Lady Andover, who had once been so proud of her beautiful daughter and who had arranged for her what had seemed to be such a brilliant match, had had the last thirty years of her life blighted by Jane's disgrace. But Jane regretted these long years of bitterness and estrangement, and longed for a reconciliation with her family. For this reason, and to settle various business affairs, in the Autumn of 1856 she decided to make one last visit to England.

Jane arrived at Folkestone on 19 December, where she was met by Miss Jane Steele, sister of the governess who had looked after her during her first pregnancy. Together they drove to Ernstein Villa in Tunbridge Wells, where her mother lived in retirement. Lady Andover was no longer the handsome woman that Jane remembered. She was eighty, gone to fat, and was worn out by the years of fretting over her prodigal daughter. But at least she was now ready to forgive and forget, and she welcomed Jane home with open arms. For Jane the homecoming was almost unreal. 'I in England!' she wrote that night in her journal.

A few days at home showed Jane that all was well so long as the conversation was kept away from her Arab husband or her life in the desert. The old governess, Steely, made it abundantly clear just what she thought about Arabs. They were 'lesser creatures, their skin especially pigmented by the Almighty that one might recognise them as inferiors.'

In January her 'dear, long-estranged brother' Edward, and his wife Theresa, came to visit. But any hopes she may have had that they might prove avid listeners to stories of her extraordinary and colourful desert experiences were soon dashed. She noted with pain that, when she showed them her sketch-books of Palmyra and the desert, the atmosphere immediately cooled. Their disapproval was apparent. Having to refrain from mentioning her beloved Sheikh, and to spend day after day indulging in endless small talk, eventually wore Jane down. She poured out her sorrows in her journal.

'My family ties burst asunder; no children; no English home! And oh, the grief I have brought upon others, on my dear kind, by my fatal misconduct. And here I am, sitting almost a stranger when I hear of my own family whom I hardly know. I am not gay as I gaze around and think of what might have been and what is.'

MAD AND SINFUL PASSIONS

A visit from her younger brother Kenelm, an Anglican clergyman, cheered her up a bit, as he had no reservations about discussing her life with Medjuel. But she was beginning to yearn once more for her spiritual home. Here in England, she was still a complete outcast from society which, if anything, had hardened still further against her. While in 1830 her sin had been that she had offended the code of society by being found out, in 1857 her sin was that she had sinned. On 3 April she celebrated her fiftieth birthday.

> 'Fifty! Triste and melancholy anniversary,' she wrote in her diary. 'All the romance and poetry in life ought to be long since past and over, and here I am still with a beating and burning heart...'

Victorian England was no longer any place for Jane. On 6 April, she kissed her mother goodbye for the last time and set sail for Calais, accompanied on board by a flock of Norfolk turkeys as a present for Medjuel.

Her first stop was Paris, and here Jane began to feel herself again, spending a wonderful, carefree few days. She bought a piano, new clothes, cloth, painting and sketching materials, a copy of Flaubert's newly-published *Madame Bovary*, and even arms and ammunition for her Bedouin tribe. Before sailing back to the East from Marseilles on 13 April, she wrote a final note to her mother:

> "I would gladly be as you are, but I cannot change my nature. I am different. How different I had hardly realised ... I regret much of the past, but over the future I feel sanguine.'

She knew that she would never see England or her mother again. She recorded her arrival home with ecstatic happiness.

> 'With a beating heart I arrived at Damascus. He arrived, Medjuel, the dear, the adored one, and in that moment of happiness I forgot all else.'

Jane never did return to England. She spent the rest of her life married to Medjuel, and living in Damascus, where her house became a Mecca for many English travellers. Barty Mitford, later Lord Redesdale, visited her in 1871, and remembered how 'her tables were covered with miniatures, knick-knacks and orna-ments indigenous to Mayfair – quite out of tune with Damascus.' Isabel Burton, wife of the famous explorer Richard Burton who, along with her husband, became a close friend of Jane's wrote of her 'suite of apartments which is elegance itself. Family and home treasures, and little reminiscences of European life, old china and paintings, are mingled with Oriental luxury, whose very atmos-phere bespeaks refinement.' She also described a unique menagerie kept by Jane, with 'curious snow-white geese with curling feathers, turkeys, ducks, poultry, pigeons, guinea-hens, and other pets.' These included numerous cats and dogs, gazelles, partridges, turtle-doves, falcons, and a tame pelican.

There is another interesting description of Jane in A. M. W. Stirling's biography of Coke of Norfolk, which suggests that England was never far from her mind.

'An English lady, who procured an introduction to her, relates how she met her, swathed in a veil and Arab garments, and riding at the head of a cavalcade of wild Arabs – a veritable Queen of Banditti – in surroundings which rendered her gracious, courteous manners, her air of grande dame and her sweet low voice more singularly impressive, even though her beauty – all but her glorious eyes – was scrupulously concealed from view. And still her thoughts turned to the life from which she was severed; all her questions were of Holkham Hall, of the relations which she was fated never again to see. Yet in her strange dual existence she stated that she found a freedom which she loved.'

That she often reflected on her past life is shown from an entry in her journal made soon after a visit from her niece Emily, Kenelm's daughter, honeymooning with her new husband. When they left on 1 May 1862, she wrote:

'I felt inexpressibly sad as I gazed at her and after her. Ah, thought I, such was I too, once, long years ago, ere mad and sinful passions blighted my existence and cast their poisonous shade on that of others ... My dear and honoured parents, my fond brothers...'

Jane died in August 1881, aged seventy-four. She was buried in the Protestant cemetery in Damascus, and Medjuel and his

Bedouins sacrificed one of their finest camels in her memory. Two years after her death her friend, the missionary Dr. William Wright, visited her grave and wrote this epitaph:

'Here lies the beautiful and cultured Lady Ellenborough, known at Damascus as the Hon. Jane Digby el Mezrab, who lost her way in London in the seething slough of fashionable society, and after a wild, passionate and reckless career closed her days in peace as the wife of a Bedawy Sheikh, and died in the Christian faith in sure and certain hope of a blessed resurrection.'

APOSTLES OF PEDERASTY

'He has gone – he is beyond punishment, or rather out of reach of the law. I only want if possible not to increase the fearful disgrace which has fallen on his family. For the man in his defence, I can only trust that he is mad.'

(SIR DIGHTON PROBYN to Lord Salisbury)

THERE is one group of black sheep which does not conform to the general pattern, but is important nevertheless. In the introduction I mentioned my mysterious Uncle Daniel, whose misfortune was to be homosexual in a world which was intolerant of such leanings, and which eventually sadly led to his turning to drink and drugs. For generations homosexuals like Daniel had been ostracised. Incredible though it may now seem, from the reign of Henry VIII until the middle of the 1960s homosexuality was regarded as a crime, the maximum penalty for which was death right up to 1861, and thereafter prison. This drove the large majority of homosexuals into the arms of a protective subculture which grew up in the great cities of Europe: 'a sect,' wrote Lord Chesterfield 'that ought to be excluded from all civil society and human conversation.' For the aristocracy things were on the whole a little easier. Their riches gave them greater access to the aristocratic societies of Europe where it was possible to move in a discreet homosexual network. Italy, for example, was described by Chesterfield as, 'le siège de l'athéisme, de la sodomie et des mauvaises manières.' If they remained at home the ease of their lives largely depended on their relations with their fathers and their wives, and the security of their social position. Lord Hervey and Lord George Germain were both homosexuals who managed well enough because they were favourite sons and had tolerant wives. Hervey had his wife's consent to set up house in London with his lover, Stephen Fox, while Lord George shared his house with his wife, his daughters and his young man. Lord Bateman was not so lucky. When his brother-in-law, the Duke of Marlborough, learned of his homosexual leanings, he was forcibly separated from his wife.

Certainly in the majority of cases the public discovery of homosexual tendencies in a man led to his disgrace, and even exile. Perhaps the most celebrated example of this in the eighteenth century was that of William Beckford. Beckford, who is best remembered today as the author of *Vathek*, was the rich and eccentric squire of Fonthill in Wiltshire, once the home of Lord Castlehaven. In the Autumn of 1779, aged nineteen, while on a tour of England with his tutor, the Reverend John Lettice, he visited Powderham Castle in Devon, home of the second Viscount Courtenay. Here he met and fell hopelessly and romantically in love with William Courtenay, the ten-year-old son of Lord Courtenay, the youngest and only boy in a family of thirteen, and a child of great beauty. The powerful feelings which Beckford had for Courtenay are well expressed in a letter which he wrote two years later to his friend Alexander Cozens, the noted water-colourist, after seeing the boy in London where he was being painted by Romney, a sitting he had himself arranged.

'O that I could snatch up some inspired pencil, and dipping it in the most vivid colours of Heaven, paint his wild roving eyes instinct with the brightest fancy and yet softened by tears ... His countenance at one moment appeared as lively as light; the next, a dark shade came over it, and those eyes, which but the last instant sparkled with vivacity, now glistened with tears.

'In this wavering state the hour he spent with me was passed; and after a thousand transitory hopes and fleeting anxieties, after confused moments of the liveliest happiness and deepest dejection, he was summoned away. I followed him wistfully with my eyes and listened till his steps grew fainter and fainter. The door closed, and the sound of the carriage which bore him from me was lost in the noise of London.

'Then returning melancholy and alone, I threw myself on the ground and wept like a poor miserable being cast away on a desert world, deprived of the best part of its existence ... all my miseries are renewed when I consider how seldom I am doomed to be with him, how little his father or mother comprehend the nature of my love.'

Though Beckford's love for Courtenay was almost entirely of a romantic nature, it was to prove disastrous to both of them. By 1784 Beckford was a fast-rising star. His family had arranged a good marriage for him, which had taken place the previous year,

26. WILLIAM BECKFORD (Romney)

27. WILLIAM, 3RD VISCOUNT COURTENAY
(Romney)

to Lady Margaret Gordon, daughter of the fourth Earl of Aboyne. He had known her from childhood, and, although he was not in love with her, it was a fairly amicable arrangement. He had been elected to Parliament as Member for Wells, and it was being openly stated in the newspapers that a peerage was imminent. The future could not have looked brighter for Beckford when the incident took place that destroyed his reputation.

In September 1784, he and Lady Margaret were invited to spend a month at Powderham. Considering that one of the other guests was Lord Loughborough, he was unwise to have gone. Loughborough disliked Beckford. He was jealous of him because he knew that, before her marriage, his wife Charlotte, who was William Courtenay's aunt, had been in love with him. He also bitterly resented Beckford's political advancement, especially since he was very much the protégé of Lord Chancellor Thurlow, Loughborough's hated political and professional rival. In addition he deplored what he saw as the unwholesome interest which Beckford took in Courtenay and had, ever since the death of the boy's mother in 1782, and his subsequent marriage to her sister, been slowly and cunningly poisoning the family's mind against him.

When Beckford left Powderham, after a somewhat tense stay, Loughborough spread the story through the family that he had been caught early one morning in William's bedroom, a story that was apparently strengthened by some kind of confession which he had forced out of William. Moreover he had in his possession various letters which Beckford had written to William, and which were expressed in the most romantic and extravagant terms. However innocent these may in reality have been, viewed in the wrong light they appeared to provide damning evidence against him. The family were naturally deeply shocked. When Beckford's brother-in-law, Lord Strathavon, heard the story, he stormed down to Fonthill to drag his sister away from her depraved husband. When she refused to go, he slapped Beckford's face hoping to provoke a duel, but without success.

Realising the gravity of the situation, for what Loughborough was accusing him of was sodomy, Beckford's immediate family and friends held a conference to decide what best to do. It consisted of Beckford, his wife and mother, Lord Chancellor Thurlow, and his former tutor John Lettice. They understood that the evidence against him, particularly the letters, was sufficiently damning to warrant serious concern about his being found guilty and sentenced to death. His mother's somewhat impractical solution was that he should go up to London and parade about with half a dozen Covent Garden whores, which action she suggested would do more than anything to remove suspicion from him!

The course upon which they eventually decided was that he should leave the country until the storm had blown over, a decision with which Beckford reluctantly agreed. He got as far as Dover, however, on 29 October, when he realised that to flee abroad was to play into his enemy's hands. It would be as good as an admission of guilt. He decided to return to Fonthill, and wait to see what Loughborough's next move would be. Loughborough took a cowardly course. Having realised that he had in fact insufficient evidence to prosecute, he set about blackening Beckford's name by vicious gossip. On 27 November, the following paragraph appeared in the *Morning Herald*:

'The rumour concerning a grammatical mistake of Mr. B— and the Hon. Mr. C— in regard to the genders, we hope for the honour of nature originates in calumny! For, however depraved the being must be, who can propagate such reports without foundation, we must wish such a being exists, in preference to characters, who, regardless of divine, natural and human law, sink themselves beyond the lowest class of brutes in the most preposterous rites.'

It was not long before London was buzzing with the scandal. The gossips thirsted for details.

'Is it true that Beckford's wife will not leave him,' wrote Lord Pembroke to his son Lord Herbert from Naples, 'and after all what was the exact business, how, when, and by whom, and with whom discovered? Who passive and who active ...? Everybody takes for granted I know all, and therefore gives me no more than the bare outlines.'

The story that was probably circulating, though highly inaccurate in detail, was that related by Charles Greville to his uncle Sir William Hamilton, in a letter written to his embassy in Naples, dated 25 December 1784:

'I did not write to you about Beckford, until I could know from some authority both the fact and his intentions. It seems young C. was put to a school with a clergyman near Fonthill; he went over very early one morning before they were up and into Courtenay's room; Mr. Moore, the tutor's name, heard a creaking and bustle, which raised curiosity, and thro' the keyhole he saw the operation which it seems he did not interrupt, but informed Lord Courtenay, and the whole was blown up. He remains at Fonthill till Lady Margaret, who it seems is with child, either lays in or miscarries. They are then to go abroad together, as he cannot brave it, and it is too public to pass as a slur. His promised honours will be withheld; he probably will be obliged to vacate his seat and retire to Italy . . .'

Despite the glaring inaccuracies of this story – it was at Powderham, not Fonthill, where the episode was supposed to have occurred; the tutor's name was not Moore but Taylor; Beckford was staying in the house and did not 'go over' anywhere – it did irreparable damage to Beckford's reputation. His mother made a desperate attempt to counter Loughborough's tale by producing her own version of the facts, as reported by Joseph Farington in his diary:

'She said the fact was that Lady Loughborough, aunt to Lord Courtenay, was in love with Beckford, and had a correspondence with him by letter, while on this visit at Powderham Castle, and Lord Courtenay, then a boy, carried the letters, one of which he so mismanaged that it fell into wrong hands, which Beckford discovering and being very passionate, he went to Lord Courtenay's room, while he was in bed, it being morning, and locking the door, he horsewhipped him, which causing the boy to scream out, his tutor came to the door and found it *locked*. This gave cause for the suspicion and the reports which were soon after circulated.'

This, however, lacked conviction, as Farington himself said:

'I could not but feel the improbability of much of the story, it not at all agreeing with many other well authenticated circumstances, and being in itself difficult to give credit to: and from all I have heard the stories told to clear Mr. Beckford have not been well considered.'

For all Beckford's continual assertions of innocence, he was a ruined man. His peerage was cancelled, and George III let it be known that in his opinion he ought to be hanged. Some years previously his friend and confidante Catherine Lady Hamilton had warned him that if he did not take care his reputation would be lost 'never, never to be regained.' That prophecy now came to pass. Society turned its back on him, and for the remainder of his life, another sixty years, he could never escape the slur on his character, being referred to by Byron as the 'great Apostle of Pederasty'. When his wife died in childbirth in 1786, the newspapers blamed him for having broken her heart. When he travelled to Spain and Portugal during his years of self-imposed exile abroad, the British envoys saw to it that he was not received at Court; and in 1796, when the Prince Regent of Portugal, whom he had befriended, entrusted him with an important mission to the British Government, the Foreign Secretary refused him the right to deliver it.

At home his neighbours cut him dead.

'Not long since,' wrote Joseph Farington in his diary of 16 October 1806, 'Sir Richard Hoare of Stourhead applied to Mr. Beckford to see the Abbey which Mr. B. granted and attended Sir Richard when he came for that purpose. These civilities which passed between them were reported to the neighbouring gentlemen who took such umbrage at it ... that a gentleman wrote to Sir Richard in his own name and that of others to demand of him an explanation of that proceeding as they meant to regulate themselves towards him accordingly. Sir Richard applied to his friend the Marquis of Bath upon it, and represented that he had no further desire but to see the Abbey and the meeting with Mr. Beckford was accidental and to him unexpected. Such is the determination of the Wiltshire gentlemen with respect to excluding Mr. B. from all gentlemanly intercourse.'

Even towards the close of his life, after he had left Fonthill and was building the Lansdown Tower, there was a moment when the workmen struck, refusing to work for a 'bugger,' and Beckford was only persuaded by the Master Builders from leaving Bath in a fury.

As for Courtenay, on his father's death he inherited Powderham where he lived for many years, alone save for one of his spinster sisters. He was however extremely indiscreet in his private affairs, and it was soon common knowledge that he was an inveterate homosexual. 'Many of the neighbouring gentlemen refuse to hold intercourse with him,' wrote Farington in 1810, going on to report that when he had almost completed the building of a house in Torquay 'the people of the place reviled and insulted his servants in terms so opprobious and this was done with such perseverance that the scheme of finishing the house was given up and it remains a monument of the public opinion against him.' He was finally driven out of the country in the Spring of 1811 when an Exeter magistrate named Morton, who had been quietly collecting evidence against him, produced statements which conclusively pointed to his guilt under the Henry VIII Statute. According to Farington, Courtenay at first believed that 'should he be accused before the Lords, they, most of whom were like himself, would not decide against him. Thus shameless was he in his mind. But when he was informed that the Officers of Justice were ordered to pursue him, he lost all resolution, wept like a child and was willingly taken on board a vessel, the first that could be found, an American ship, and passed there under a feigned name. After he had been on board some time, he asked whether he might not be called by his own name but was told it would be dangerous on account of the sailors whose prejudice against him might have had bad effects.' The Will that he made before he left, leaving a thousand pounds a year to his sister, provided that she was never to marry, was cited by Farington as being 'a strong trait of his disposition and mind.' Courtenay eventually landed in France where he spent the remaining twenty-four years of his life, living in relative obscurity in a small house in the Place Vendôme in Paris.

George Ferrars Townshend, 3rd Marquess Townshend, later Lord Leicester, was a younger contemporary of Courtenay's who gained equal notoriety. At Cambridge, where he was known by his courtesy title of Lord Chartley, he was regarded as something more than just eccentric. First of all he took with him up to Trinity College an Italian named Neri, who had formerly been a waiter at the Coca Nut Coffee House in London. When these two were not shut up alone in Chartley's rooms, sometimes for as much as a week at a time, they occasionally emerged to give guitar concerts which were attended by 'most of the nobility and many of the seniors of the College.' He also spurned the purple

28. GEORGE FERRARS TOWNSHEND, 3rd Marquis

gown traditionally worn by noblemen at College in favour of a
pink one and 'dressed his hair effeminately, and was called Miss
Leicester, Lady Chartley, etc., in derision.' According to the
Annual Register there were 'notorious reports' circulating freely
during his Cambridge days accusing him of 'infamous and
unnatural crimes.' Certainly he was next heard of handing out
gold watches and fine clothes to various privates of the first
regiment of Guards, with whom he was openly seen walking
arm in arm, and whose commander, Colonel Rainsford,
confirmed that, for over three years, he had heard nothing but
'vile reports' of Chartley.

In 1807 Chartley was styled Lord Leicester, and Farington
recorded in his diary of 25 November that he was a 'very effemi-
nate young man – sometime he wore pink ribbons to his shoes.'

He also noted that 'having married a young lady only a few months ago, he is said to be on the point of separation from her.' How he came to be married is not known, but it may well have been a desperate attempt by his father to set him on a straight course. Needless to say the union was a disaster, and in June 1808 Lady Leicester made an official application for a divorce on the grounds that her husband was impotent, and was 'not formed as a man should be.' It later transpired that 'Three sleepless nights were all they passed together, and after that time they were never in bed and seldom at board together.' On the few occasions when they were actually together Lady Leicester 'had been obliged to sit down at the table of her Lord with wretches that are a disgrace to human nature, and who ought not to be permitted to live. There was Neri, the Italian secretary, Hayling, Playfair, and other wretches of that description ...' In the end she was 'banished from his house by such conduct.'

All this was too much for Leicester's father who disinherited him, and threatened to cut him off completely unless he retired abroad. He fled to Italy.

'The wretched son of an English Marquess,' commented the *Morning Herald*, 'has absconded on a charge which Lady Leicester has exhibited against him. A special warrant has been issued for apprehending this Lord, whose infamies have long rendered him a disgrace to human nature.'

This newspaper openly claimed that Lady Leicester had accused her husband of sodomy, a charge which was in fact quite untrue. Leicester, in his absence, sued for libel and won his case, but, because his reputation was so bad and there were so many 'flying rumours' about his character, he was awarded only £1,000 damages, rather than the £20,000 he had claimed.

Leicester remained abroad for the rest of his life, settling at the Villa Rostan at Pegli, near Genoa. Here he lived under the name of 'Signor Compton', which had been his grandmother's maiden name. The cellars of the Villa Rostan are said to have been filled with a great supply of wine, which he gave away freely at a time when wine in the Liguria was very scarce; and at dinner he always sat with his hat on. He died on 31 December 1855, and was buried in the Protestant cemetery of San Benigno.

The eighth Duke of Beaufort had two homosexual sons, both

of whom died in exile. The eldest of the two, Lord Henry Somerset, known in the family as 'Penna', was married to Isabella, the daughter of the last Earl Somers, who, as well as being a great heiress, was a woman of the highest moral standards. After five years of marriage however, his homosexual leanings drove her to throw all her puritan principles to the wind and leave him, taking with her their only child. 'We have nothing whatever to say in defence of Penna,' wrote Henry's mother to her daughter-in-law, 'and unless he is mad cannot understand his behaviour,' while the Duke told his son that 'a man may get tired of his wife, but your conduct and language is not that of a gentleman.' Lord Henry retired abroad in 1879 after losing a long, drawn-out legal battle for the custody of his son. He resided first in Monaco, and then in Florence, where he made something of a name for himself as a writer of sentimental songs for the Victorian drawing-room, amongst which some of the most popular were 'Hush me, O Sorrow', 'Dawn', and 'All through the Night.' A book of poems he wrote called *Songs of Adieu* was said to have been inspired by his love for a young man called Henry Smith, who was the cause of the break-up of his marriage, and who subsequently emigrated to New Zealand.

If the Duke and Duchess were horrified by the revelations about Lord Henry's private life, those concerning Lord Arthur as good as broke their hearts. Lord Arthur, who was the Duke's third son, was a close friend of the Prince of Wales, who had recently appointed him as Extra Equerry, and superintendent of his stables, with an office in Marlborough House. It was said that the Prince relied greatly on his judgement in buying horses both for racing and for breeding. 'He is the best of sons,' revealed a profile of him which appeared in *Vanity Fair* on 19 November 1887, 'a true Somerset, a gentleman, a good sportsman, good natured, and of much solid sense. He is favourably regarded by the fair sex . . .' How these words must have caused his parents to glow with pride, especially after all their troubles with Penna. Their joy in Arthur was, however, to be short-lived.

In July 1889, while investigating reports of the existence of a male brothel at a house in Cleveland Street, owned by a professional male prostitute named Charles Hammond, the police received a statement to the fact that the house was frequently visited by 'men in high positions,' two of them were alleged to be Lord Euston, eldest son of the 7th Duke of Grafton, and Lord

29. LORD ARTHUR SOMERSET

Arthur Somerset. Hammond fled on hearing about the police enquiries, but a man who lived with him under the name of the Reverend G. D. Veck, a quite bogus clergyman, and a confederate named Henry Newlove, were both arrested and committed for trial. When the police searched Veck on his arrest, they found letters on him from a teenage youth named Algernon Allies begging for money and mentioning a certain 'Mr. Brown,' who had been helping him financially. Allies eventually confessed that 'Mr. Brown' was in fact none other than Lord Arthur Somerset, who had been supplying him with money for services rendered. He told of how he had been previously employed as a house boy at the Marlborough Club, which was where he had first attracted the attention of Lord Arthur. He had however stolen money from the club, for which he had been arrested and charged with theft. Lord Arthur had helped him, and instead of being sent to prison he was bound over, Lord Arthur going surety for his good behaviour. He had been sacked from his job at the club, and had had nowhere to go, as his disgrace had made him ashamed to go home. Lord Arthur had written to Hammond in Cleveland Street asking him to accommodate Allies, who had been put up there as 'a friend of Mrs. Brown's.' As well as being thus linked to Allies, Lord Arthur was also positively identified as being a client of Hammond's by two other boys who worked at the house in Cleveland Street.

The Home Secretary, after reading the statements of Allies, and various other evidence, was unwilling to prosecute Somerset, as he considered the evidence against him to be insufficient. The trial of Veck and Newlove went ahead, and they were found guilty and sent to prison. Lord Arthur, however, as well as his solicitor, Newton, naturally assumed that he would be next, especially since he had been interviewed by the police on at least two occasions. He panicked, and fled abroad to Dieppe on 27 September. From there he wrote an account of his hurried journey, from Newmarket, where he had been attending the Autumn Sales, to his close friend the Hon. Reginald Brett.

'I had an awful drive to Cambridge, the axle heated and I had to take off the wheel. Of course it ran very heavy in consequence and the horse stopped a mile out of Cambridge and I had to run with two bags and a rug in a very thick coat a mile at least. However I just caught the King's Cross train, took a ticket to

Hitchin but travelled on to Finsbury Park and paid excess there and thence to Brondesbury by road and thence by train to Willesden and thence to Addison Road, thence to Clapham Junction and so to Newhaven and Dieppe and was not sick once – too much worried. I had a fright at Clapham, a man with black whiskers in a grey coat and white hat walked up to a policeman near me and said, "I am not sure whether I shall want you or not" – but nothing happened.'

As soon as he realised that any rumours that he was about to be arrested were false, at least for the time being, Lord Arthur returned to England on 30 September by the night boat to Newhaven. The very act of running away in the first place had, however, been a bad mistake. It had set the tongues wagging. The case had been widely reported in the newspapers, and his name was now being whispered in society as being one of the 'noble Lords' involved in the affair. He ignored Newton's advice to stay put. 'I cannot stay away without exciting curiosity,' he wrote to Reginald Brett. 'For the first time in the memory of man the stables don't know where the Master of the Horse is and they can't get a brush or an oat without my initials.' He travelled from Newhaven to his father's house at Badminton, using a route which avoided London, where he apparently managed to satisfy the Duke as to his reasons for having left Newmarket so suddenly.

On 9 October Lord Arthur returned to London where he was informed by Newton that, in spite of the Home Secretary's reluctance to proceed any further, the police and the Director of Public Prosecutions were determined to prosecute him and that it was their avowed intent to apply for a warrant for his arrest.

'I am afraid things look as black as it is possible for them to do,' he wrote to Brett. 'So much so that Newton is very anxious that I should go abroad again for a good long while. But of course I might as well cut my throat at once. The only thing is whether everything is not really over and that I should just as well make up my mind to it and be off. A very kind letter from H.R.H. but of course he says he must know why I left Newmarket without letting my father know and why I went to Dieppe just when he particularly wanted to see me.'

When the Prince was finally informed of his friend's involvement in the Cleveland Street affair, he was incredulous. 'I don't believe it,' he wrote to Sir Dighton Probyn, his Comptroller. 'I won't believe it any more than I would if they had accused the Archbishop of Canterbury.'

Although Lord Arthur had consistently vowed to his friends that he would stay and fight any accusations that were made against him, as the pressure mounted it became too much for him to bear, and on 18 October he left England again. He wrote to his father explaining 'that his brain could not stand the anxiety of this awful scandal, that he feared he would be prosecuted and that even if he got off with flying colours he could never, having been accused of this awful crime, live in England again.' The Duke was reported by Sir Dighton Probyn to have been 'brokenhearted' at the news. 'I know not what to say to you,' he wrote in reply to his son's letter. 'God help you. What will you do?' I must go to Badminton tomorrow and break it to your mother.' Lord Arthur confided to Brett: 'That is an awful thing to read and know one is the cause of. Poor dears, and they have always been so good to me.' A few days later Lord Edward Somerset, the youngest son, reported to Brett that his father had decided after all not to tell his mother as her heart was in a particularly weak state, and he felt that the shock might kill her. 'You can't think what an awful state of suspense and misery we are all in,' he said.

Probyn felt strongly that, now that Lord Arthur had gone, further publicity could do nothing but harm, and he wrote to the Prime Minister, Lord Salisbury, begging him to have the case dropped. 'It can do no good to prosecute him. He has gone and will never show his face in England again. He dare never come back to this country.' He continued:

'I think it is the most hateful, loathsome story I ever heard, and the most astounding. It is too fearful, but further publicity will only make matters worse. I have of course telegraphed to the Prince, and am writing full particulars of this disgusting calamity to H.R.H.

'The Prince will be terribly cut up about it . . . I felt that in writing to you I am only doing what the Prince would wish.

'I do not write with a view of trying to save the man. He has gone – he is beyond punishment, or rather out of reach of the law. I only want if possible not to increase the fearful disgrace which has fallen on his family.

'For the man in his defence, I can only trust that he is mad.'

Salisbury did evidently write to the Prince of Wales giving him the impression that it was his intention to drop the case, as he received a letter on 25 October in which the Prince stated that he was 'glad to gather ... that no warrant is likely to be issued against the "unfortunate lunatic" (I can call him nothing else), as, for the sake of the family and society, the less one hears of such a filthy scandal the better.'

Meanwhile Lord Arthur was in Rouen pondering on the grim realities of life as an exile.

'I have wandered about all day for two days,' he wrote to Brett on 24 October, 'trying to think what employment I am fit for and am still undecided. You see, if I got a promise of any employment, I should require a reference. To whom am I to refer? ... My poor father and mother, it is too awful for them and I suppose I shall never see them again nor shall I see any of my many friends...'

He outlined the various options for a man in his position.

'I don't much fancy the idea of the Cape, as I know a lot of people out there. I think I shall make my way to Eastern Europe as soon as things are settled, but of course I must know what my financial prospects are before I go anywhere. Perhaps Drummond-Woolf [Sir Henry Drummond-Woolf was British Envoy in Tehran] could get me something in Persia. At this moment I know the Sultan wants a man to look after his horse breeding. I had arranged with Marcus Beresford about a man. Ask him if he accepted the berth. If not I might get it. I really could do it, and the place is worth £800 a year. I don't fancy the Sultan would have any prejudice, would he? But of course I shall want letters before I could get the place, but I suppose no one would give me any. Another thing I might do is teach English in a school or to any private pupils, but it is one thing knowing English and another to try and teach it.'

The following day he wrote rather pathetically that he had tried the local tramway company and also the Commercial Union Insurance branch for employment, masquerading under the name of Arthur Short, 'but could not get any.'

On 4 November the Duke of Beaufort finally decided that his wife had to be told about their son. He began by pretending that Arthur had had to go abroad as a result of some trouble with a woman. The Duchess was, however, no fool: she realised that 'no entanglement with a woman would oblige him to go abroad and give up his Regiment.' The Duke then told her 'we thought he had been decoyed to a house by some woman and the people of the house threatened him, and having no rebutting evidence to bring against any accusations they chose to make would not face the horrors of a trial.' Her immediate reaction was to try and persuade her husband to go and bring back Arthur to face any charge that might be brought against him.

'It is so difficult to say, "He can't meet it," ' the Duke wrote to Brett, 'and yet that is practically what his going has done, as I explained to his lawyer. He avoids the exposé of the Police Court and all the horrors of the newspaper reports and remarks – but going like this and leaving his office and his Regiment are, with the above exceptions, as hard as being found guilty. Everybody says the same thing, he must face it. Why don't you make him?'

Lord Arthur never did return. On 12 November the police, having gathered overwhelming evidence against him, issued a warrant for his arrest, and four days later his name was actually published in the pages of a London weekly newspaper, the *North London Press*. These events merely confirmed him in his belief that any life he might face abroad was better than the shame he must endure were he ever to return home. It was a bitter disappointment to his family.

Christmas found Lord Arthur alone in Vienna.

'All last night and all today,' he wrote to Brett on Christmas Day, 'it has been and is snowing. The awful melancholy when one has no one to speak to and nothing to do, and when one cannot even walk about and get exercise, is not to be told.'

He spoke of his intentions of going to Gardone on Lake Garda.

'It is between that and Africa or Asia to my mind. In many ways I should prefer the latter as life is too utterly hopeless as it is.'

He also wrote of being harassed by the local police.

'The Vienna police have made a fox of me for two whole days.

I cannot move but I am pursued by armies of plain clothes police aided and abetted by small boys. At all events I have given them some exercise and I don't suppose they have any right to touch me. But of course they might embroil me in some row and I suppose they are like their English compéres. What one lies, all the rest swear to, so I must clear out of this.

Early in January he moved to Paris, a city he hardly knew, from where he wrote to Brett asking him if he could help him find somewhere to stay.

'For a few days a hotel does very well,' he told his friend. 'But as no one stays more than two or three days it would be best to get rooms somewhere in that city . . . I don't know the place at all. But if I could get an airy room in the suburbs (like Hampstead or Fulham) I should be comfortable and my friends might come and see me sometimes, if they would.'

With Brett's help he eventually found a quiet pension in Passy, 40 Rue Copernic. 'This house is full of Americans and children,' he wrote on 11 January, 'but I never speak to any of them, and there are two old Spanish ladies.'

In the latter part of March Lord Arthur was visited by his sister Blanche Waterford in the Paris suburb where he had settled under another name. She 'found the poor dear very much aged, but very quiet and natural and cheerful, and if only no one molests him to signify – i.e. if they don't insist on his moving on – he is better here than anywhere, and is nearly as happy as one could hope. This is such a snug rabbit hole, and he has done it up capitally and made all his surroundings as cheerful as possible.' For the rest of his life his whereabouts were to remain a closely guarded secret known only to his family and intimate friends like Brett. On her way back home from Paris Lady Waterford visited her parents at Badminton to give them the latest news of their son, and wrote to Brett.

'I left my poor dear Friday night, and we made up our minds to behave well. Poor thing! What a life – but he gets used to it, he says, and except for the misery to father, mother, etc. could get on if he could presently find something to do. Perhaps later he may manage some buying of horses for dealers, but I have told him he must be patient. So he is, I must say, poor heart . . . My people are going out very soon in bits, – not all at once – so as to spin themselves out, and I hope to go again in July. Arthur looks 1,000 but won't turn grey which is a pity and would disguise him better than anything. I will look for some stuff that would turn his hair gradually. It must not be done at once or the few people (shopkeepers) who know him in his new name would become suspicious. Of course, the most pitiable thing of all is my Mother's state – no wonder. She is as good and plucky as she can be; but her misery is so far beyond description that I don't see how her brain can stand it. However, God knows, and it is no use my bothering who don't know anything. It is the knowledge of this misery that kills Arthur – for himself he says he is getting used to this wretched life.'

Lord Arthur's long and dreary exile lasted for another thirty-six years, all of which he spent living incognito in France, eventually moving from his rooms in the Paris suburb to a villa in Hyères on the French Riviera. Here he lived out his life in the Villa Sophie looked after by a French cook and servants, and an English companion named James Andrew Neale. He died on 26 May 1926, and was buried in the 'English section' of the town cemetery. Unlike his life, his death passed unnoticed by the English newspapers.

Considering the horror with which the revelations of such a scandal as the Cleveland Street affair were received, the reaction of the Duke of Beaufort to his son was really remarkably restrained, certainly in comparison with that of another famous father when he heard of his son's homosexual liaison. The story of Lord Alfred Douglas and Oscar Wilde is too well known to bear repeating, but it is worth quoting from two letters written by Lord Alfred's father, the 8th Marquis of Queensberry, to his son as being good examples of disgust, felt by a father for his son's behaviour, at its most extreme. The first is dated 1 April 1894:

'Secondly, I come to the more painful part of this letter – your intimacy with this man Wilde. It must either cease or I will disown you and stop all money supplies. I am not going to try and analyse this intimacy, and I make no charge; but to my mind to pose as a thing is as bad as to be it. With my own eyes I saw you both in the most loathsome and disgusting relationship as expressed by your manner and expression. Never in my

experience have I seen such a sight as that in your horrible features. No wonder people are talking as they are. Also I now hear on good authority, but this may be false, that his wife is petitioning to divorce him for sodomy and other crimes. Is this true, or do you not know of it? If I thought the actual thing was true, and it became public property, I should be quite justified in shooting him at sight. These Christian English cowards and men, as they call themselves, want waking up. Your disgusted so-called father,
                    Queensberry.'

By 28 August he was well into his stride:

'You miserable creature,
I received your telegram by post from Carter's and have requested them not to forward any more, but just to tear any up, as I did yours, without reading it, directly I was aware from whom it came. You must be flush of money to waste it on such rubbish. I have learned, thank goodness, to turn the keenest pangs to peacefulness. What could be keener pain than to have such a son as yourself fathered upon one? However, there is always a bright side to every cloud, and whatever is is light (sic). If you are my son, it is only confirming proof to me, if I needed any, how right I was to face every horror and misery I have done rather than run the risk of bringing more creatures into the world like yourself, and that was the entire and only reason of my breaking with your mother as a wife, so intensely was I dissatisfied with her as the mother of you children, and particularly yourself, whom, when quite a baby, I cried over you the bitterest tears a man ever shed, that I had brought such a creature into the world, and unwittingly had committed such a crime. If you are not my son, and in this Christian country with these hypocrites 'tis a wise father who knows his own child, and no wonder on the principles they intermarry on, but to be fore-warned is to be fore-armed. No wonder you have fallen prey to this horrible brute. I am only sorry for you as a human creature ... You must be demented; there is madness on your mother's side, and indeed few families in this Christian country are without it, if you look into them. But please cease annoying me, for I will not correspond with you, nor receive nor answer letters, and as for money, you sent me a lawyer's letter to say you would take none from me, but anyhow until you change your life I should refuse any; it depends on yourself whether I shall ever recognise you at all

again after your behaviour. I will make allowance; I think you are demented, and I am very sorry for you.
Queensberry.'

Lord Alfred Douglas was also to spend many years in exile, along with countless other homosexuals who considered it wise to leave the country after the Wilde trials. According to Frank Harris, 'Every train to Dover was crowded, every steamer to Calais thronged with members of the aristocratic and leisured classes, who seemed to prefer Paris, or even Nice out of season, to a city like London, where the police might act with such unexpected vigour ... Never was Paris so crowded with members of the English governing classes; here was to be seen a famous ex-Minister; there the fine face of the president of a Royal society; at one table on the Café de la Paix, a millionaire recently ennobled, and celebrated for his exquisite taste in art; opposite to him a famous general ... the majority of the migrants stayed abroad for some time. The wind of terror which had swept them across the Channel opposed their return, and they scattered over the Continent from Naples to Monte Carlo and from Palermo to Seville under all sorts of pretexts.'

This book began with a story of exile, and it will end with such a story. It was a fate that was common to many black sheep. In the nineteenth and early twentieth centuries, when England was still expanding her Empire, young men who disgraced their families were often paid to go to the Colonies in order to avoid any scandal.

'My dear son,' wrote Edward Stacey, a highly respectable Ordnance Clerk in the Tower of London, to his son George in March 1836, 'After much consideration Mr. Dobson, your poor wife's anxious father, and myself, your distracted parent, agree that you should immediately go to Canada. I have mortgaged my future in borrowing several hundred pounds to keep you out of the Debtor's Prison, and I am determined for you to leave England in order to keep you out of the clutches of that wretched woman in whose toils you so foolishly became entangled ... You will have no more money from us if you remain in England. I am satisfied that your only chance is in the colonies ...'

Society coined a term for young men like George Stacey. They were known as remittance men. In a book called *The Pioneer*

BLACK SHEEP

Years 1895–1914, about the opening of the American West, there is a good account of what must have been a typical group of such scallywags.

'Just about this time I was cooking for four remittance men near Kindersley ... I tell you they were quite a crew. They weren't wanted at home in England. Paid to stay in Canada. They had been Oxford and Cambridge men. Oh my, let me tell you, we lived high. Peaches and cream for breakfast. We never wanted for nothing. Anything I asked for cooking they'd get. They paid me twenty-five dollars a month and that was all I wanted. I was living just like a king, nothing to spend it on, and I was high, wide and fancy free and if I wanted a drink why I'd just take one. The bottles of whisky just came in a steady flow from Kindersley.

'The way they worked it, my remittance would run out but yours would be coming in, and when yours was gone then the other fellow's cheque would come in. It worked out fine. They never ran out of money.

'Oh, they had homesteads but ... they never did any work on them. Nothing. All they ever did was go out in the bush and bring in poles and set them up as steeplechase. They all had real good horses and they'd spend a lot of time jumping, riding. They rode to foxes. Except their foxes were coyote, chasing them across the hills.

'This Chris Murr. He decided he was going back to the old country for Christmas. Well, he went back and he said he'd be gone three or four months. Well, before the end of January he was back in the shack.

'"Well, what happened, Chris? How come you're back so soon?" somebody said.

'"Well," he said, "I'll tell you. We're sitting at breakfast one morning and I turned my head to say something to my sister sitting next to me just at the time a maid put a cup of coffee between us and my head hit the coffee and spilled all over her and I yelled out: 'Jesus Christ!' Well, my mother fainted, and my father jumped out of his chair, and he ordered me out of the house and when I went back to get my things they ordered me never to come back again. And I got an increase in my remittance."

'Yes, they lived good. They all had big remittances and they weren't afraid to spend it. I'll tell you what they did once. I had a mouth organ and I was sitting outside the shack once, playing away on the old thing, and one of these fellows came out and he said, "For God's sakes, throw that bally thing away." I said something about it's nice to have music around the place, and you know what they did? They all piled into the wagon and they went to Kindersley and they were gone about a week. When they came back, do you know what they had in the wagon? A player piano and a big box of rolls.

'But they never had to earn a living. Their folks just sent them money to stay away. They didn't farm, they didn't do a thing but drink and ride their horses and eat my good food. They were fine fellows.'

Legends of remittance men appear in all stories of colonial life, whether it be Australia, India, Africa, or other far reaches of the British Empire. My favourite is the following, again about Canada. A certain gentleman was travelling through the back-woods of Canada, when he came across a man felling a tree, dressed in full evening dress. Naturally curious as to why the man was thus attired he engaged him in conversation. It transpired that the man, who was English, having committed some misdemeanour at home, had been banished to Canada by his family, and had arrived with nothing but a suitcase of clothes to his name. Gradually over the years he had worn through all these, until the day had finally arrived when he had nothing to wear except his evening dress.

> 'The Duke – his aged grand sire – bore
> The shame till he could bear no more.
> He rallied his declining powers,
> Summoned the youth to Brackley Towers,
> And bitterly addressed him thus –
> "Sir! You have disappointed us!
> We had intended you to be
> The next Prime Minister but three:
> The stocks were sold; the Press was squared;
> The Middle Class was quite prepared.
> But as it is! ... My language fails!
> Go out and govern New South Wales!"'

ILLUSTRATIONS

ILLUSTRATIONS

BIBLIOGRAPHY

AILESBURY, 7th Marquis of: *The Wardens of Savernake Forest*. Routledge, London, 1949.

ALEXANDER, B.: *England's Wealthiest Son*. Centaur Press, London, 1962.

ANGLESEY, Marquis of: *One Leg*. Jonathan Cape, London, 1961.

The Anglesey Papers.

The Annual Register of World Events. Longman & Co.

AUSTEN, JANE: *The Letters of Jane Austen*. Edited by Lord Brabourne. R. Bentley & Son, 1884.

BLAKISTON, GEORGIANA: *Woburn and the Russells*. Constable, London, 1980.

BLANCH, LESLEY: *The Wilder Shores of Love*. John Murray, London, 1954.

BLUNT, REGINALD: *Thomas, Lord Lyttelton*. Hutchinson, London, 1936.

BREASTED, BARBARA: *Comus and the Castlehaven Scandal*. From *Milton Studies III*. University of Pittsburgh, 1971.

BROADFOOT, BARRY: *The Pioneer Years 1895–1914*. Doubleday, Canada, 1977.

BRODRICK, G. C.: *English Land and Landlords*. Cobden Club, 1881.

BRYANT, ARTHUR: *The Age of Elegance*. Collins, London, 1950.

BRYANT, ARTHUR: *The England of Charles II*. Longman & Co., London, 1934.

BURFORD, E. J.: *The 'orrible Synne*. Calder and Boyars, London, 1973.

BURKE, SIR J. B.: *Anecdotes of the Aristocracy*. Henry Colburn, 1849.

BURKE, SIR J. B.: *Romances of the Aristocracy*. Hurst and Blackett, 1855.

BURKE, SIR J. B.: *Vicissitudes of Families*. Longman & Co., 1859.

Burke's Genealogical and Heraldic History of the Peerage, Baronetage and Knightage. Edited by Peter Townend.

BURNET, GILBERT: *Life of Sir Matt Hale and John, Earl of Rochester*. London, 1829.

CADOGAN, DR. WILLIAM: *An Essay on the Nursing and Management of Children*. London, 1750.

CASTLEHAVEN, Earl of: *The Arraignment and Conviction of Mervyn Lord Audley, Earl of Castlehaven...* London, 1699.

CASTLEHAVEN, Earl of: *The Case of Sodomy in the trial of Mervyn Lord Audley, Earl of Castlehaven...* London, 1708.

CECIL, E.: *Primogeniture*. John Murray, 1895.

The Chatsworth Papers.

CHESTERFIELD, PHILIP STANHOPE, 4th Earl of: *Letters of Lord Chesterfield to his Son*. J. M. Dent & Sons, London, 1929.

CLARENDON, EDWARD, Earl of: *Life of Clarendon*. Oxford, 1759.

COBBETT, WILLIAM, M.P.: *State Trials*. London, 1809.

COCHRAN, C. B.: *A Showman Looks on*. J. M. Dent, 1945.

COKE, LADY MARY: *Letters and Journals 1756–74*. David Douglas, 1896.

Complete Baronetage. Edited by G. E. Cokayne.

Complete Peerage. Edited by G. E. Cokayne and Hon. Vicary Gibbs.

COMTE, EDWARD LE: *The Notorious Lady Essex*. Robert Hale & Co., London, 1970.

CROFT, SIR HERBERT: *The Abbey of Kilhampton*. London, 1780.

CURLING, J.: *Edward Worthey Montagu, 1713–1776*. Andrew Melrose, Hutchinson, London, 1954.

DANGEAU, MARQUIS DE: *Journal du Marquis de Dangeau*. Paris, 1854–1860.

DELANY, MRS: *The Autobiography and Correspondence of Mary Granville, Mrs Delany*. Edited by Lady Llanover. London, 1862.

DEVONSHIRE, ELIZABETH, Duchess of: *Anecdotes and Biographical Sketches*. London, 1863.

ELERS, GEORGE: *Memoirs of George Elers*. Edited by Lord Monson & G. Leveson-Gower. Heinemann, 1903.

BIBLIOGRAPHY

EMDEN, P. H.: *Regency Pageant*. Hodder and Stoughton, London, 1936.

EVELYN, JOHN: *Diaries and Correspondence of John Evelyn*. Edited by W. Bray. Bohn's Historical Library, London, 1859.

D'EWES, SIR SIMONDS: *Autobiography of Sir Simonds D'Ewes*. London, 1845.

FARINGTON, JOSEPH: *The Farington Diary*. Edited by James Grieg. Hutchinson, 1922.

FOTHERGILL, BRIAN: *Beckford of Fonthill*. Faber, 1979.

FROST, THOMAS: *The Life of Thomas, Lord Lyttelton*. London, 1876.

GARDINER, S. R.: *History of England*. London, 1863.

The Gentleman's Magazine.

GIBBS, SIR PHILIP: *King's Favourite*. Hutchinson, 1909.

GIBBS, the Hon. Vicary: *Peerage Cuttings*. London Library. n.d.

GOODY, THIRSK AND THOMPSON: *Family and Inheritance, 1200–1800*. Cambridge University Press, 1976.

HALIFAX, GEORGE SAVILE 1st Marquis of: *Advice to a Daughter*. Cayme Press, Welwyn Garden City, 1927.

HAMILTON, ANTHONY: *The Memoirs of the Count de Grammont*. London, 1890.

HATTON, Family of: *The Hatton Correspondence*. Camden Society, 1878.

HERON, SIR ROBERT: *Notes by H.* Grantham, 1851.

HERTFORD, FRANCES, Countess of: *The Hertford Correspondence 1738–41*. Edited by W. Bingley. London, 1805.

HERVEY, LORD JOHN: *Lord Hervey and His Friends*. John Murray, 1950.

HERVEY, LORD JOHN: *Some Materials Towards Memoirs of the Reign of King George II*. Edited by R. Sedgwick. Eyre & Spottiswoode, London, 1931.

HEWETT, O. W.: *Strawberry Fair*. John Murray, 1956.

HIBBERT, CHRISTOPHER: *The Grand Tour*. Weidenfeld & Nicolson, London, 1969.

HOLLIS, CHRISTOPHER: *Eton, a History*. Hollis & Carter, London, 1960.

HYDE, H. MONTGOMERY: *The Other Love*. Heinemann, London, 1970.

HYDE, H. MONTGOMERY: *The Cleveland Street Scandal*. W. H. Allen, London, 1976.

JENKINSON, C.: *Life of Simon Lord Irnham*. London, 1769.

JONES, L. C.: *Clubs of Georgian Rakes*. Columbia University Press, New York, 1942.

KAY, J.: *Free Trade in Land*. C. Kegan Paul & Co., 1879.

KENNY, C. S.: *The History of the Law of Primogeniture in England*. J. Hall & Sons, 1878.

KENYON, J. P.: *Robert Spencer, Earl of Sunderland*. Longman & Co., 1958.

KETTON-CREMER, R. W.: *Norfolk Gallery*. Faber, London, 1948.

KETTON-CREMER, R. W.: *Horace Walpole*. Duckworth, London, 1940.

LAMINGTON, LORD: *Days of the Dandies*. W. Blackwood & Sons, 1890.

LEWIS, W. S.: *Horace Walpole*. Rupert Hart-Davis, London, 1961.

LILLY, WILLIAM: *A True History of King James I and King Charles I*. J. Roberts, 1715.

LONGFORD, ELIZABETH: *Wellington, Pillar of State*. Weidenfeld, 1972.

LONGFORD, ELIZABETH: *Wellington, the Years of the Sword*. Weidenfeld, 1969.

McELWEE, W.: *The Murder of Sir Thomas Overbury*. Faber, 1952.

MONTAGU, LADY MARY WORTLEY: *The Complete Letters of Lady Mary Wortley Montagu*. Edited by R. Halsband. Oxford University Press, Oxford, 1966.

NEVILL, RALPH: *Light Come, Light Go*. Macmillan, 1909.

NICOLL, SIR W. R.: *Literary Anecdotes of the Nineteenth Century*. Hodder and Stoughton, 1895.

NOBLE, P.: *Anne Seymour Damer*. Kegan Paul, London, 1908.

NORMAN, CHARLES: *Rake Rochester*. Crown, N.Y., 1954.

Notes and Queries (Periodical) 1849–.

O'BYRNE, W.R.: *Naval Biographical Dictionary*. London, 1849.

ODDIE, E. M.: *Portrait of Ianthe*. Jonathan Cape, 1935.

OGG, DAVID: *England in the Reign of Charles II*. Clarendon Press, Oxford, 1934.

PARSONS, WILLIAM: *A Genuine Account of the Life and Transactions of W. Parsons, Esq.* London, 1751.

PARSONS, WILLIAM: *Memoirs of the Life and Adventures of W. Parsons, Esq.* London, 1751.

BIBLIOGRAPHY

PEACHAM, HENRY: *The Compleat Gentleman.* London, 1634.

PEPYS, SAMUEL: *Diaries of Samuel Pepys.* J. M. Dent, London, 1924.

PIGOTT, C.: *The Jockey Club.* London, 1792.

PINTO, VIVIAN DE SOLA: *Enthusiast in Wit.* Routledge & Kegan Paul, 1962.

PINTO, VIVIAN DE SOLA: *Restoration Carnival.* Folio Society, 1954.

PINTO, VIVIAN DE SOLA: *Sir Charles Sedley.* Constable & Co., London, 1927.

PLUMB, J. H.: *Sir Robert Walpole.* Cresset Press, London, 1956–61.

The Pembroke Papers. Edited by Lord Herbert. Jonathan Cape, 1950.

RODERICK, COLIN: *John Knatchbull: From Quarterdeck to Gallows.* Angus & Robertson, 1963.

ROUGHEAD, W.: *The Fatal Countess.* W. Green & Son, 1924.

ROWLAND, D.: *A History and General Account of the Family of Neville.* London, 1830.

ROWSE, A. L.: *Homosexuals in History.* Weidenfeld, London, 1977.

SCHMIDT, M. F.: *Passion's Child.* Hamish Hamilton, 1977.

SEDGWICK, ROMNEY: *History of the House of Commons.* H.M.S.O., London, 1970.

SHARP, DR SAMUEL: *Letters from Italy.* London, 1767.

STONE, LAWRENCE: *The Crisis of the Aristocracy, 1559–1641.* Oxford University Press, Oxford, 1965.

STONE, LAWRENCE: *The Family, Sex, and Marriage in England 1500–1800.* Weidenfeld, 1977.

SURTEES, VIRGINIA: *A Beckford Inheritance.* Michael Russell, Wilton, Wiltshire, 1977.

TAYLOR, GORDON RATTRAY: *Sex in History.* Thames and Hudson, London, 1953.

TIMBS, JOHN: *Club Life in London.* London, 1872.

The Times newspaper.

TREVELYAN, G. M.: *English Social History 1304–1901.* Longman & Co., 1940.

TREVELYAN, G. M.: *England Under the Stuarts.* Methuen, London, 1924.

TREVELYAN, SIR G. O.: *The Early History of Charles James Fox*. Longman & Co., 1880.

TRUMBACH, R.: *London's Sodomites*. From *Journal of Social History*, Vol. II. Edited by Peter N. Stearns. Carnegie-Mellon University Press, Pittsburgh, 1968.

TRUMBACH, R.: *The Rise of the Egalitarian Family*. Academic Press, London, 1978.

TUCKER, W. H.: *Eton of Old*. London, 1892.

TURNER, ROBERT: *Truth Brought to Light*. London, 1659.

VULLIAMY, C. E.: *Aspasia. The Life and Times of Mary Granville, Mrs Delany, 1700–88*. Geoffrey Bles, London, 1935.

WALDEGRAVE, MARY, Countess of: *Waldegrave Family History*. Privately published.

WALKER, OBADIAH: *Of Education, Especially of Young Gentlemen*. Oxford, 1673.

WALPOLE, HORACE: *The Yale Edition of Horace Walpole's Correspondence*. Oxford University Press, 1937–1980.

WEDGWOOD, J.: *The Economics of Inheritance*. Routledge & Sons, 1929.

WELDON, SIR ANTHONY: *A Secret History of the Court of James I*. London, 1811.

The Wellington Papers.

WHITE, BEATRICE: *Cast of Ravens*. John Murray, 1965.

WHITE, T. H.: *The Age of Scandal*. Jonathan Cape, 1950.

WILLIAMS, SIR CHARLES HANBURY: *Works*. London, 1822.

WILSON, ARTHUR: *History of the Reign of James I*. London, 1719.

WILSON, J. H.: *Court Wits of the Restoration*. Princeton, 1948.

WILSON, J. H.: *A Rake and His Times*. Frederick Muller, London, 1954.

WOHL, ANTHONY: *The Victorian Family*. Croom Helm, London, 1978.

WOOD, ANTHONY A.: *Athenae Oxonienses*. London, 1721.

WOOD, ANTHONY A.: *The Life and Times of Wood, 1632–95*. Oxford History Society, 1900.

INDEX

INDEX